JUSTICE IN LÜRITZ

JUSTICE IN LÜRITZ

Experiencing Socialist Law in East Germany

Inga Markovits

PRINCETON UNIVERSITY PRESS

PRINCETON AND OXFORD

English translation copyright © 2010 by Princeton University Press
German edition © Verlag C.H. Beck oHG, München, 2006

Published by Princeton University Press, 41 William Street, Princeton, New Jersey 08540
In the United Kingdom: Princeton University Press, 6 Oxford Street, Woodstock, Oxfordshire OX20 1TW
press.princeton.edu
All Rights Reserved

Library of Congress Cataloging-in-Publication Data
Markovits, Inga.
  [Gerechtigkeit in Lüritz English]
  Justice in Lüritz : experiencing socialist law in East Germany / Inga Markovits.
    p. cm.
  ISBN 978-0-691-14347-7 (hardcover : alk. paper) — ISBN 978-0-691-14348-4 (pbk. : alk. paper) 1. Law—Germany (East)—History—Case studies. 2. Justice, Administration of—Germany (East)—History—Case studies. I. Title.
  KKA890.M3713 2010
  349. 43'1—dc22
                                                                                2010012558

British Library Cataloging-in-Publication Data is available
This book has been composed in Times
Printed on acid-free paper. ∞
Printed in the United States of America
10 9 8 7 6 5 4 3 2 1

Again, for Dick

"Bei hellem Tageslichte
  hab ich es anders gesehn."
"Gewiss. Geschichten und Geschichte
  wachsen und wechseln schon im Entstehn."
    —THEODOR FONTANE

"In broad daylight
  I have not seen it so."
"I know. Stories and histories
  shift and change as they grow."

TABLE OF CONTENTS

Acknowledgments ix

CHAPTER 1
The Files 1

CHAPTER 2
The Beginning 8

CHAPTER 3
People 16

CHAPTER 4
Property 26

CHAPTER 5
Work 42

CHAPTER 6
Families 69

CHAPTER 7
Punishments 92

CHAPTER 8
The Party 141

CHAPTER 9
Hopes and Lies 182

CHAPTER 10
The End 219

Notes 243

ACKNOWLEDGMENTS

I have spent an embarrassing amount of time and effort on this book and, in the process, relied on the help and advice of more people than I was entitled to expect. Supportive representatives of the East German Administration of Justice provided access to the Lüritz records. Experienced colleagues mediated during my negotiations with data protection officials. Patient archival staff fetched one bundle of files after the other from their cellars and deposits. At the Lüritz Magistrate Court and the Prosecutor's Office in Neuburg, I graciously was provided with the space, the explanations and the help I needed to find my footing in an unfamiliar work environment. The many partners to my interviews—above all, Frau Rüstig, Frau Walter, and Frau Neuman—described as honestly and as precisely as they could what it meant to be a judge, and to be judged, under Socialism. The German Volkswagen Foundation generously financed my many trips to Lüritz, to Neuburg, and to Potsdam. And my family, throughout all these years, bore up with loving equanimity under my many journeys to the sources.

If I misread my data, misunderstood my witnesses, or missed out on important aspects of my story, I have only myself to blame. I have tried hard to get things right. There were times when I thought that this book never would get done. Here it is.

JUSTICE IN LÜRITZ

CHAPTER 1

THE FILES

There is no Lüritz. But the place hiding behind this name exists: a town of about 55,000 inhabitants in that northern part of Germany that not so very long ago belonged to the German Democratic Republic (GDR), now deceased. Lüritz is a pretty town with a big market square, two or three beautiful churches, the remnants of two city gates, a once busy port, a shipyard (now also much reduced in size and workforce), an engineering school, and a number of splendid Renaissance buildings in front of which the tourists study their travel guides. One of these buildings houses the city's magistrate court. Of its eight judges, seven are West Germans.

There always was a courthouse in this place: under the Archduke, the Weimar Republic, the Nazis, the Socialists, and now, finally, under the rule of law. Most of the times it was called, as it is today, the "magistrate court." Only under the Socialists it was a "district court," in which, during the last years of the GDR, a crew of five judges decided together about a thousand cases a year: a potpourri of civil litigation, labor and family law disputes, and criminal cases. Today, four of those judges are attorneys in town; only the fifth, still young and inexperienced when the Wall collapsed, was kept on the bench after what the Germans call *"die Wende"*—the Turnabout. In the court's archive, Socialist and rule-of-law case files are peacefully united on shiny metal shelves (the old wooden shelves, all solid oak, were thrown out soon after the reunification), and only the changing colors of the folders and their suddenly increasing bulk would tell a curious visitor that around the year 1990, the town's legal life must have experienced an important change.

It was no accident that I discovered the Lüritz courthouse. Soon after the demise of Socialism, an East German colleague had hinted at possible archival finds in the former GDR: there must be courthouses, he said, that had preserved almost their entire output, because the East German administration of justice was notoriously short of staff and would not have managed to always properly weed out its superannuated records, as the law required. With a little luck, I might find a court that had held onto most of its files since the early postwar years.

So I went on a search in Mecklenburg, that part of Germany where Bismarck had said he wanted to be when the world came to an end, because in Mecklenburg everything happened fifty years later than elsewhere. Hopefully, that would

CHAPTER 1

include the cleansing of archives. Inquiries at twenty-four brand-new magistrate courts (erstwhile district courts) finally led me to Lüritz. I remember well how the sight of the Lüritz courthouse stirred my hopes: a grand affair with two broad wings, built more than four hundred years ago as a wedding present for the daughter of a duke and surely big enough to have had room to preserve the court files of four decades. And indeed: the shelves in the court's archive contained case law from the very beginnings of the GDR until its end—not without gaps, but complete enough to trace the life course of a legal system that started out with the hopes of a few believers and that collapsed under the suspicion and disappointment of so many.

As I left the Lüritz courthouse after that first visit, I noticed a little door in the curved wall of the circular staircase, too low for an adult to enter without stooping. "That is the wood cellar," I was told. "That's where we keep our waste paper." After the Turnabout, the court had not yet found the money to hire a hauling company to carry off its waste. The wood cellar turned out to be a dark and chilly vault filled to shoulder height with the byproducts of forty years of judicial administration: registers and ledgers of all sorts, personnel files, search and arrest warrants, citizens' letters and complaints, desk diaries, communications between the district court and the superior judicial bureaucracy, judges' notebooks covering briefings and training courses, work plans—a veritable garbage pile of legal history and a gold mine for me. I asked for a delay in its disposal and returned during my spring break to spend a week under the dangling light bulb of the wood cellar, sorting with freezing fingers through the treasures. As a child, I had sometimes played with the idea of stealing the contents of a mailbox at a busy intersection in town and, by reading every letter in it, discovering what life was all about. Now I had found my mailbox.

This book is based on my Lüritz discovery and on conversations with many people in town who, in one way or another, came into contact with the law: judges and prosecutors; plaintiffs and defendants; party functionaries, city officials, *Stasi* collaborators. With the help of my files and interviews I want to reconstruct the rise and fall of a totalitarian legal system from the vantage point of ordinary citizens. I am not interested in the big and important happenings in East German legal history: the plenary sessions of the Central Committee, the pronouncements by the Party leadership, the major decisions of the Supreme Court. We know enough about those. Legal sociologists have often told us that even under the rule of law, there are wide gaps between the law on the books and the law as practiced or not practiced in real life. Under Socialism, too, the legal prescriptions of the powerful had to be obeyed and carried out by those at the bottom. What did law made in Berlin look like by the time it was applied in Lüritz? How did Lüritz notables and ordinary citizens deal with it? How did the law affect them, and how did they affect the law? The legal institutions of Socialism in the GDR are dead. But the past is still alive in the minds of those who lived it. It is their experiences that are the subject matter of this book.

It will not be easy to extract from my files and interviews what Leopold von Ranke optimistically described as "what really happened." In Lüritz, too, there won't be one but several pasts, the products of the convictions and the vantage points of their respective observers. Moreover, I am an outsider, accustomed to legal conventions that may lead me to misinterpret GDR events and the reports of my informants. And can I trust even the files? Can I trust the memories of my conversation partners? Do I have to worry about being lied to? Or will I rather be misled by being too suspicious? The past is an uncertain territory. Some readers may remember it differently from the way I will describe it. To not appear unduly confident of my own impressions, I will present not only the facts, as I see them, in this book, but also some of my doubts and the mistakes I made on my search for what Socialist justice meant in Lüritz. I hope that in this fashion my excursion into the past may appear credible even to those who have experienced it differently.

But legal history written "from the bottom," as it is attempted in this book, is harder to justify than "top down" history that focuses on those canonical events and people on whose significance we all agree. My Lüritz story deals primarily with everyday events. It is true that the sky will be reflected even in a village pond, and I claim with this book that "justice in Lüritz" can also stand for "justice in the GDR" and, reaching even further, for "justice under Socialism" with all its failures and, who knows, successes. But I will persuade my readers of the justification of this claim only if I succeed in describing my protagonists in ways that not only depict their own everyday hopes and experiences with the law but that also show the imprint of the political system which gave rise to them. I must make visible the general underlying the specific. I must endow my Lüritz actors with the credibility of Socialist everymen and women. And I must put together the many parts of my historical puzzle in ways that produce a portrait consisting not only of many specks of color but also displaying the shades and contours of an image that allows us to recognize and, hopefully, to understand its sitter.

I am not worried whether Lüritz, as a law-town, can serve as a useful model of adjudication in the GDR in general. The economic make-up of the city, with its mixture of heavy machinery and service industries, communal administration, tourism, and an agricultural hinterland, showed enough variety to allow its legal disputes to stand for disputes litigated elsewhere in the GDR. Moreover, the East German administration insisted on the uniformity of Socialist justice and constantly compared the output of its trial courts, calling those courts to order whose arguments or sentencing habits deviated too much from the national mean. As a result, my Lüritz files will be more representative of the work of trial courts everywhere in the GDR than the files, say, of a Bavarian or Bremen magistrate

CHAPTER 1

court might be of West German judicial practice. But the grand lines of my Lüritz portrait will be harder to draw than if I tried to paint a history "from above." Seen from up high and at a distance, the directions of developments are easier to recognize than when blocked by the obstructions of the grassroots level. The big events that we all read and heard about seem to legitimate themselves: since they happened in this and in no other fashion, they appear endowed with a developmental logic that needs no further explanation. But the details of my Lüritz story will make historical sense only if I manage to arrange them in meaningful fashion. But how? It will not do to simply string them on a time line. Instead, like an archeologist assembling the shards of a shattered clay pot, I must move around the pieces of my puzzle, arranging them first in this way, then in that, in order to discover the fit that best reveals the former contours of the artifact.

I have other problems, too. This will be a book with few footnotes. Their absence is due to the facts that, in Germany, court files are not publicly accessible (I needed the permission of the state's Minister of Justice to gain entry to the Lüritz archive) and that I do not want to identify by citations even those bits of information gained from books and public archives open to all, because I want to preserve the anonymity of my town and of my story's protagonists. But footnotes make a text appear trustworthy by demonstrating outside support for the author's statements. I must find other ways to convince my readers that my account is sticking to the truth as best it can. "How can she know that?" might be asked by someone who learns of decisions and events that people usually do not know about unless they were involved in their occurrence. That means I have to talk about my sources.

First, the files that are the main foundation of my story. GDR district court files looked very different from the output of West German magistrate courts. West German judicial records are produced by lawyers for lawyers. They focus only on those issues that are disputed between the opponents at a trial; discuss these issues not in plain German but in legalese punctuated by references to code sections or case law; give voice to laypeople only in their occasional and curtailed role as witnesses; ignore the human conflict underlying a dispute and illuminate only that specific point at which a complex web of social relationships has torn apart. Since all the legally nonessential pieces of a human puzzle are lacking, it often is difficult to compose from the remaining pieces the picture of an everyday event. What actually happened? The reader, looking up from her lecture of the transcript, rarely has seen enough of the protagonists to feel sympathy with one or the other side. A West German court record is uninterested in the human dimensions of a legal conflict. What matters is who is in the right.

GDR court files tell a story. They begin at the beginning and often do not even stop at the end, perhaps because the judge may have to help solve some remaining problems of a party (such as finding a job for someone who was fired) or because a criminal sentence is discussed (*"auswerten"* it was called: "evaluated" or, in literal translation, "made use of") in the defendant's work collective. Because it was the court's task to resolve not only individual disputes but also the collective tensions that had caused them, others than the immediate participants were given voice in the proceedings. Neighbors commented on the pedagogic talents of both parents in a custody dispute; co-workers assessed the work ethics of a criminal defendant; court-appointed "social defenders" or "accusers" described the collective's sympathy for or anger at a delinquent's deed. Trials were conducted not in experts' legal Mandarin but in workaday German. GDR judges were expected to instill respect for state and law in every person present in the courtroom and therefore had to be intelligible to all. Given the few attorneys and the many laypeople who participated in the process, East German court language was largely de-professionalized. What it gained in comprehensibility it lost in legal precision.

But to a reader of these files, their language is more colorful and humanly more informative than the professional lingo of West German records. In civil litigation, many parties to a dispute wrote their own briefs, and their outraged descriptions of why they were right and their opponents wrong help me to understand what mattered to Socialist citizens and what they expected from the law. The judges' admonitions and objections reflect the obsessive pedagogic urges of this legal system. The questionnaires that husbands and wives had to fill out in every divorce suit demonstrate the planners' belief in social management and provide me with information I would otherwise have missed, such as the division of household tasks in Socialist marriages or the differences in education and income between men and women in the GDR.

Even the paper used in the Lüritz records tells a story. In the immediate postwar years, when new paper was not to be had for love or money, the Lüritzers would use whatever could be squeezed into a typewriter or written on to compose their briefs, and if I turn around an early page, I might find a decision from the Weimar years or the clenched fist of a Socialist poster hero, now cut down to page size. No text from the Nazi years, though—after Germany's collapse, the Lüritz archive must have been well swept. With the gradual establishment of the new regime, civic order returned to Lüritz, and paper became again available. Already now, the stationery that Lüritz citizens selected for their missives to the court reflected something of their strangely trusting dependence on a state that did not like to see a lawyer step between it and its children. Early briefs usually are handwritten and look more like family letters than like business mail. Polite petitioners send best birthday stationery, filled in Sunday script and with a picture of a flower in the corner; obstreperous ones send a few pages torn from notebooks, hastily covered in pencil scratch. The tone is human rather than official.

CHAPTER 1

By the 1970s and 1980s, however, most of the briefs in the Lüritz archives are typed. Now I can tell by the quality of their paper which rank the senders hold in this society. The paper used by legal actors in the Socialist economy is smooth and firm. Communications sent by city administrators or other representatives of state officialdom look a little grainier and yellowed but still reasonably smooth. The letters coming from the Socialist judiciary are typed on miserable stock: thin and porous, in a smudgy beige. Occasionally I detect a few snow-white sheets among all the poor man's gray. They tell me that a West German attorney must have played a role in the proceedings.

I have spent so much time describing the Lüritz files because I want to show how much life may be hidden under the dust of long forgotten paper mountains. Besides the Lüritz archive, I have used other depositories of East German records: the Federal Archives (formerly in Potsdam, now in Berlin, which hold the files of the GDR Ministry of Justice and the Supreme Court, many of which contain reports on the country's district courts); the State Archive in Gronau (which keeps the records of the Lüritz District Leadership of the Socialist Unity Party [SED]); the *Stasi* Archive (for reasons that need no further explanation); the Lüritz City Archive (which holds a complete collection of the local newspaper—the *Lüritz Sentinel*—since 1947 that can tell me how the weather changes in East German politics affected my town). Now that the book is written, I find it difficult to leave the romance of the archives for everyday life at a university. Archives offer more sensual experiences than those provided by law libraries or search engines on computer screens: the rustling of brittle papers as you carefully loosen the string that bundles them together; their slightly musty smell of mushrooms and raked leaves; the golden shimmer on the ink of signatures that have dried long ago. Research becomes adventure. Like the discoverer of a city long lost under sand dunes or volcano ashes and now finally dug out again, I look for footprints of its citizens; try to guess from the objects that they left behind what might have happened in their daily life; rejoice if some unexpected find (the police photo of a fugitive, a newspaper clipping that somebody forgot among the pages) shines some extra light into a corner.

Because this legal system only recently was buried under the rubble of the ages, I have an advantage over the archeologist: I can test the information gathered from the files by way of interviews with the former inhabitants of my Atlantis. Since unemployment, the fear of an unknown Federal Republic, and sometimes even surprising success under the new system kept most of them at home after the Turnabout, I have been able to find eyewitnesses to events that happened many years, sometimes even decades, ago. Their reports will not always coincide with the information that I gather from the files. The files are more precise: their data on things that actually happened (such as the severity of penalties or the percentage of defendants represented by a lawyer) will be more reliable than the accounts of those immediately involved in the proceedings, whose memories may be refracted in the prism of the political changes they have since experienced. But my conversation partners may be able to explain the human implications of a dispute; they can talk about their hopes and worries at the time, throw light on everyday practices that might mystify me, provide me with biographical information, and in many other ways infuse the sometimes cryptic summaries of Socialist court reporters with sense and life. One of my witnesses has even taken me along to visit the Socialist corner of the city's cemetery: once a resting place of honor, now dusty and overgrown with weeds. On a few gravestones I recognize the names of early postwar judges from my Lüritz courthouse. Only an occasional bunch of recently cut flowers reveals that one or another of the dead assembled here must still have relatives in town.

So these are the materials that went into the construction of this book. It is very likely that another author would have used the same sources I read to compose a very different tale. History is made not only by those who live it but also by those who, with their very own expectations, sensibilities, and limits, write about it. I catch myself continuously talking about "my town," "my courthouse," and "my judges." They are mine: I discovered them, I saved them from oblivion, I decide in which way to arrange my data to give their story meaning and direction. I will try to exercise the power of the narrator as honestly and as precisely as I can. Apart from the names of persons and of places, nothing in this book has been made up. If I often write "it seems" or "I assume" it is because I often am not fully confident of a particular interpretation. All sentences contained within quotation marks have been said or written just the way I cite them. I cannot claim to offer the only truth about what justice meant in Lüritz. Nevertheless, this is a true story, or at least one among several true stories. Was it worth all the effort? This book deals with a small section of life in a small town in a small country that you can't even find any longer on the map. And yet: justice and injustice under Socialism have affected the lives and minds of millions of men and women and have left their mark on peoples' expectations, reflexes, and memories for many years to come. I know no better place to gain access to the daily life that formed these habits and beliefs than the Lüritz archive.

CHAPTER 2

THE BEGINNING

Where shall I start? Why, at the beginning, which in this case also means the end or, as the Germans called it in these years, "the zero hour." But I could find no evidence as to the very first postwar months of my Lüritz story. The earliest case record in the Lüritz archive comes not from Lüritz but from Dorndorf, a little town in the vicinity, in which in August 1945, three-and-a-half months after Germany's unconditional surrender, a "people's court" of unknown provenance resolves two farmers' dispute over the use of a meadow with a sound talking-to and a resulting settlement. Nothing besides the court's unusual name hints at the confusion of the war and postwar years. In fact, Lüritz and its surrounding areas have been under Soviet military administration only since July 1, 1945, when the Western Allies, who arrived here first, agreed with the Russians on the final delineation of their Occupation Zones. The Lüritz museum holds a photograph in which a little girl hands a gigantic bunch of flowers to a Soviet soldier who with a friendly smile bends down to her. The idyll is not persuasive. Everyday postwar life in Lüritz must have looked different. More like this:

The city is overrun by treks of refugees who on their westward flight are looking for food and shelter. A quarter of all living accommodations in Lüritz is destroyed by bombs, another quarter is damaged. The stream of refugees does not flow only from East to West: the city bursts under the back and forth of people who on the other side of their respective border are looking for family members or some other foothold after their world collapsed. Sanitary conditions are faltering: in 1945 and 1946, Lüritz counts 1678 cases of typhoid. In 1947, more than a third of the town's inhabitants are "migrants," most coming from the former Eastern provinces of Germany. The Russians, terrifyingly strange, undisciplined, and unpredictable, are in control. It is hard to imagine how law and the courts might restore order in this chaos.

What law? What courts? On September 4, 1945, the Soviet Military Administration in Germany (SMAD) had ordered the dismissal of all Nazi judges and the reconstruction of the judicial system in its zone, four months before the Allied Control Council decreed a similar policy for all of Germany. But unlike the Western Occupation Forces, the SMAD actually carried out the goal of excluding all former members of the Nazi Party (NSDAP) from the judiciary. For the Russians, the radical cleansing of the courts could serve a double purpose: it removed all supporters and fellow travelers of Hitler from the bench and it made room for a new generation of judges who would not stand in the way of building Socialism but rather support and accelerate the coming of a new society.

For the time being, though, these judges did not yet exist. Before Germany's capitulation on May 8, 1945, of the approximately 2500 judges and prosecutors in the area that was now the Soviet Occupation Zone, about 80% had been members of the NSDAP or its auxiliary bodies.[1] Even of the roughly 500 judges and prosecutors who had managed to stay away from the Nazi Party, not many conformed to the Socialist ideal of a judicial functionary. In the immediate postwar years, most of these "untainted" bourgeois judges absconded to the West. In any case, there had been way too few of them to staff the East German judiciary. On December 17, 1945, the SMAD thus ordered the creation of training courses that in six months (later extended to one and, eventually, two years) would turn capable and, above all, politically reliable, men and women of the people into Socialist judges and prosecutors. Until enough new "people's judges" had been trained, one would have to make do with substitutes: politically "clean" former judges and attorneys now recalled from retirement; judicial trainees preparing for their bar exam; paralegals of all sorts; policemen and other guardians of law and order; and, since the numbers still did not add up to what the state required, "experienced anti-Fascists, workers, and other toilers"[2] without any legal education. One of these stand-in judges must have chaired the "people's court" in Dorndorf when in the fall of 1945 it resolved that dispute between two farmers claiming ownership of the same meadow.

By January 1946, however, that "people's court" no longer exists. On the civil law case records, "Dorndorf" has been crossed out and replaced by "Magistrate Court Lüritz." By now, enough men (they're still all men) could be found in Lüritz to serve as temporary judges at the court. Most of them are familiar to me from the files. There is, first of all, Herr Curtius, the most permanent among a colorful and changing crew. He is sixty-eight years old when the court first opens its doors; shows up first as "Magistrate Judge," then, in 1947, as "Senior Magistrate Judge"; and is apparently a trained attorney now resurrected from retirement who is not compromised by previous NSDAP connections but who— to judge by his decisions—cannot in good faith be called a man of progress either. He remains on the bench until the reorganization of the GDR court system in 1952 and in the next few years occasionally reappears in my files as counsel for one or the other party. Two bourgeois colleagues of Herr Curtius, also trained lawyers and, if their spindly Gothic handwriting does not mislead me, even older than he is, spend a few months each on the Lüritz bench and thereafter vanish. In the spring of 1946, a self-styled "legal advisor" for a short time functions as "judge by designation." Various "judicial trainees" with unspecified training turn up, again "by designation," do primarily divorces, and disappear

CHAPTER 2

again—presumably in the Western direction. A "paralegal assistant" in 1946 has a short walk-on part and returns two years later as "Magistrate Judge": it is Herr Kellner, the first newly trained "people's judge," of the court and in the years to come its self-appointed chief ideologue. In 1950 he is joined by two further "people's judges" and even then the comings and goings at the Lüritz court do not yet quiet down: new judges arrive (from where?), get sick or vanish for other reasons (where to?), are delegated to other courts or borrowed from them. The GDR Administration of Justice cannot afford to be too finicky in its appointments of new staff. Even obviously "bourgeois" judges are tolerated for a while and, to judge by the accounts of their barely trained proletarian colleagues, are much appreciated as helpful sources of legal learning. After all, the work has to be done.

The Lüritz court, in the late 1940s, has indeed a lot of business. That is not so surprising in the area of criminal law: in times that want to bury an old world and create from scratch a new one, neither state nor citizens pay much attention to the "dos and don'ts" of ordinary civil life. The earliest criminal case files in the Lüritz archive date from 1952; my criminal law data on previous years are indirect and patchy. But I have no doubt that those were years in which the criminal law played a visible and scary role. A Lüritz newspaper report from the fall of 1948 speaks of "1138 criminal cases handled by the magistrate court" in the third quarter of the year. Projected onto the whole year, the figure would imply that roughly 4500 crimes were adjudicated in Lüritz in 1948, ten times as many as in 1978 and at this dramatic level not quite plausible, even if the *Lüritz Sentinel* reports that "only 10%" of the offenses were "committed by the local population." Maybe the story can partially be explained by the resentment the good citizens of Lüritz feel towards the hordes of refugees now inundating their town.

Even the civil law files in the archive reveal the extraordinary hold the criminal law has over Lüritz lives in these early years. And if it's not the law, it is the Russian Occupation Force's power to use the law at its pleasure that is reflected even in the records of private law disputes. A surprising number of direct or indirect participants in the proceedings are listed as "in prison." "By judgment of March 7, 1950, the defendant's entire assets have been confiscated," states a brief in a contract case. A woman in a 1947 inheritance dispute writes that in December her husband "was taken by the NKWD" (the Soviet Commissariat for Internal Affairs) and has not yet returned. Another woman is more hopeful: she asks for the postponement of a trial because her husband, a prisoner of war, "is likely to return in the near future." Even in seemingly harmless civil disputes, poverty and grief, like Banquo's ghost, are guests at the court's table. Their miseries do not keep Lüritz citizens from turning to the law for help. In 1946, about 350 civil cases are filed in the Magistrate Court; in 1947, that number has grown to 500; and by 1950, the court has to resolve 788 civil law cases, most of them disputes between citizens. The litigation wave does not last long: in 1953, only 328 new civil cases are filed, and ten years later, only a bare 90. As Socialism in the GDR consolidates, the law loses its usefulness as a protector of private claims. But in its very first years, the court is still a place where Lüritz citizens fight for the few possessions they have left. Destitution and hardship have not dulled the law's usefulness as a weapon, but rather have sharpened it. "I have lost everything," a refugee writes in 1946 in her self-composed brief. "The defendant has been cleaned out by requisitions," a local litigant complains. People go to court in the hope of keeping or regaining possession of one of those few things they have left.

In 1946, about half of the civil suits in Lüritz do not ask for money (which is not worth much in these topsy-turvy times) but for the restitution of objects: maybe a bicycle (the most reliable means of transportation) or a sewing machine (to keep the family clothed). Brothers sue sisters over a wristwatch or some sheets; house owners and the tenants assigned to them by the housing authorities fight over crockery or a piece of furniture; and again and again I encounter suits over livestock between long established farmers and the "new farmers" (*Neubauern*) created by the drastic land reform that assigned tiny land holdings to thousands of refugees and to the local poor. Lawsuits are fought intensely and, at times, with more than a hint of desperation. In 1946, 43% of all civil litigants are assisted by counsel (as conditions settle, those figures will soon drop: in 1950, only 27% of Lüritz litigants are represented by an attorney, and by 1985 representation has dwindled to 11%) and almost half the lawsuits end not in settlements but in a contested judgment (by 1979, that figure, too, has dropped, to 19%). The judges take these fights as seriously as do the parties. In 1946, the court needs several sittings to decide a dispute over a thirty-four-year-old sewing machine and in 1950, it questions nine witnesses about a 125-meter metal cable. Precious possessions!

As it does in criminal matters, the Soviet Occupation Force plays an important role in civil matters, too. It controls not just the social background of these disputes but often is their cause as well. What happens to the legal claims of the sequestered Lüritz carriage factory about to become a victim of the Allied policy of *démontage*? Who owns a cow that a group of Soviet soldiers first took along and then passed on to another German farmer? I catch a lot of glimpses of the Occupation Forces in these files; by plaintiffs and defendants always called "*der Russe*" ("the Russian"), in the singular, which reminds me of that photograph of the Soviet soldier in the town's museum, with his belted jacket and his Cossack's boots (but without the smile). "The Russian" is everywhere and meddles with everything: abducts horses and cows, requisitions cars and leaves them by the roadside when no longer needed, redistributes the taken livestock, and leaves it to the Lüritz court to figure out what in the end is owned by whom.

CHAPTER 2

Herr Curtius and his frequently changing crew of colleagues thus must satisfy the wishes of many different clients and authorities: the citizens who insist on claims to which they still feel themselves entitled; the Occupation Force whose orders and decisions cannot be ignored; the new East German government (I discover the first reference to a plaintiff's Party membership in a brief from August 1946); the letter of the law (mostly old bourgeois statutes from the prewar years); and the demands of a destroyed or impoverished economy in which the loser in a conflict, if not taken care of, might well be unable to recover from his loss. "The urgency of need speaks both for plaintiff and defendant," Herr Curtius writes in a 1949 judgment that tries to resolve a dispute between a mother and a son over the use of an oven in a way that will leave neither party without at least some source of warmth. He must not only find the answer to a legal question but also deal with vital social problems.

Where to find the criteria that could provide some guidance for this kind of emergency- and transition-jurisprudence? While the trained lawyers among the Lüritz judges might apply an inherited bourgeois law in the formalistic fashion they once studied in university, their proletarian colleagues would consider the same text baffling and forbidding. Both the decrees of the Soviet Occupation Force and those of the new East German government are numerous, complex, and frequently, it seems, not even available in printed form. Often, they are only cryptically alluded to. "According to a decree by Marshal Shukov ...," one brief, for instance, claims without any further details, and in another brief a lawyer asserts "that the administration, not very long ago, issued a circular" that would confirm his legal view of the dispute or at least "come close to confirming it." Who knows what's right? ... and so the parties settle. Sometimes, the new local Party authorities (with more or less tact) make their preferences known, and the case file in these instances suggests that the court may be annoyed but that it also may not want to alienate the Comrades.

And so the judges muddle through their cases as best they can. Sometimes it takes a while before they realize which way the wind blows. In March 1946, for instance, Herr Curtius rules that a horse that had been shooed away by Russian soldiers had, in the sense of §935 of the German Civil Code of 1900, been "lost" by its original owner and therefore could not be purchased in good faith by a third person. But already in August 1946 he abandons the unrealistic notion that legal rules are weightier than the acts of the Occupation Powers. "§935 is a provision meant for peace times that does not fit in with conditions caused by war," he now writes. The owner of the horse in question lost his rights solely "due to the fact that members of a foreign army took possession." If the animal is later sold to someone else, the purchaser obtains new and unburdened property. The unfortunate original owner protests against this interpretation of the Code: "Law must stay law, just as injustice will remain injustice, even in times like ours.

Indeed, it should be said that especially in times like ours, it is important to pay extra attention to the law."

Who would not wish it? Like everybody else in the land longing for permanence and order, the judges, too, in many of these cases show sympathy for the former owner. The legal rule—acts of the Occupation Powers create new and unencumbered property—will soon be undisputed judicial practice in the entire GDR. But courts try to soften its harshness, if they can: push for settlements that also leave the loser with some benefit or award him a consolation prize to compensate a little for the loss of ownership rights that virtually everyone in the courtroom still appreciates. In our horse case, the original owner appeals Herr Curtius' decision and manages, at the appellate level, to obtain a settlement that leaves the horse with its new purchaser but that awards the first foal the mare will bear to its original owner. In a similar dispute about a cow, decided—also in 1946—by one of Herr Curtius' colleagues, the cow remains with the farmer who received it, out of the blue, from some Russian soldiers, but the court also obligates him to assume some of the milk delivery obligations of the loser, also a farmer, who now, with one cow less, has trouble fulfilling his targets.

There is something down to earth and old-fashioned about these decisions; a whiff of Grimms' fairy tales. The world is out of joint, but its inhabitants continue to hold on to the values they were raised with: property, authority, tradition, discipline, order. In the civil law records of the early years, plaintiffs and defendants are identified by their occupation: "the cartwright Müller," "the farmer Schulze." Women are defined by the men in their lives: "Frau Lehmann, a civil servant's daughter"; "Frau Meyer, a baker's widow." As I can tell by his child support and paternity decisions, Herr Curtius views women with the eyes of a patriarch from the Kaiser's days. But his colleague Herr Kellner, one of the new people's judges and a noisy Socialist, is not much better. Both men are bourgeois moralists and easily shocked by bohemian life styles. The language of the early files uses a mixture of old and new. I find virtually no citations of code sections or of previous case law. If nothing else avails, the court appeals to "today's democratic legal values." But it may also, without embarrassment, use judicial formulas from the preceding years: references to "the convictions of the *Volk*," its "healthy sense of law," the "healthy *Volk* view." The court's model citizen is "a decent fellow."

Above all, the judges in these years are practical. "There is no point in stumbling over sections of the code," Herr Curtius writes in a 1948 case that also has attracted the attention of the Lüritz SED Leadership and comes out in favor of that side which is supported by the Party. But mostly it is not politics but ordinary plain good sense that motivates the court's decisions. "No one will be so stupid as to pour valuable sugar into some other person's gas tank," I read in a tort suit of 1949. Or in a 1947 judgment: "These days no reasonable person will

CHAPTER 2

give away valuable objects without getting something in return." Maybe I find so relatively few references to ideology in the very early case law because nobody is certain of the future. Change lies in the air. But change in which direction?

Everything seems uncertain and contradictory: like the Lüritz bench, with proletarian and bourgeois judges working side by side; like the hodgepodge of confusing laws and edicts on which they base their case law; like the court's staff and like its litigants who any night might disappear by going West. Everyday political life in Lüritz is no exception from the general uncertainty. In August 1947, the SED arranges in Gram, the district's capital, a meeting at which (if the local newspaper's report is to be believed) more than 1000 citizens protest against "too lenient" sentences for speculators and demand to know "who is responsible for the release from prison of the fence and swindler Bergeman." The Party seems to threaten and to warn the courts in order to ensure their good behavior. But seven months later, again in Gram, the very same newspaper reports on the first decision of the district's new Administrative Court that in a bourgeois craftsman's suit against the Ministry of Agriculture sides with the plaintiff. We know today that this and other administrative courts that in the early postwar years were established in the Soviet Occupation Zone did not survive for long. But Lüritz citizens (Herr Curtius not excluded) who read their paper over breakfast in those days could be forgiven for wondering whether, maybe, East German courts might not soon gain in influence. Most newspaper reports dealing with law describe criminal trials for sabotage. But in the late 1940, the penalties for economic crimes were still measured in prison-months, and not, as the 1950, in years of hard labor. Occasionally, a story might add some silver lining to the political clouds on the horizon, such as an article of March 1949, announcing an amnesty for farmers who had underreported their land holdings. In 1946, the Lüritz defendant in a suit for child support lists among his expenses the same amounts for church tax as for Party dues: 1.50 Marks a month. Can anybody at this time predict how the situation will develop?

Herr Curtius and his frequently changing staff at the Lüritz *Amtsgericht* cannot, and so they live, in legal terms, from hand to mouth and fashion their decisions to suit the moment. But there is one constant factor, after all, persisting in the general disorder. I notice it while reading a brief from 1946 complaining about the freezing of the writer's bank account because of her alleged close connections to the Nazis. It was not she who had a Nazi past, it was her sister; her own political behavior was beyond reproach. "It cannot be," the plaintiff writes, "that the Party should cause me to lose all my money." For a second I am puzzled. Should the SED have intervened in the affair? But then I realize: it was not this party the plaintiff had in mind. She meant the other one: the NSDAP. But the matter-of-factness of the woman's choice of word—just "Party," as if no further adjective was needed to describe such a manifest and powerful reality—makes me understand how seamless Lüritz citizens' transition from one to the other "Party" must have been; how little time they had to catch their breath between one and the next totalitarian government, and how inexperienced in the practices of self-determination that are a precondition for the rule of law they were. Socialism left them far more room for human kindness than Hitler's National Socialism had done. But the individual's subjection to the state shaped the law in Lüritz for more than half a century.

CHAPTER 3

PEOPLE

By 1950, and certainly no later than 1952 (when the SED at its Second Party Conference decided to launch "the construction of Socialism"), people in Lüritz can no longer have had doubts about the future direction of their country. But before continuing my story, I want to pause to introduce some of its protagonists. Imagine looking at the cast list before the curtain rises on a play. In our case, it is the judges of the Lüritz district court who give some continuity to a long and uneven sequence of developments. Over time, their values and their legal arguments will change. But their human relationships and problems will remain.

The judges are not the only actors in my story. There will be parts for others, often continuing over many years. The lawyers, for example, play important roles. For decades, two attorneys had their offices in Lüritz, with a third joining them in 1984—today, there are over fifty. Even without looking at their letterheads or signatures, I know them well enough to recognize their work just by their reasoning styles. Then there is Herr Kosewitz, for twenty-eight years First Party Secretary in the district, whom everybody is aware of even if he plays his role largely behind the scenes. As plaintiffs and defendants, Lüritz citizens have mostly walk-on parts, although often at crucial moments of the action. But it is the judges whom we will encounter at every turning of the road: as symbols, as actors, occasionally as victims, and, always most important, as sources of information for my story.

I can't claim to know all the judges equally well. Those who spent just a short time at the court often are no more than names for me: Frau Dörig, for example, who in 1953, after no more than a year in office, lost her post because her daughter had absconded to the West; Herr Hansen, who in 1971 came from Berlin, was housed in a storeroom in the courthouse's gigantic attic, drank more than he should have, and soon disappeared; or Herr Kleinfeld, according to a people's judge's report "one of the old guard" with "beautifully manicured hands" and "very gentle" in his criticism when one of his proletarian colleagues on the bench had made a legal blunder. But the main actors, those judges who stayed on for many years, seem like old acquaintances even if I met them only in the files. One cannot read innumerable judgments of a person without forming an impression of his or her character.

There is Frau Christiansen, for example, a people's judge since 1951 and a war widow with two small children. In her first year in office she rejects the alimony claim of a divorced woman who has moved to West Germany and now sues for the support that under the law of both Germanies her adulterous husband owed her at the time. Because women now have equal rights, they should be obligated to support themselves, writes Frau Christiansen. Neither the East German Court of Appeals (that overruled Frau Christiansen's judgment) nor her own later verdicts stuck to this uncompromising notion of gender equality. But Frau Christiansen's reasons in this early case reflect the convictions of a woman who had to learn to stand on her own two feet and therefore can encourage another women who, like herself, has to learn to master her own problems: "The plaintiff will only find true happiness in life if she applies her own abilities to a kind of work that suits her."

Frau Christiansen speaks from the heart. The ideological admonitions of her colleague, Herr Kellner, a people's judge since 1948 and always handy with political platitudes, do not sound warm and human, but didactic. In November 1958, for instance, he complains in a letter to the Ministry of Justice that a recent shipment of instructional materials had arrived late and, worse, had contained some serious errors. "On page 6 paragraph 3, there is mention of the fact that the Vth Party Congress decreed the construction of Socialism. This, too, is evidence of sloppy work. The Vth Party Congress decreed the victory of Socialism."

And finally there is Frau Rüstig, a people's judge since 1953 and a third-generation Communist, who speaks of Socialism as the gospel of good tidings. In a 1963 judgment that declares void a farmer's attempt to rescind a contract by which he had acquired membership in an agricultural cooperative, Frau Rüstig advises the defendant not to let the collective's present messy state overshadow its rosy future. Instead of "focusing on current conditions, he should put his whole strength at the service of the collective's program for the future. Then the defendant, too, would soon enjoy the benefits of agricultural innovation under Socialism."

Three different forms of reasoning, three different Socialists. Like the reader of a novel, I discover likes and dislikes for the protagonists of my files. Frau Christiansen, self-confident, unsentimental, her handwriting round and firm, elicits my respect. When writing to superiors, she speaks of herself without embarrassment as "I." Frau Rüstig is more eager and more pious, and worries more whether she does things right. In letters to those above her she refers to herself as "the undersigned." Herr Kellner, self-righteous and authoritarian, seems to doubt neither himself nor the true doctrine. I cannot stand him.

What I learn about Lüritz judges in the files I supplement with narratives from eyewitnesses. By far my best informant is Frau Rüstig: originally a cigar maker by training; then a student at the last (now two-year long) instruction program

CHAPTER 3

for people's judges in Bad Schandau, and from her graduation in 1953 to her retirement in 1980, a judge at the District Court in Lüritz. She is seventy-four when we first meet in 1994: a small and wiry woman, with unstoppable energy, still fully convinced that Socialism got it right and yet curious and eager to learn about the new times that have overtaken it. Frau Rüstig knows everything and everybody. It is she who tells me about Judge Kleinfeld's manicured hands: as in other revolutionary times, the proletarian had remembered the smooth, uncalloused hands of privilege. I know from Frau Rüstig that both Herr Kellner and Herr Teubner, another early people's judge in Lüritz, under the Nazis had spent several years in prison. Frau Rüstig has even shown me a photograph of Frau Christiansen: a beautiful, tall, heavy woman, exuding strength. We will meet her repeatedly in these pages.

Not all the Lüritz people's judges were working class; Frau Christiansen, for example, by training a secretary, seems to have come from a middle-class family. But all were linked by an education that was firm on politics though wobbly about the law. The fact that they had lived together, boarding-school style, during their training courses may have created further ties between them. Frau Rüstig got to know her later husband (for a while also a judge in Lüritz) during her training course, and friendships from those years also existed between other Lüritz judges and prosecutors. In many ways the people's judges remind me of the kibbutzniks of the early years in Israel: a sworn little group of likeminded people with the unshakeable belief of being in the right. They miss no chance to praise the accomplishments of Socialism in their judgments: "It must be borne in mind that due to our toilers' reconstruction efforts our workers' and farmers' state has seen a considerable drop in prices" (1953). They do not hesitate to reject claims that they disapprove of for reasons of political morality. In 1952 Herr Kellner dismisses the suit of a restaurant owner for payment of 69.85 Marks that the defendant spent on drinks as immoral "exploitation": "Innkeepers should offer their clients rest and relaxation; not cause them misery just to turn a profit. Society will need a person's labor power also the next morning." Herr Curtius, only three years earlier, had had no qualms enforcing the alcohol debt of another tippler (at 890.20 Marks more than twelve times as high) by classifying it as a "loan." But people's judges believe in the utopia of a new and better world. Or is it not utopian if Frau Christiansen, in 1958, applies to the authorities for the installation of a central heating system in the gigantic, icy, and completely unheatable Lüritz courthouse? As to be expected, the central heating stays a dream. More than thirty-five years later, when I first come to Lüritz, in winter, buckets full of coal are carefully aligned on the steps of the entry hall so that the janitor, at the crack of dawn, can feed the large tiled stoves dispersed throughout the building.

PEOPLE

The early people's judges struggled not with politics but with the law. Although she attended not one of the very early training courses but the final one, which lasted two full years, Frau Rüstig never lost her fear of the Civil Code. The German *Bürgerliches Gesetzbuch* (BGB) of 1900 stayed in force in the GDR until its own new Civil Code was passed in 1975. With more than 2400 highly abstract sections, the BGB is the very model of bourgeois conceptual perfectionism. It gave not just Frau Rüstig trouble. People's judges did not like to get involved in questions of jurisdiction, subsumption or concurrences and found it much easier to warm to legal concepts with some obvious human meaning, such as the general provisions of the BGB that speak of "good faith" or "immorally inflicted harm" that they could reinterpret to fit new proletarian values. Most court decisions in these years were sweet and short, often filling no more than half a page. A Lüritz plaintiff, whose sixty-three pages of detailed legal arguments the District Court had dispatched with a mere third of a page of reasons, complained in 1953: "The court's arguments for rejecting my suit are extraordinarily skimpy." Upon appeal, he obtained at least a settlement. The courts of appeal, too, often were dissatisfied with the performance of their trial courts; pre-1952, the old Appellate Court in Gram no less than, post-1952, the new Regional Court in Neuburg (both courts located, by the way, in the recently re-christened *Stalin-Strasse* of their towns). Judicial inspectors kept complaining about the many professional and ideological shortcomings of the people's judges: too short decisions, too lax accounting practices, too mild (or, occasionally, too severe) sentences, too unreliable orthography, too many ideological confusions. "District Judge Schlumm has to be tightly supervised," I read in the 1953 report of one of the revisors. "Needs guidance," is his assessment of one of Herr Schlumm's colleagues. In 1954, an inspector from the Regional Court in Neuburg comes once a week to review Frau Rüstig's work and, if necessary, to correct it.

I don't get the impression that the Lüritz people's judges resent the supervision as illegitimate interference with their own affairs. It is not their "own affairs," after all, that are at stake, but the construction of a new society that must be planned and carefully controlled by people more experienced than they are themselves. If I read the files right, the Lüritz judges of these years do not think of themselves primarily as jurists (which they are only to a limited extent) but as handmaidens of a new age. When their work is done, they don't go home but travel the countryside to recruit new members for the agricultural cooperatives, encourage women to find outside work, or explain to baffled parents at a village meeting that physical punishment will harm their children. People's judges are missionaries of Socialism. They see to it that nobody will stray from the right path. When in 1962 at one of the District Court's weekly advice evenings someone complains about a neighbor who every night goes out to live it up in town, Frau Christiansen writes into the court's log book: "It must be ascertained how the woman makes her money." The judge is not embarrassed to also serve as a policeman. People's judges served the Party in whatever capacity and place they could be useful.

But they served the Party for the noble goals that it pursued. Because they believed in the righteousness of Socialism, people's judges were dependent on the ideological authority of their superior comrades. "I've always thought of it as a kind of pyramid," Frau Rüstig once explained to me. "Those higher up than I could see much farther." But their belief in their good cause also gave people's judges a sense of self-security and a fund of moral values that, paradoxically, made them far less dependent on those above them than their better educated and less faithful successors were. In the late 1950s and early 1960s, for example, Frau Rüstig and Frau Christiansen frequently tussle with the Lüritz prosecutors and police over the accuracy and legality of criminal investigations. In 1958 Frau Rüstig finds herself at odds with the Supreme Court because she is not willing to convict a defendant *in absentia* (he had since managed to escape to the Federal Republic) without inquiring into the fact (well known by all in Lüritz) that he had been brutally beaten by the police. The Supreme Court wanted to leave this aspect of the story uninvestigated. A report by an inspector from the Ministry of Justice criticizes "the dismal lack of Party spirit" at the Lüritz District Court in this and other cases. Frau Rüstig, when I ask her about the matter, does not at all remember it as political confrontation between a young people's judge and the highest court in the land. "Oh yes," she says, when I finally show her the copy of a scathing letter from the Supreme Court that is part of the case file. "I got into a lot of trouble with this case." But why? Because, as she remembers it, she had referred to the police unit involved not with its official title—"Rapid Response Squad"—but with the popular term—"mugging squad" (*Überfallkommando*). The trusting memory of the loyal Socialist had expunged her superiors' illegality and retained only her own linguistic blunder.

It was to be expected that the simple straightforwardness of the early people's judges could not for long resist the pressures from above. Their world view was grounded in human experience and proletarian solidarity, but it was vulnerable because the people's judges lacked the professional tools they would have needed to defend their gut reactions with jurisprudential arguments. I can trace the loss of proletarian spontaneity by looking at the criminal law statistics. In 1952, Lüritz judges deviated in 49% of all criminal cases from the prosecution's penalty suggestions—virtually always in favor of the defendant. Already in 1959, that figure had dropped to 15% and by 1979, Lüritz judges handed out different penalties than those suggested by the prosecution in only 9% of all criminal cases (still almost exclusively to the defendant's advantage). As people's judges at my Lüritz courthouse are replaced by professionals trained at the new law faculties of the GDR, their case law becomes technically more proficient, less colorful, and better adapted to the political conventions of the moment.

In 1965, Rolf Taddäus is appointed head of the District Court: its first university-trained director. Already the previous year, a professional jurist had been delegated to the Lüritz bench and from now on, professionals are slowly replacing the crash-course people's judges. By 1976, Frau Rüstig is the only people's judge left on the court. Like all her other colleagues from the training courses, she had to take correspondence courses in order to earn, by 1960, her university diploma. But even the new degree could not eliminate the whiff of proletarian directness and simplicity that the newer judges did not have. Until her retirement in May 1980, Frau Rüstig remained the representative of a heroic time that with great effort tried to change the world. The new professional judges at the Lüritz District Court seem pleased to have escaped these arduous years.

I know several of them from personal conversations: Herr Taddäus, a tall and brooding man who makes life difficult for himself and others; Frau Walter, judge since 1973 and director of the District Court since 1984, a smart, critical, and acerbic woman; Frau Neuman, labor law specialist and a sensible and skillful judge. But despite having met them all in person, I find it difficult to describe this middle generation of Lüritz judges as a group. They did not share the common boarding-school experience of the people's judges; they also, or so it seems to me, did not share their uncomplicated and unquestioned faith in Socialism. The biographies of the judges from the 1960 and 1970 look smoother, easier, but also more confined than those of their predecessors from the immediate postwar years. The people's judges came to office before the Berlin Wall was built: they joined the bench because they had decided not to run away but to commit themselves to the service of a new society. The post-Wall judges entered their careers in a state that would not let them leave. Where should a shared political belief have come from?

As a result, these judges mostly seem the product of their personal histories. Frau Walter, the only Socialist in a Catholic worker's family, was drawn to law by her sense of justice and her gratitude toward a state that enabled her to be the first member of her family to get a university education. Frau Neuman was won over by the solicitude of Socialist labor law. I cannot tell what fueled Herr Taddäus' choice of a profession. He left the judiciary in 1984 at his own initiative— as he describes it, because he was "fed up with everything"—but his departure could not have succeeded without the Party's help and was at least partially motivated by Herr Taddäus' conflicts with his colleagues and his animosity toward the director of the Regional Court in Neuburg, an able, bright, and bossy woman. Still, there are some commonalities even among the judges of the middle generation. They all grew to adulthood in a Socialism that seemed to gain in

CHAPTER 3

strength and permanence and shared, I think, its basic faith in social justice and in the authority of the Party and the state.

The youngest generation of judges at the District Court, who at the time of the *Wende* had held their office for only a few years, believed in not much more than that it was the obligation of the state to provide for the basic creature needs of its citizens. To me this generation appears more professional and flexible, but also more materialistic and cynical than the generation of their parents. Take Gisela Nissen, for example, a Lüritz judge since 1981 and the daughter of Ruth Nissen, who since 1978 has been director of the Neuburg Regional Court and in this capacity embodies the authority on which my Lüritz judges are most dependent and of which they, probably, are most afraid. The mother, intelligent, energetic, and demanding of herself and others, is the product of a Socialism that with its benign and its malign characteristics was focused on the *longue durée*. In our conversation we talk about the hopes and disappointments of a legal system insistent on achieving utopian goals. The daughter is softer than her mother, more adaptable and with less sense of direction. She does not give the impression that the collapse of Socialism caused her to lose something close to her heart. I have difficulties steering our conversation to topics other than the sales prices for television sets. The junior Frau Nissen and her young colleague, Herr Rodewaldt (judge since 1987 and the only one to survive the Turnabout professionally), are the children of a tired, disappointed, and discontented Socialism. They no longer see why their own hopes and plans should be subservient to those of society. They are sick of their restrictions. Herr Rodewaldt tells me how in the summer of 1989 he had been entangled in a dispute with a neighbor over the use of a garage. When negotiations failed, he had brought suit against him. But Frau Walter, as the District Court's director, had simply removed his complaint from the docket. "A judge does not bring suit," she had said: a functionary of the state does not engage in fights with other citizens but serves as role model to all. There had been a Party meeting at the courthouse at which Herr Rodewaldt was told " to not push his personal interests into the foreground." That lesson has since become outmoded. Herr Rodewaldt and Frau Nissen seem relieved.

I have drawn the portraits of judges from three different generations, who over the years defined what justice meant in Lüritz and who, together with their definitions, changed themselves. But I should not exaggerate the differences between the periods. Almost more important than the ideological shifts and changes was the permanence of their practical surroundings, which for forty years determined the existence of all Lüritz judges, whether young or old, faithful or not: the poverty, privations, and constrictions of the East German judiciary. I don't know where to begin. There were the worries about the courthouse building. In 1956 parts of its roof cave in. Even twenty years later the damage is only provisionally patched because there are either no funds or—even if funds are provided in the annual plan—no building capacities to allow for a proper restoration. The bricks that would match the old building are unavailable; the chimneys are at the end of their life span; the gutters can no longer hold the rain. "Greenland on the courthouse roof," the *Lüritz Sentinel* reports in November 1962. In 1977, the timber to repair the roof has finally been delivered but the beams lie rotting in the courthouse yard because no roofers can be found to do the work. A patch-up job of 1979 proves useless when after the first rainstorm the roof leaks worse than ever. Herr Taddäus threatens the city's building department with a petition to the Ministry of Justice. Only in 1980 is part of the attic structure replaced—the complete rehabilitation of the building will have to wait for the arrival of Capitalism. The Lüritz District Court is not the only crumbling courthouse in East Germany. In 1988, GDR Minister of Justice Heusinger complains that the condition of 248 judicial buildings in the country is "close to intolerable."

There are also the heating problems. The damp and drafty Lüritz palace of justice is impossible to warm. In 1963, coal is still rationed in the GDR. The court hoards its "precious coke" for the periods when the thermometer dips below the freezing point. On other winter days, the courthouse ovens are stoked with brown coal and with peat. "Please store your combustibles early in the year," the Lüritz city council advises the court in May 1962; "any demands for additional provisions during the heating period are pointless." When it becomes obvious that Frau Christiansen's dream of a central heating system was indeed just a dream, the court in 1973 is finally allotted 30,000 Marks for night-storage heaters. In 1976 it seems that the units have arrived. But electricity is in short supply. "The storage hours for electric heaters are to be reduced from eight to seven hours a night," a circular from the Ministry of Justice prescribes in October 1979. Another circular from 1981: "In preparation for the weekend, the temperature of e-heaters is to be turned down to level I already on Friday mornings." Fortunately, the Lüritz court has kept some of its old tile ovens. One of them stands in the corner of the room in which, in the winter of 1996, I brood over my case files. From time to time, I rise from my cold desk to warm my back against its toasty wall.

What else is lacking? Even in 1959, the court does not have access to its own car; if necessary, judges are given rides in the car of the district prosecutor and pay for gas. A shipment of 1500 arrest warrants is damaged in the post because for want of packing paper, the printing office could not wrap it properly. My files do not reveal how many of the warrants have gone missing. In 1960, the court's vacuum cleaner breaks down; a new one is not to be found for love or money. By 1979, the court owns its own car, an old Moskowitch, but it cannot buy new tires for it because "under current conditions, the court cannot draw on tire allotments assigned to the general public." In the same year, the court's secretarial office is ordered "to issue new ballpoints only upon return of empty ballpoint leads." As late as September 1989, the Lüritz police apply for the extension of the deadline in a criminal investigation because the necessary copying of documents "due to technical difficulties cannot be carried out on time." In other words: the only Xeroxing machine has broken down again.

Can it be a surprise that in this poor man's world the GDR courts are permanently understaffed? They are short of bailiffs, secretaries, cleaning ladies, custodians. Even state-owned enterprises pay more than the Administration of Justice. In 1983, the court's typing office lacks half its regular employees; civil litigants have to wait months to receive copies of their judgments. In December 1988 the Regional Court directs its district courts to advertise, for want of cleaning staff, their unfilled housekeeping jobs among the courthouse colleagues; the offered payments are 10.00 Marks per toilet, 50 Pfennig per square meter of mopped floor.

Judges, too, are in short supply. They earn less than legal counsel in the state-owned economy or than attorneys. When Frau Walter joins the court as a young judge in 1973, she makes 900 Marks, before taxes, a month; by 1980, her pay has risen to 1320 Marks and by 1985, in her new job as director, to 1500 Marks. By GDR standards, judges' working hours are long: they have to be present in the courthouse from 7 AM to 4 PM, often followed by additional obligations such as conducting training sessions for lay assessors, public relations work, or visits to enterprises. Add to that Party meetings and the regular attendance at legal education and training sessions of all kinds. Thus, since the days of the people's judges, the Ministry of Justice had difficulties rounding up sufficient candidates for a career in the judiciary. It offered too little room for developing one's own strengths and ambitions. Young people with drive preferred jobs in the state economy; the most energetic and capable law students hoped to join one of the fifteen attorneys' collectives (*Rechtsanwalts Kollegien*) in the country. In 1972, a working paper of the Ministry of Justice complains that "what used to be called the 'solid type of judge' has almost disappeared" in the GDR. "Solid"? East German judges, in their own way, seem "solid" enough: diligent, cooperative, disciplined. But they are not imaginative; they have learned to adapt to the limits of their world; they don't glitter. Again, the working paper of the Ministry of Justice: for young people currently leaving high school, "admission to law school often is a second choice because the more desirable places of study have already been taken by the most gifted applicants." The paper's author, in bemoaning the loss of the "solid type of judge," seems to miss the self-confident and independent members of the bench whom East German legal policy itself by way of bossing, spoon feeding, and keeping its judges on a tight leash and a meager budget, reduced to the modest functionaries now in judicial office. "We were nothing special," an East Berlin judge once explained to me. Adjudication was a social service job.

The various directors of the Lüritz District Court thus did not find it easy to round up enough candidates to fill the posts. In the GDR, law students were recruited before their graduation from high school but began their studies at Humboldt University in Berlin only after completing their mandatory military service. Young women usually had to take up some industrial job before they could enter university. It was the district courts' task to identify suitable candidates for the judiciary among the local high school leavers. Herr Taddäus, and after him Frau Walter, explored the Lüritz schools for likely prospects. Ideally, judges should come from working-class families (so the share of judges with a working-class background matched the share of workers in the entire population); they should be male (because the number of women in the GDR judiciary began to outpace that of men); they should be Communists (or at least ready to join the Party); have no connections to West Germany (because a judge ought to have no "contact problems"); and, to top it all, they should be less interested in money than in their service to society. Where to find such people? In May 1978, Herr Taddäus responds with obvious annoyance to a renewed request by the Regional Court for still more names: "In view of the fact that in the past, I have found applicants willing to study law in almost every year, I consider the most recent demands for additional recruits to be moot." But he is lucky: four months later, a young mechanic from the Lüritz shipyard who, simultaneously with his apprenticeship, was working for his high school graduation and who had no links to the FRG, had unexpectedly turned up. "He is willing to join our Party of workers and farmers," Herr Taddäus proudly reports to the Regional Court. No, this was no dream job. And yet judges had important roles to play in the dream that Socialism had set out to realize: the dream of a more just society.

CHAPTER 4

PROPERTY

I will organize my search for justice in Lüritz by areas of law, just like an archeologist will rope off individual areas of his terrain before beginning with the digging, in order to make sure that none of the artifacts that may be buried in the ground will escape him. The corner where my own search should begin, I think, is property law. Socialism was focused, or maybe I should say fixated, on property in ways that remind me of Christianity's preoccupation with sin. Without sin, no need for salvation. Without property, or without the kind of property that Capitalism had produced, no need for a social system that would undo its aberrations: the exploitation of those who owned nothing but their ability to work by those who owned the machinery to work with; the schizophrenic split of human beings into a self-possessed private and a public persona; a concept of freedom that, in Marx's words, seemed to delineate "the elbow room of the individual Capitalist." And just as the wordly law for Christians, in the words of Martin Luther, was meant "to keep sin in check," the law under Socialism had the task of keeping its citizens' possessive greed in check.

It's not as if the war had not already wrought havoc on the distribution of property in Lüritz. But it had not changed the fact that this was still a small-town, partially agrarian society in which property and order were close cousins. Ownership legitimated. Those who had lost everything hoped to regain it in the future. The tensions between the locals and the refugees in Lüritz were also tensions between people with and without property. In the beginning, Socialism's attacks on property seemed to favor the refugees who had lost everything. In the end, Socialist law assaulted the rights and possibilities of all citizens in Lüritz to accumulate and use property according to their own abilities and plans.

The incursions came in waves: the expropriations of Nazis and war criminals (and of those who might fit that description) soon after the war had ended; the nationalization of the most important industries; the Land Reform that by early 1949 had seized more than three million hectares formerly belonging to the large estates of aristocracy and gentry, redistributing more than half that land among 210,000 *Neubauern* ("new farmers") who each on average received a plot of eight hectares.[3] The intrusions of the planning system made it increasingly more difficult for private enterprises to compete with the state economy. The criminal law became an important ally in the transformation of society and, especially in the first years of the new plans, punished even minor violations of state property with lengthy prison terms. Rent control and the new landlord-and-tenant law transformed house ownership from an asset into a financial burden.

To what extent did law and its application by the Lüritz court help to change people's everyday experience of their "property"? Was law still useful to defend it against invasions by fellow citizens or by the state? Did state property rank higher than an individual's personal property? Did the law succeed in collectivizing the concept of property: did individual possessions lose in attractiveness and did the property that served general social interests gain in citizens' esteem?

What law? The expropriations and the Land Reform were outside the reach of law and courts. The Central Administration of Justice (which in the early postwar years organized and steered the judicial system of the Soviet Occupation Zone) did not even attempt to domesticate the enormous transformation of the East German economic system with the help of law. "The Central Judicial Administration has no jurisdiction in these matters," its eighty-five-year-old chief executive Dr. Eugen Schiffer (by political affiliation a Liberal) wrote in response to a letter by a lawyer from a town near Lüritz who had requested that his client be allowed to keep at least a tiny portion of his estate that had just been expropriated. Even a younger man than Dr. Schiffer would have been unable to resist the pressures that politics exerted on the law. The Land Reform "is part of a revolution that cannot be regulated by the sections of a code," an expert opinion issued by the Saxon Ministry of Justice declared in 1948. I find some 1949 and 1950 case law in the Lüritz archive in which the court, in disputes between citizens who obtained their land through the Land Reform, does not directly question the reassignment of land by state authorities but nevertheless tries, as it were, to redirect a public-law dispute onto a civilist track by enforcing claims based on contract law or on a plot's entry in the official land registry. "I don't quite understand who has the final say in these matters: is it the Land Commission or the court?" a *Neubauer* writes in 1950. A proper child of his times, he does not want to pay for a cow that had belonged to the small land holding he had just acquired from its previous owner, also one of the "new farmers." And the court gives him the answer that he wants to hear: not the judges, but the Land Commission is in control. Herr Curtius dismisses the previous owner's contract suit for lack of jurisdiction. In August 1951, a decision of the East German Supreme Court settles for good the question of who is competent to resolve disputes connected with the Land Reform: the state economic agencies. Not only the administrative expropriation and redistribution of property is outside the courts' control but also "the resolution of all disputes connected with these government decisions."[4]

That means that a "new farmer" cannot, through litigation, enforce a legal claim that might arise from his succession to a farm that had been created by the

CHAPTER 4

Land Reform. He certainly can't sue the state for any illegalities occurring in the process of transferring the farm from one *Neubauer* to the next. But that does not mean that the law no longer plays a role in the farmer's life. The debts that he incurred by borrowing from state and collective service organizations and money lenders in order to keep his little farm afloat continue to be legally enforceable: payments for seeds or fertilizer obtained from state or collective bodies specializing in farm supplies; the costs of threshing or plowing services provided by the new "machine and tractor stations" that, Soviet-style, offered help to farmers who did not own agricultural machines; loans from the (state-owned) "German Farmers' Bank." Most *Neubauern* managed only with great difficulty (and often only temporarily) to keep their modest enterprises in the black. Their holdings of roughly eight hectares usually were too small to be cultivated at a profit. The "new farmers" lacked farm hands, livestock, and the most elementary machinery. Those who had come as refugees from the former Eastern provinces of Germany (about a third of all "new farmers") often also lacked the good relationships with local farmers who otherwise might have provided advice and help. Twenty-nine percent of all *Neubauern* had no agricultural experience. Many were women who had lost their husbands in the war or who were still waiting for their return from military prison camps.[5] As a result, a large number of "new farmers" ran up debts that led to litigation many years after the original loans—comparable to the fall-out of a big explosion whose sound and fury has abated long ago but whose rubble still clogs roads and sidewalks.

The Lüritz files from the *Neubauern* years make the new "property" look more like a burden than a right. The self-made proletarian farmers struggle to survive: if someone's husband runs away or if his wife dies, the person left behind can no longer manage on his or her own. They do not make enough to pay their bills. "I ask the court to forgive my debt because I have nothing left," writes an old woman who from her monthly pension of 75 Marks is expected to pay arrears of 698 Marks for fodder that she bought years ago from the state-owned agricultural clearinghouse. Many *Neubauern* flee West. "I, the farmer Walter Arnold, erstwhile from Birkenhof near Dornburg, have left the GDR for economic reasons because after my wife's death I am no longer able to farm my land," one of the fugitives writes to the court in 1955. Many "new farmers" simply capitulate or lose their run-down farm when the authorities transfer it to another candidate. "They took my farm just before harvest time," somebody writes in 1955 to challenge a four-year-old debt allegedly owed a machine and tractor station for past repairs, and another debtor states: "The local agricultural authorities repossessed my farm. They also assumed the debts."

But often, such excuses do not pass legal scrutiny. The court is finicky if public money is involved and accepts debt assumptions only if there is a proper contract of transferal to which the old owner of the farm, its new owner, and the creditor all must have consented. I find very few contracts of this sort in the Lüritz records. The government agencies administering the "new farmers" program show no more understanding for legal formality and precision than the farmers do. In the resulting muddle it can happen that someone is sued for debts related to a farm that he had long since handed over to another farmer or the state. "Up to this day I never saw a bill or any other form of accounting," complains a butcher who in 1955 is sued for a debt for fertilizer that he incurred four years ago during a short and chaotic spell as a "new farmer." In 1958 the German Farmers' Bank wins a suit to retrieve an agricultural loan from a woman who after her divorce in 1954 abandoned her "new farm" that since had been assigned to two new owners, both of whom in the meantime had absconded to the West. None of the re-assignments had been documented by a proper "protocol of transferal." But the original recipient of the farm was still recorded as its "owner" in the Land Registry, and the court, when it comes to the enforcement of state interests, is quite willing to treat *Neubauer* "ownership" according to the rules applying to old-fashioned bourgeois real estate. But from the viewpoint of the farmers, the "ownership" of their Land Reform allotments looks more like an inferior kind of service property that brings more responsibilities than rights. It cannot even be abandoned at will. When in 1952 a settler, after six years of hard labor on his plot, "renounces" his property rights and moves to Lüritz because his wife refuses to any longer struggle with the work, he is prosecuted under the "Decree on Economic Crimes" of 1948 for "willful desertion" of a "new farm" and sentenced to six months in prison. "It is unacceptable if a farmer, just because he feels like it, casts off his settlement," the outraged judge says in his decision.

But even the criminal law cannot prevent the collapse of the *Neubauern* program. Exhausted farmers leave their settlements with or without obtaining the permission of the authorities, who then proceed to reassign the land and livestock with or without the proper legal documentation, until no one can tell any longer who is responsible for the accumulated bills. Here is a description of a woman who in 1959 is sued by the German Farmers' Bank for payment of five years of interest on a loan:

> I bought on credit a heifer, a cow, and also a horse. The horse died soon thereafter. The two cows I handed over together with my farm in 1952. I didn't get any payment for the cattle. I don't know what happened to the buildings on my settlement. I wasn't remunerated for the buildings either. There never was a protocol of transferal. No officials from the district council or the village were present when I handed over the land. I sent all the documentation that I had to the district council. Since then, I haven't heard from them. My land was divided up between several farmers; I did not ask for the deletion of my

CHAPTER 4

name in the Land Registry because I thought the district council would take care of that."

And so she is still listed as the "owner" in the Registry: a sixty-four-year-old housewife who had a short and bygone walk-on part in the GDR's dramatic enterprise to create landownership for everyone.

But now, in 1959, even the court does not attempt to save the "new farmers" policy: the bank's suit is dismissed for lack of evidence. By now, the establishment of new agricultural cooperatives (LPGs) is running at full steam that had been initiated in 1952—first on a voluntary basis, then increasingly with psychological and economic pressures and the occasional physical intimidation—and is soon to be completed. Despite the rough tactics of the agitators, many "new farmers" join the new cooperatives with a sigh of relief. The collectivization of East Germany's agriculture distributes the previously lone work of the *Neubauern* onto many shoulders. It offers a regular workday and a number of household services (attractive to the women) and promises a way out of the hopeless indebtedness and over-extendedness of small-lot farming. On February 22, 1960, a proud report in the Lüritz *Sentinel* announces that the district is first in the entire region to be "fully collectivized." The last new farmers to join the agricultural cooperatives have brought on average ten hectares each into their LPG. Theoretically, even in the cooperative the land remains their individual property for which—again: purely theoretically—they would receive a comparable piece of land on the LPG's outskirts should they ever decide to leave. But practically, the establishment of the agricultural cooperatives signals the end of an agriculture based on the individual ownership of land. The *Sentinel* describes the new approach on its front page: "New human beings have developed. Overnight. The new production relationships have created a new spirit. Socialism has won over the heads and minds of individual farmers."

Did the demise of individual ownership of land indeed transform citizens' attitudes toward their own and other people's property? The criminal case records in the Lüritz archive paint a different picture. East German criminal law, too, had an important role to play in the redefinition of ownership: it had to protect and strengthen "people's property" and reduce individual property to the mere satisfaction of consumption needs. In the first postwar years, GDR criminal law, understandably, was preoccupied with the protection of the new economy: nationalizations and the planning system had been more or less forced upon a reluctant population and were attacked and questioned from many sides. The first East German legislation protecting the economy—especially the Decrees "On Economic Crimes" of 1948 and "On Penalties for Speculation" of the following year—focused on activities that might endanger the new planning system and the supply of foodstuffs for the population and provided severe penalties for such offenses as the violation of delivery quotas and the unauthorized slaughtering of livestock or, worse, "diversion" and "sabotage." In many instances, the confiscation of the defendant's assets could be added to his punishment.

The Lüritz archive holds no criminal case records from the late 1940s and the early 1950s. The *Sentinel* carries a number of stories about "severe but just" sentences for saboteurs, black market dealers, and speculators in these years, but I find it difficult to gauge their tone. The harsh sentences, those for lengthy prison terms and for hard labor, seem to affect primarily defendants whose acts of theft or embezzlement might also have offended the sensibilities of a bourgeois judge, and the new-style sinners who did not fulfill their delivery quotas, used too little seed when sowing their fields, or sold cigarettes on the black market usually get off with a few months rather than years in jail. Two decades later, Hilde Benjamin, notorious GDR Minister of Justice from 1953 to 1967, complained about the "generally too lenient practice of the courts" during this period,[6] and her criticism might also have described the case law of my Lüritz court. I cannot tell.

But with the establishment of the new German Democratic Republic in October 1949 (five months after the foundation of the West German Federal Republic), East German plans to build a new kind of society are beginning to take shape. At the SED's Second Party Conference in July 1952, Walter Ulbricht announces that the country will now embark "on the planned construction of Socialism." The year 1952 is also the first year covered by the criminal case records in the Lüritz archive. It is amazing how their nature changes in the short span of twelve months. At the beginning of the year, the criminal law judges of my court (primarily Herr Teubner, officially acknowledged as a "victim of the Nazi regime" and by now director of the District Court) are still ready to accept excuses for certain violations of state property. "We must consider the great difficulties that still are caused by the electric black-outs," Herr Teubner writes in January 1952 in a case in which on a dark winter evening the use of candlelight in a barn had caused a fire, and two months later, in defense of an employee of the state's *Handelsorganisation* (trade organization, or HO) prosecuted for embezzlement: "The court assigns much of the blame to the HO management. Unfortunately, it must be noted that the trading organization's business practices leave much to be desired. It is time for the HO central administration to put their house in order." At the beginning of the year 1952, the prison sentences handed out by the Lüritz District Court usually can be measured in months, and in many cases are shorter than the sentences suggested by the prosecutor.

But as the year progresses, the Lüritz penalties for offenses against "the people's property" (*Volkseigentum*), now clearly marked by a VE label on the case file's cover, become increasingly severe. In December 1952 a farmer who tried to hide sixty cent weights of grain and two of his pigs and calves from the authorities is prosecuted for "concealment" and sentenced to four-and-a-half years hard labor. His defense counsel had pointed to the judgment of another district court that in January 1952 had called a very similar case of concealment "less serious." But Herr Teubner waves the comparison aside. "It is clear that today, we can no longer use the same yardstick as last year," he says. On October 2 1952, the East German People's Chamber had passed the "Law on the Protection of People's Property" (*Volkseigentums-Schutzgesetz*, or VESchG), which punished theft and embezzlement of state property with between one and five years (and, in "aggravated" cases, with twenty-five years) of hard labor. According to an article by Hilde Benjamin, published in the spring of 1953, the law was intended "to put a stop to the conciliatory attitudes" that GDR courts until then had shown in their treatment of attacks on people's property.[7] The *Volkseigentums-Schutzgesetz* "must be applied in its full severity" Benjamin (then Vice President of the Supreme Court) had written. The Lüritz farmer who had "concealed" his sacks of grain had not been prosecuted under the VESchG (which at the time of the offense had not yet been passed) but under the Decree on Economic Crimes of 1948. But both laws were fueled by a policy of malign neglect of individual property rights that the VESchG brought to ideological perfection and that for the next years shaped the court's reaction to all attempts to use people's property for individual purposes or to shelter remnants of individual property against the state's grasp. "We must try, through strict sentencing, to force citizens to respect the people's property," Herr Teubner writes in one of his decisions. In May 1953, the leaseholder of a Lüritz cinema is punished for tax arrears of 3700 Marks with two-and-a-half years of hard labor. "Tax evasion is a crime against the people's property," the *Lüritz Sentinel* pronounces.

The radical protection of social property caused a redefinition of individual property. Under the pressure of the Decree on Economic Crimes and the VESchG, personal ownership of land and of production tools (that is, of assets that might also serve collective interests) increasingly is no longer treated as a person's "own" but, even without preceding nationalization, as a public good. To cut down one's own trees without prior permission by the state thus becomes an economic crime. The court rates the negligent causation of a fire on a farmer's own estate as "arson," even though the German Criminal Code of 1871 (in 1952 still in force in the GDR) in its §308 defined "arson" only as setting fire to other people's property. A recidivist is punished for the theft of four bicycles with two years hard labor, because the personal property he took also had to serve important public functions: bicycle theft "makes it impossible for many toilers to show up for work and thus is likely to cause losses in production."

The law on economic crimes in the early 1950s strips the distinction between one's own and others' property of its bourgeois matter-of-factness and respectability. It expects its citizens to be un-acquisitive and selfless. In the spring of 1953, a carefully synchronized campaign called *Aktion Rose*[8] intensifies the criminal law attacks on private property by depriving hundreds of hotel and restaurant owners along the Baltic Coast of their inns and taverns not by way of *nationalizations* but through *criminal prosecutions* that result in the confiscation of the owners' properties. Under the law on economic crimes, the pretexts for the prosecutions were easy to fabricate: black-market purchases, tax arrears, "concealment" of provisions, and the like by which the owners of the hotels, in times of scarcity, had tried to feed their guests and to keep their businesses afloat.

The very worst excesses of this period last only for about a year. Crucial events occur in 1953: Stalin dies on March 5; on June 11, the GDR Council of Ministers resolves to launch a more moderate "New Course"; six days later, the easing up of pressures is followed by the popular uprising of June 17. The new liberalization continues nonetheless. On October 28, 1953, the Supreme Court issues a "Guideline" that restricts the application of the "Law on the Protection of People's Property" to "grave attacks" on public assets. The next day, the East German People's Chamber passes legislation to relax the Decree on Economic Crimes and repeals the Decree on Speculation. More than two decades later Hilde Benjamin speaks of a "serious lesson" that East German criminal law had to draw from "having overshot the mark" with its early attempts to safeguard people's property.[9] Already in 1954, many of the businesses confiscated during *Aktion Rose* are returned, not necessarily to be owned, but at least to be managed by their original owners. In 1956, there is not a single prosecution for the nonfulfillment of delivery quotas in the Lüritz District.

As the years wear on, East German legal policy on economic crimes becomes increasingly more differentiated and relaxed. The Law on the Protection of People's Property and the Decree on Economic Crimes saw everyone who stole a pound of sugar or a bag of coals from the state trade organization as an enemy of Socialism. The Supreme Court Guideline of 1953 and, four years later, the Criminal Law Amendments of December 23, 1957, still divided the world into friend and foe but also conceded that not every little swindler intended an attack on Socialism and thus reserved the most severe penalties for serious violations of state property. The new East German Criminal Code of 1968 continued to distinguish crimes directed against collective property from crimes against personal property and dealt with the two offenses in different sections of the code. But both those sections were structured, under the same criteria, to sanction three different levels of intensity of each offense and both provided for the same variations of penalties. That means that the people's property, in fact, was no longer privileged under the criminal law.

The equal treatment of social and personal property under the new East German Criminal Code may also have been something of a capitulation. The Lüritz people's judges of the 1950s still tried (by way of admonitions or, if necessary, penalties) to persuade those who infringed upon state property that they had violated an asset that was the basis of their own well-being; not to say: their salvation. In 1958, for instance, Frau Christiansen tries to explain to two collective farmers who had put aside one of their collective's piglets for a wedding feast that thefts like these were silly and unnecessary in a Socialist society. The defendants had been driven "only by their backwardness," she says. "With careful and thrifty use" there easily would be enough for everyone. But it appears that neither the people's judges (who, I assume, believed in their own message) nor later generations of judges in the GDR succeeded in persuading their audiences that "people's property" was actually the property of the people. In my files, the protestations of the "new quality" of people's property always come from the bench. Lüritz citizens seem unaware of their new role as owners.

On the contrary: my criminal case records reveal that Lüritz citizens show more respect for personal property than for the property of state-owned enterprises and cooperatives, and that theft from individuals meets with far more moral disapproval than theft from "the people." Since many of the defendants in my files are opportunists who are uninterested in the legal classification of an object and simply steal those things that are easiest to pocket on the sly, statistical distinctions between the theft of "social" and "personal" property are not very reliable: most thieves have stolen both. Nevertheless, the records hint at significant distinctions between both offenses. At least since the 1960s, infringements of people's property are far more frequent than theft, embezzlement, and fraud affecting individual owners: consistently throughout the decades, roughly twice as many Lüritzers illegally help themselves to assets owned by the state than to things belonging to their neighbors. In the eyes of my judges, too, theft from fellow citizens often seems more blameworthy than theft from the state: in many years, the average penalties of thieves of personal property exceed those of thieves who have stolen public goods. The profiles of both kinds of perpetrators differ. Someone who filches from other people usually is poor, run down, without a steady job, and a social outsider on more than one account. Someone who fleeces the state is frequently an ordinary citizen, usually an insider in the cooperative or enterprise whose property he makes away with, and often even a particularly capable, esteemed, and decorated employee of the very enterprise that he defrauds. The most energetic and gifted culprits come up with the cleverest thieving schemes and the biggest booty because they are most able to spot the weak points of state accounting methods and controls and know how to manipulate them to their advantage and also, I would guess, because they are looking for an outlet for their entrepreneurial energies for which a rigid and authoritarian planned economy provided little room. Under Socialism, intelligence, imagination, and the willingness to take risks were not the kind of qualities that made you rich. So these defendants used their abilities for the illegal acquisition of property. Some of these crimes involved large sums. In 1975, the dispatcher of a state-owned transport company in Lüritz uses accounting tricks to embezzle 95,000 Marks; in 1986, an employee of the Lüritz post office defrauds the state lottery to the tune of 130,000 Marks by manipulating winnings.

Not only the Lüritz thieves and frauds are lacking in respect for the people's property. The civil case files, too, reflect the almost contemptuous insouciance with which many of the inhabitants of Lüritz treat the state's assets. Tenants of state-owned or cooperative apartments do not pay their rents; consumers are in arrears with their electricity bills; fare dodgers cheat the state on public transport; couples default on generous state marriage loans. Confusing accounting methods, patchy monitoring, and sluggish debt enforcement on the side of public creditors suggest that for their part, state-owned enterprises, too, are not particularly scrupulous about protecting the people's property. Ideally, everyone should see himself as owner. But in reality, nobody treated people's property with the same care and solicitude as his personal belongings. At a legal conference in July 1988 in Neuburg, the regional capital, Frau Walter writes into her notebook: "Ownership consciousness needs strengthening." And again in May 1989 at a meeting for criminal law judges: "Ownership consciousness of our citizens must be strengthened."

A cynic might suggest that the daily little acts of stealing from the state that had for many become second nature under Socialism did in fact reflect a new consciousness of ownership: if the state-owned Lüritz City Transit Company lost 20,000 unpaid fares per year it might have been because Lüritz citizens considered the city's trams and buses as their own and therefore saw no need to pay for using them. But it is much more likely that the protagonists of my Lüritz files did not see people's property as their own but rather as nobody's property. "Since all this material was just lying about I thought that I could take some of it, too," an auto mechanic said in 1975 at his trial. He had used 300,000 Marks worth of his enterprise's tools and supplies to run a private after-hours service for car repairs. No, this was not the kind of "ownership consciousness" Frau Walter had in mind. Instead, I detect the traces of another kind of "ownership consciousness" in my files, also not in line with Frau Walter's notion, that throughout the entire life span of the GDR prompts my protagonists to defend what they possess with hand and tooth and to this purpose, turn to the law for help.

At least during the early years of their republic, East German private owners had little reason to expect the law to come to their defense. The earliest attempts of civil litigants to rely on legal reasoning in order to curb state assaults on their possessions end in pathetic, sometimes desperate, defeats. The case law shows that between the immediate postwar years and the Berlin Wall of 1961 my judges are increasingly reluctant to listen to legal arguments against the enforcement of state interests. When in 1950 a teacher's widow sues for the return of furniture

CHAPTER 4

that the mayor had distributed among the local needy (including his own brother-in-law) during the plantiff's fortnight absence from her village, Herr Curtius initially treats the suit as a conventional restitution claim under the Civil Code. But he gets cold feet when the district council intervenes: the furniture had been assigned to "impoverished refugees" and "we are of the opinion that Frau Lehman because of her flight from the village [she had left, temporarily, at the arrival of the Soviet Occupation Forces] has no further claims. We ask to treat this matter accordingly." Herr Curtius is still hesitant; tries to arrange a settlement between the parties that Frau Lehman angrily rejects (she wants *all* her furniture back), and after one more letter from the district's "Department for the Protection of the People's Property" throws in the towel in this uneven struggle between law and might and dismisses Frau Lehman's suit for want of jurisdiction. "In the GDR I will never be able to get my property back," Frau Lehman (whose lawyer meanwhile has deserted to the West) writes in a moving protest letter to the court. She is not quite right: a few wedding gifts among the requisitioned objects—a grandfather clock, a few smaller items—are in the end returned to her. But it is the mercy of an administration that does not want to seem inhuman that grants her the consolation prize—not the power of the law.

Some years later, a similar attempt to appeal to the law for help against the state's ruthless exploitation of private property not only demonstrates the hopelessness of the endeavor but also illuminates the social costs of a legal system that wants to restrain its citizens but not the state and its economy. The plaintiff, Frau Hille, is owner of a warehouse that she has let to the Lüritz state-owned VEB Fishing Company (VEB stands for *Volkseigener Betrieb*, that is, an "enterprise owned by the people") for 150 Marks a month. Since the VEB has stored its salt-fish so imperfectly that puddles of salt brine have begun to cause the wooden planks of the warehouse floor to rot away and since Frau Hille's complaints receive no answer, she finally gives notice and requests the VEB to leave the premises by the end of the contractual notice period, that is, by June 1, 1959. The Fishing Company replies with a blank refusal: "After consulting with the SED District Bureau/Divison Fishing Industry and the district council we reject your notice for economic and technical reasons." Frau Hille (who handles her own case) responds with a letter (written in a trembling hand) that tries to relocate the dispute under the umbrella of the law: "In my opinion, contractual duties must be carried out. A change of contract would have needed the consent of both parties." But the Fishing Company again replies with arguments that reflect the practical constraints of an economy that respects the market just as little as the law: the East German fishing industry had caught more codfish than East German citizens would buy; accordingly, "emergencies" in the entire GDR led to the surplus being salted; state economic agencies, moreover ("for reasons not of our making") had imported large quantities of salt herring that also "do not conform to popular demand" and thus could not be sold, and all this unwanted salt-fish needed to be stored. If the District Court chose to decide in favor of the plaintiff, "we will, for want of other storage space, place all our salt-fish barrels in the street."

The judge in the case (Herr Steinmetz, a people's judge, carpenter by training, under Hitler imprisoned for three years and only recently at an inspection of the District Court accused of "inactivity") must have felt himself between a rock and a hard place. What was he to do? He did not want to pass a judgment that resulted in leaky codfish barrels standing on the sidewalks. In any case, the neighbors of Frau Hille's warehouse already had complained about the stink of fish in the vicinity. The VEB had informed the court in writing that its decision not to vacate its storage space also was supported by the Party's "Division Fishing Industry." Moreover, the plaintiff, who had not even managed to find a lawyer to represent her case (because no one dared? because the matter was hopeless?), belonged—in the words of the defendant—"as owner of a former wholesale trading company," to "an epoch we have left behind." "This lawsuit must not cause any damage to the state economy," writes the VEB. Herr Steinmetz does not find it in him to disagree. He persuades Frau Hille to withdraw her suit.

If legal arguments had counted in this dispute it would have ended differently —without the fish barrels having to end up in the street. As a matter of GDR law at the time, Frau Hille was in the right (which may have been the reason why Herr Steinmetz did not dismiss her suit but disposed of it by way of a withdrawal). The prospect of a certain defeat in court might have persuaded the VEB Fishing Industry to offer Frau Hille an acceptable compromise: maybe the repair of the storehouse floor coupled with a rise in rent. Already at an earlier stage of the salt-fish story, fear of receiving notice or requests for damage payments from their landlady might have caused the VEB to repair its barrels and thus prevent the damage in the first place. And worries about additional storage costs might have kept GDR economic functionaries from importing large quantities of unmarketable salt-fish. Herr Steinmetz's refusal, however motivated, to help the plaintiff to obtain what was her right did not only impair Frau Hille's property but also helped to disable East German law (at least, East German civil law) as an instrument of steering and monitoring the economy. "Hille vs. VEB Fishing Industry" is only a little pebble in a large mosaic depicting an economy that by flaunting private rights also undermines its own legal self-control. One easily could collect more pebbles of this sort in the Lüritz archive.

They usually stem from the years before the Berlin Wall. After the Wall, the situation changes. By 1961, the collectivization of East Germany's agriculture essentially has been completed; economic planning has become the norm; the closing of the border has stopped the drain of citizens and assets flowing West, imparting an air of inevitability and permanence to Socialism in the GDR in which individual property no longer seems to provoke and undermine the dignity of people's property. Almost all productive assets are owned either by the state or by social organizations. If an individual owner now calls for law to ward off collective invasions onto his territory, Lüritz judges can listen to his arguments with greater equanimity than before. For a state that has appropriated all productive property within its borders, the civil law no longer is a threat. As a result, I find a number of trials in the post-Wall years in which individual owners use the law, not to win brilliant victories over collective interests, but at least to bargain for acceptable compromises.

"Lüritz Consumers' Cooperative vs. Böhnke" is such a case; begun in 1963 under Herr Steinmetz's direction and concluded in 1967 with a settlement under Herr Taddäus. At stake is the "Cooperative Hotel" in Lüritz; in earlier days— and again after the *Wende*—as "Hotel Stockholm" the best address in town, but by 1963 already so run down that I have encountered it repeatedly in Lüritz police reports as "the most disreputable hotel in the area." Herr Böhnke, the owner, let it in 1953 to the Lüritz Consumers' Cooperative, which changed its nostalgic name to "Cooperative Hotel" and assumed its management. In 1958, Herr Böhnke has to take out a loan of 150,000 Marks to finance the many improvements required by the Lüritz City Building Division to keep the crumbling edifice in working order. In February 1960, when the repairs are done, Herr Böhnke enters into a new agreement with the Cooperative under whose terms the rent is raised to 2400 Marks a month and the Cooperative, as lessee, assumes responsibility for all future repairs needed to keep the hotel "in suitable condition for its contractual use."

The Cooperative would have done better not to sign this contract. Already by 1963, the hotel is, again, in deplorable condition: the roof leaks; the window frames are rotting away; the electric wiring is a fire hazard. Who should pay for the repairs? The Cooperative demands that Herr Böhnke, as owner of the building, reduce the rent, take out another loan, and carry out the necessary work. Herr Böhnke, understandably, declines by pointing to the contract of 1960 under which it is the Cooperative, as lessee, that has to keep the building in working order. After much to and fro and a barrage of new demands for further restorations by the City Building Division, the Cooperative in May 1963 brings suit against Herr Böhnke, demanding that he undertake all necessary work to keep the "Cooperative Hotel" in a habitable state.

It promises to be an uneven fight. The Cooperative represents society's interest in providing accommodation for its travelers. It can enlist support from other public institutions that further the Cooperative's case by pestering Herr Böhnke with additional demands: the Lüritz Price Office reduces the rent Herr Böhnke is allowed to charge for the hotel; the Work and Health Inspection requires new ventilation for the kitchen and the installation of new food lifts. The Consumer Cooperative raises the possibility of buying the hotel but suggests a price that lies below the 1960 mortgage with which the owner financed the original repairs.

But Herr Böhnke is not to be intimidated. For four long years—and with the help of two attorneys--he resists attempts to browbeat him into submission until the Cooperative is willing to buy the hotel at twice the price that it originally offered. Even after subtracting the mortgage and the value-added tax (negotiated by Herr Böhnke's lawyers with the city) he is left enough to buy a car and start a new, and under GDR conditions, lucrative, career as taxi driver. As the new owner, the Consumer Cooperative, in an economy of scarcity, struggles until the final days of Socialism to keep the hotel from disintegrating altogether. Herr Böhnke, who only has a taxi to look after, must have been glad of having gotten rid of his dinosaur. As I learn many years later from one of his nephews, Herr Böhnke bore no grudge against the system. He remained a Party member all his life.

It would be misleading to call "Lüritz Consumers' Cooperative vs. Böhnke" a triumph for the legal institution of private property. But the case shows that by 1967, the law, again, had a say if individual and collective interests collided. The four-year-long fight over the "Cooperative Hotel" was structured by legal arguments and strategies to an extent that ten years earlier would have seemed impossible. Herr Böhnke's lawyers negotiated not only with the plaintiff and the court but also with the city's Work- and Health Inspection, the Lüritz mayor, the Central Organization of Consumers' Cooperatives in Berlin, and, when it came to taxes, the GDR Ministry of Finances. The plaintiff's and defendant's moves were plotted by their lawyers: affidavits, expert opinions, changes of pleadings, many motions to suspend or to reopen the proceedings. Even though it would have preferred to see the matter dropped, the Lüritz court treated the dispute as a conflict that ought to be decided by the law. In May 1966, Herr Taddäus writes in a "for-internal-use-only" message to the Regional Court: "In my opinion, the Consumers' Cooperative's suit is without legal merit and should be dismissed. If the Regional Court shares this view, it might be useful to ask representatives of the regional consumers' cooperative to attend a conference at which the court informs the cooperative accordingly." Even thirty years later, the cooperative's attorney, Herr Bleibtreu, then a young man with ideological convictions, remembers the confrontation with the obstinate Herr Böhnke not as a victory but as a defeat. Considering the constellation of opponents and the asset at stake, it had far more decisively been shaped by legal arguments than I would ever have assumed.

The change reflects a new and more relaxed understanding of property. To own things and to defend one's own possessions seems no longer morally suspicious. In the Böhnke case, attorney Bleibtreu (maybe remembering his days at university) had tried to argue that the cooperative's interests affected "economic, technical, and social developments" and thus mandated "a dialectical interpretation of the lease" that must serve "progress." But Herr Böhnke's lawyer rejects that notion with a candid and unembarrassed defense of individual self-interest. "The plaintiff's view that the defendant should renovate the hotel's kitchen solely for the purpose of protecting and improving Socialist property is totally incomprehensible. Why would the defendant enrich Socialist property at the expense of his own?"

The fight over the "Cooperative Hotel" is unrepresentative of East German property law in the post-Wall years because it concerned an object far more valuable than the average issue-in-controversy of an ordinary civil suit. In 1966, 82% of all Lüritz civil litigation turned on values under 500 Marks; and even in 1988, 55% of all disputed values did not exceed this sum. But the "Cooperative" case is representative because it shows that a robust concern for individual property was no longer anathema in the GDR. Lüritz judges no longer based their decisions on the implausible assumption that plaintiffs and defendants should care less about their own possessions than about those of the state. Law was again permitted to protect a citizen's self-interests. It seems likely that the rehabilitation of property rights was assisted by the fact that most property suits in Lüritz concerned negligible sums: the Socialist state had no reason to fear its subjects' economic competition. But as the "Cooperative Hotel" case shows, the law's new respect for property held up even in those instances were a lawsuit's outcome mattered to the state.

Most Lüritz civil litigation, however, turned on petty-bourgeois personal possessions. The parties fought over gardens, rooms, garages, furniture, cars—over often tiny enclaves of self-determination in a close and regimented world. Lüritz citizens turned to the court for help in order to ward off intrusions on their territory. Usually, the fattest case files deal with disputes between neighbors. In many quarrels, the bone of contention is a key: a symbol of control over a bounded space to which the plaintiff wants to gain entry, or whose invasion by others he wants to prevent. As late as 1989, about a quarter of all civil suits aim for the restitution of specific objects that, unlike money, are not fungible, but to which the parties, as it were, claim a personal relationship. And a growing number of civil cases deal with cars, the most Capitalist objects of desire, that represent not only a monetary value but also the chance to break out and increase the radius of one's life. As the low values in most controversies suggest, Lüritz plaintiffs and defendants, as a rule, are anything but wealthy. While in Capitalist civil courts the "haves" usually sue the "have nots" who cannot pay their debts, in Lüritz "have nots" tend to sue each other. There is a whiff of poverty to many of these records: the values of the disputed objects are so low, the parties' room to maneuver is so narrow, that the property that is protected by the court despite its obvious meaning to those immediately concerned seems socially banal and insignificant.

But it is the subcutaneous rehabilitation of ownership I am concerned with in this chapter; its growing assimilation to familiar bourgeois notions such as *"klein aber mein"* ("small but my own") or "everyone for himself and God (or the Party) for us all." A legal system that set out to tear down the divisions between "mine," "yours," and "ours" so everyone would live together in collective brotherhood ended up by reinforcing the determination of its citizens to hold on all the more tightly to the few possessions they had left. GDR owners were no more self-centered than owners everywhere. But their property was more narrowly defined, restricted to their personal use, and without the entrepreneurial possibilities that under Capitalism makes property also a medium of freedom.

One of my most illuminating Lüritz conversations was with a master plumber who only a few days before the collapse of Socialism had fled to West Germany (and returned two weeks later) because he was not willing to let a state-assigned tenant occupy two unused rooms in his own house. My conversation partner was a Party member, had never felt politically alienated, ran his own flourishing little business for bathroom installations, and even drove a car imported from the West. But he did not see why he should lodge a stranger in his house. His opposition to the request by the Lüritz Housing Office had brought him into an open confrontation with the Party. I would guess that the Party—at least among comrades still unwilling to tolerate too blatant an exhibition of self-interest—wanted to set an example in his case. "What do you want," the First Party Secretary had said to him, "you've got it much too good. We're short of housing." When no protest availed, my conversation partner in early November 1989 managed to escape to the Federal Republic by way of Poland. "What else could I do," he said to me; a martyr to the belief in a free housing market. "It was my property. Do you give in when you are in the right?" A house owner from 1900, the year in which the German Civil Code, the Song of Songs of market Capitalism, entered into force, could not have spoken the words with more conviction.

CHAPTER 5

WORK

If, under Capitalism, the quintessential legal actor is the owner, his counterpart under Socialism, one would think, must be the worker. And, indeed, East German labor law—or at least, East German labor law as reflected in my Lüritz files—was, in a way, the most "Socialist" branch of this legal system. Not the most important, far from it: in Lüritz and elsewhere in the GDR, labor law disputes made up only a small part of the courts' yearly business. But the fundamental values of Socialism were demonstrated in more unadulterated form in this than in other areas of the law. It was less blemished, if you want, by ideological betrayals. When deciding labor law disputes, Lüritz judges spoke in a more creditable voice then when they dealt with civil or criminal law matters.

Admittedly, it took many years of false starts and detours before the labor adjudication of my court turned into a method of resolving conflicts that Lüritz citizens, after the Turnabout, occasionally would mourn. When the Lüritz Labor Court decided its first case in May 1946, the East German legal landscape looked no different from that on the other side of the border. In the Federal Republic, labor law primarily protects the legal interests of employees. Employers do not need the law to safeguard their financial interests against the people they employ—they can rely on their market power to get things done their way. More than ninety-five percent of the plaintiffs in labor court are workers who use the law to challenge decisions of employers that affect their work. The state of the economy determines what aspect of their jobs needs the protection of the law: in times of full employment, suits about salaries and wages tend to rise; in times of unemployment, more people will sue to contest dismissals.[10]

In the early postwar years, Lüritz labor law litigation followed this traditional pattern. More than 90% of the plaintiffs were employees. Most lawsuits involved controversies over pay or firings. Until 1952, the frequency of labor litigation rose despite the fact that private employment in the GDR was in decline. But then, the picture changes. The labor law caseload of the Lüritz court begins to shrink: from 255 suits in 1952 to 111 suits in 1958 and a mere fifty-one labor law disputes in 1960. The distribution of plaintiffs and defendants changes, too. In 1952, 96% of labor plaintiffs had been employees. By 1960, their share has been reduced to 65%. Parties begin to go to court for different reasons than before. If in 1950, litigation was either about pay or about dismissals, beginning in 1952, a new type of labor suit appears in which *employers* pursue claims for compensation against their employees. By 1960, these suits make up more than a third of the Lüritz labor law caseload. What happened?

Maybe the creation of the new conflict commissions (*Konfliktkommissionen*, or KK) in the spring of 1953 can explain the changes. These were lay tribunals set up within the enterprises and charged with the task of resolving disputes between Socialist workers and their employers in straightforward, practice-oriented, educational proceedings. The KK judges were elected by the workforce, trained by the unions, and supervised by the prosecutor's office. They had authority to adjudicate most simple labor law disputes and thus, in fact, took over the first-instance trials that had previously been handled by the district courts. Only if no conflict commission existed in the parties' enterprise or if a plaintiff or defendant repeatedly refused to appear before the commission would a dispute go directly to the court. Otherwise, the labor courts served only to decide appeals. In the early 1980s, when roughly 27,000 conflict commissions in the GDR decided a caseload of about 51,000 labor disputes every year, no more than 10% of their decisions were challenged by one or the other party. At the trial level, the KK had taken over. Is it surprising that the labor docket of the Lüritz court shrank in significance?

East German jurists were proud of their conflict commissions. Even after the *Wende*, when former Socialists were looking for at least one or the other legal institution of the GDR that might survive under a Capitalist rule of law, the social courts and their uncomplicated, user-friendly method of resolving labor disputes were mentioned as likely transplants. Admittedly, the social-court decisions that I encounter in my Lüritz files show the KK in a less than flattering light. After all, only their least convincing judgments were appealed and so showed up in the records of a district court. Particularly in the early years of the commissions, their lay judges could arrive at quite adventurous decisions not backed by any section of a code. In 1970, for instance, a Lüritz KK sentenced a layabout to three charitable work shifts benefiting North Vietnam, and a year later another conflict commission sent someone who had missed fifteen days at work for "lack of contrition" to a labor camp. All the way up to the collapse of Socialism in the GDR, the social-court adjudication of labor conflicts was marked by the—understandable—incomprehension of some laypeople of the importance of legal formality and precision. Conflict commissions occasionally sat for trial without the required number of members present; imposed penalties inspired by their own pedagogic urges rather than the law; and generally made the kind of legal blunders that carpenters or construction workers might be forgiven for. The prosecutor would check up on those decisions and the district court would either send them back, with explanations, or correct the faults itself and thus preserve the law. The vast majority of labor law decisions by the KK were in conformity with legal rules and were not appealed.

And yet, the fact that most first-instance labor litigation in the GDR never made it to the district courts cannot, all by itself, explain why my court's labor law caseload shrank the way it did. For one thing, East German labor litigation dropped even *before* the KK were introduced in 1953. Throughout East German legal history, the caseloads of the conflict commissions themselves remained—by West German standards—astonishingly low. While in 1982, one in fifty-five employees sued his employer in the Federal Republic, only one in 433 workers did so in the GDR.[11] This was a country in which labor conflicts usually were not translated into litigation. Why not?

For one thing, because the planned economy had removed many issues that feed the dockets of Capitalist labor courts from the control of those immediately involved. Planning decisions such as wage categories, the definition of labor tasks, performance targets, and the like could not be subject to contractual agreements and could not be questioned by legal arguments. The wage issues that were litigated in East German labor courts concerned primarily rewards for individual performances that exceeded the set expectations of the plan: premiums, bonuses, innovator compensations. Even these types of claims were litigated less and less. In 1952, the labor law division of the Lüritz court had to decide 156 disputes over pay. By 1960, that number had dropped to fifteen suits, and even in the (slightly more litigious) 1980s the court was rarely faced with more than twenty lawsuits over pay a year. It is unlikely that most Lüritzers were pleased with what they earned. But there was nothing the law could do about their discontent.

The other major subject of West German labor litigation—dismissals—with the consolidation of the planned economy also melted away like snow in the month of March. In 1960, there had been sixty-four dismissal suits in Lüritz. In 1960, there were thirteen, and by 1980, no more than six. Socialism disliked dismissals. One reason was its notion of a human right to work: to punish a transgression by depriving the culprit of his job seemed unproductive and immoral. And even if his enterprise might want to rid itself of an unreliable and inefficient employee, the economy as a whole would be better served by keeping a good-for-nothing at his old place of employment (where his weaknesses were known and could be kept in check) than by transferring him to another enterprise (whose management still had to wise up to his iniquities). Thus, during the entire lifetime of the GDR, most suits by which a Lüritz employee contested his dismissal were successful. Even if someone no longer could be used at his particular place of work, his employer had to retool him or transfer him to another section of the enterprise rather than let him go. "Dismissals are easier to bring about than the reeducation of a worker. The management should have investigated the source of the worker's troubles and should have eliminated their causes," says a labor law judgment of 1958. And two years later, another decision states: shirkers "must be taught through persistent efforts of persuasion to consciously observe the demands of labor discipline." When my court, for once (in the fall of 1988, close to the end), does actually approve of the dismissal of a butcher at the local meat factory who had been sentenced to fifteen months in prison for "rowdiness" and "theft," the Regional Court in Neuburg overrules the Lüritz decision. True, the Supreme Court had allowed dismissal for cause in cases in which an employee had been sentenced to more than a year's imprisonment. But that did not relieve an enterprise from its obligation to investigate whether a particular defendant with an even lengthier term could not be usefully reintegrated in the enterprise. Indeed, in Lüritz as elsewhere in the GDR, the chances to get rid of even a serious slacker by dismissing him were fairly slim.

Add to that the perennial shortage of labor in East Germany, and workers' labor rights seemed pretty much immune against invasions by employers. Most state-owned enterprises could not afford not to respect them. They were more likely to cover up for a worker's misstep than to punish it. For instance, employers commonly made up for work days lost through someone's truancy by subsequently granting him additional vacation time. Lüritz employees learned to take their bosses' leniency for granted. Some of the workers' lawsuits in my files reveal a stubborn refusal to accept a superior's authority that resembles the contrariness of children challenging the grownups. In 1985, for instance, an employee in an auto repair shop sues her enterprise because she does not want to turn her desk in the shop's office by 90 degrees and move it 20 cm to the side. She loses her case. But reading the court's record of the office battle, I'm equally amazed by the woman's gall and by the enterprise's longanimity. In 1989, a cloak-room attendant goes to court because she doubts the veracity of her enterprise's pay-slip, can't understand the firm's accounting methods and, to judge by her dogged refusal to listen to the enterprise's spokesman in the courtroom, does not want to understand them. "We have explained and explained," says the union representative, exhausted from his efforts, at the hearing. Bringing a lawsuit was cheap and easy in the GDR, and labor court judges had a lot of patience even in trivial matters. But in the working life of most Lüritz citizens not many enterprise infringements of their rights occurred that warranted going to court.

Under Socialism, labor courts had other uses besides the protection of workers' rights. They enforced not only monetary interests but also claims to good behavior. In those labor law cases that actually reached the district courts (because a KK decision was appealed or because no KK existed in the parties' enterprise), the majority of plaintiffs were not workers but employers. They sued their employees to enforce an enterprise's claim to diligence, to punctuality, to orderliness—to all those virtues that under Capitalism are impressed upon a worker by his knowledge that bad work will very likely mean less pay and possibly, dismissal. In an economy that does not allow its workers to be fired, the only way of dealing with a shirker is to reform him. East German labor courts played an important role in the attempts to do so.

The Labor Code provided an employer with several means of reeducating a deficient worker: official reprimands, monetary claims for the (partial) compensation for damage caused by the worker to his enterprise, claims for the repayment of wages for days or hours missed by absenteeism or by lateness at work, and, not very promising and reserved for the most outrageous cases, immediate dismissal. The application of these methods changed over time. A pedagogic system that began with self-righteous and exploitative severity ended with lenience and solicitude. I will trace the changes by following the development of one legal claim that plays next to no role in Capitalist labor litigation: the employer's claim to compensation for losses caused by a worker's violation of his duties. Capitalist bosses will bring damage claims—even if they have them—against a worker only in the unlikely case that the worker is insured. But under Socialist law, the purpose of the claim was not just monetary compensation but moral betterment. An employee who failed to live up to his obligations was supposed to learn discipline and diligence by bearing "material responsibility" for the economic losses he had caused. What did that mean?

In my Lüritz files, the first damage suits by enterprises against their employees show up in 1952: the year in which the GDR resolved to embark on "the construction of Socialism," the year of the "Law on the Protection of State-Owned Property," the year which saw the first steps toward the collectivization of East Germany's agriculture—a year of ideological designs and hopes of which the reeducation of man with the help of law was an important part. This also was a year, it must be said, in which the state-run food industry in the GDR had to record losses of 59 million Marks instead of the expected gains of 48 million Marks.[12] That may explain why almost all of the lawsuits charging workers with "material responsibility" in this and the following years were brought either by Socialist trade organizations (*Handelsorganisationen*, or HOs) or by the *Konsum* (a chain of collectively owned grocery stores and supermarkets) against members of their staff who had supposedly caused losses of merchandise or deficits in the store's cash register. Both HO and *Konsum* were creatures of an economic revolution that set out to replace the private property of bourgeois merchants with the collectively administered property of all. East Germany's consumer industry would no longer be fueled by Capitalist competition but by state plans that would assess citizens' needs and structure the production and distribution of consumer goods to ensure their satisfaction. Socialist shopping centers replaced the mom-and-pop stores in the villages and the department stores in the big cities. Many of the old owners of these stores fled to the West. They were replaced by state-employed "outlet managers," whose administration of their store no longer was supposed to be driven by the hunt for profit but by feelings of responsibility toward the collective. Even so, the balance in the till had to be right. It was so less and less. In 1952, Lüritz judges handled fourteen employer damage suits against their employees; by 1956, that number had risen to forty-eight—29% of the labor law case load of my court. Most suits claimed discrepancies in the balances of department stores, food stores, or restaurants.

The files provide a vivid picture of the economy that produced litigation of this sort. It is a picture of poverty and disarray. Socialist consumer trade was short of everything: cash registers (which had to be imported from the West and, up to the very end, counted as luxury items in the GDR); freezers; scales; wrapping materials; adhesive price tags that would actually stick to the merchandise; storage room (to say nothing of desirable goods to be stored); and, above all, personnel and expertise. Most of the experienced shopkeepers had gone West. In any event, their way of doing business would have been out of synch with Socialist commercial practice. When, in 1954, a particularly enterprising manager of a village store raised his volume of sales by 12,000 Marks by selling drinks and hot dogs at Sunday soccer games (and in the throng of customers and fans surrounding him also lost 567 Marks through theft), his boss, the HO, charged him with "reckless intent" and sued him to retrieve the loss. In 1958, the *Konsum* brought suit against a shop assistant for losses caused by the faulty weighing of groceries: because the shop's scale had long been lacking proper weights, the woman had used candy and packs of margarine to determine the weight (and price) of loose foodstuffs, such as flour or sugar. With many grocery items not pre-packed, weighing in East German food stores was risky business.

There was so much that could go wrong in Socialist trade. Up to 1958, when the last bits of rationing were phased out in the GDR, a salesperson could confuse *Konsum* merchandise (rationed and cheap) with HO merchandise (unrationed and expensive), with the result that, at the end of the day, her register would contain either too little money or too few food coupons. Old habits like the chalking up of food expenses, or the small-town familiarity between shopkeeper and customer, would often make it difficult to insist on immediate payment, and the sales staff had to keep track of what was owed. Without cash registers, receipts had to be written by hand. Many shops operated with the "shoebox method" and kept money and business records in a cardboard box under the counter. Many did not write receipts. That was against the rules, but every HO or *Konsum* manager knew very well that it was almost impossible to stay within the rules. Check-ups by supervisors from the central office were haphazard and superficial. " I asked for help but nobody ever came," said a butcher who was sued by the HO in 1956 for compensation for state-owned meat that had spoiled because his freezer had been on the blink. The inspectors "would just look in and leave again," said a salesgirl who found herself in court because 1600 Marks were missing in her cash register. Often, *Konsum* and HO would bring their suits for compensation only after *repeated* audits had shown faulty balances without, at the first sign of difficulties, having offered their staff some supervision and advice. Truth to tell, under the "shoebox method" even audits were unreliable. Sometimes there was too much money in the till, sometimes too little, and everyone had gotten accustomed to the mess. "Every evening we counted and the figures never matched," said a store manager in 1958 who had been sued by her superiors for a balance missing 1047 Marks. Nowhere in the GDR did the figures match. In some years, in the state-owned trade, the unexplained surpluses on the nation's balance sheet were even higher than the losses that were not accounted for.[13]

The practice of suing cashiers and other employees responsible for state-owned merchandise or money for their loss was meant to teach East German employees the social costs of personal disorder at the workplace. But I cannot find any pedagogy in these trial records. Rather, the files suggest that HO and *Konsum* functionaries would wait with their lawsuits until they themselves got into trouble with their own revisors. The people who supervised the state consumer trade in the GDR were not merchants but bureaucrats. They had to find excuses if the stores and restaurants under their control were in the red. For the defendants, who had to compensate the state for the money missing in their shoebox tills, a verdict of 500 to 1000 Marks (the sums that usually were at stake) was a real hardship. For the plaintiffs, their superiors, a litigation victory meant that their own balance sheets were now in order.

Until the passage of the first East German Labor Code, the *Gesetzbuch der Arbeit* (GBA) of 1961, damage claims for accounting losses were governed by the old German Civil Code of 1900: the enterprise, under §276 of the BGB, had to prove that the employee was at fault for not having protected the assets that were entrusted to his care. The conflict commissions that were the first to adjudicate the matter usually were quick to find the employee responsible. Most losses occurred in small, poorly equipped stores or restaurants with little staff or—even more frequently—in so-called one-man outlets: tiny shops in which that one man (or woman) in control had to keep an eye on the customers, the merchandise, the till, and everything else needing attention, and in which unexplained losses were particularly prone to happen. Those one-man outlets mostly could be found in the rural areas surrounding Lüritz. The members of the conflict commissions who ruled on the defendant's guilt or innocence, on the other hand, were city people, employed by the central offices who administered the HO and *Konsum* stores in the district. I can't discover any proletarian comradeship or pedagogical concerns in their resolutions. The mere fact that money was missing in a till was usually enough to blame its cashier. After all, *someone* had to be responsible. Often, the KK did not even try to establish the defendant's fault. The manager of a village grocery store, for instance, is sentenced to repay a sum of 1543 Marks missing on his balance sheet because "the colleague probably did not exercise the necessary care in supervising the delivery of goods." "Colleague W. evidently lives above her means," says another KK resolution, obligating a saleswoman to pay at least 100 Marks of a sum of 430 Marks that somehow had disappeared from the store's intake—she must have used at least this much of the missing money for herself. Am I too suspicious in reading a threatening subtext into some of these decisions? "Count yourself lucky not to stand before a criminal judge," they seem to say.

Maybe fear of the prosecutor is the reason why many of the defendants in these cases, even in the face of uncertain evidence, were willing to sign acknowledgments of debts that the KK (as far as I can tell, without legal scruples) would confirm, and that committed the obligor to indemnify his enterprise by installment payments that could last for years. Some store managers had to endure several "material responsibility" proceedings in the course of their professional lives. In 1960, the manager of a radio shop in Lüritz quits his job when his employer, the *Konsum*, after two previous suits in 1957 and 1959, sues him again for the compensation of losses supposedly caused through the negligence of the defendant. This time, he is accused of having let some customers take home television sets so that they could try them out. The sets could not be tested in the store—it had no reception.

Under this case law, working as a Socialist salesman or saleswoman became risky business. Sales staff were well aware of it. In the year 1956 alone my labor law files mention no less than fifteen HO or *Konsum* employees in Lüritz who, either before or after a financial audit, fled to the West: restaurant managers, cashiers, salesmen—all people who knew that as the last ones caught in a long chain of insufficiencies, they would be the ones who would go to the wall for them. If I add to these fifteen escapees those employees fleeing *criminal* prosecution for audit deficits (because they were accused of criminal negligence, embezzlement, or fraud) the number of fugitives from the world of Socialist trade rises considerably. The borderlines between both types of cases could be blurry. Like all other salespeople thought responsible for faulty balances, those who in time absconded to the West nevertheless were sued by the state trade organization and the *Konsum* for compensation under "material responsibility" rules. Even if a successful plaintiff could not collect on a verdict, he *could* place the blame for unaccounted losses on his (now absent) employee and, in this fashion, clear his own name. This strategy, too, was part of a labor case law by which Socialist trade functionaries protected themselves at the expense of their less well-heeled workers. At least as far as I can tell from the records of my Lüritz

CHAPTER 5

labor court, the conflict commissions, conceived as institutions based on workers' input and trust, blithely played along with the employers.

And with whom, in these collisions of employee and functionary interests, did Lüritz labor judges side? They had to assign blame for the loss of public money at a time when defending the "people's property" was thought to be one of the law's essential tasks. East German criminal law in these years ruthlessly came down on those who in any way infringed upon state ownership. *Konsum* and state trade organizations had the *Zeitgeist* on their side when they sued their managers and cashiers for compensation for the money missing on their balance sheets. "Both the *Konsum* board and the conflict commission share the view that the Cooperative must minimize its losses by all necessary means," said one of their briefs from 1956, and one might expect that the labor judge who read it would agree with them. After all, "people's property," in these years, was sacrosanct: it embodied Socialism's promise of a better future.

And yet, I find most Lüritz labor judges on the side of the defendants in these cases. Despite their shaky legal education, my judges think like lawyers. Small-fry lawyers, admittedly. Nevertheless, they argue like people who believe in the importance of legal formality and precision. They overrule conflict commissions on appeal not just for factual mistakes but also because KK decisions violated formal rules: because the defendant's enterprise did not properly apply for a hearing, for example, because the commission meeting was not recorded in a protocol, or because the protocol did not show that the defendant was informed of his rights. My judges show annoyance when confronted with unproven assertions or with cheap excuses. When, in 1958, the *Konsum* once again based its compensation suit against a hapless saleswoman on the fact that she had not recorded customers' payments with receipts, the labor judge lost patience. "It is well known to the court that both in the plaintiff's grocery and in all other *Konsum* food or vegetable stores sales staff habitually do not write receipts," she wrote. "Since this practice has continued to this day, the court assumes that the defendant never has been instructed otherwise." Sometimes, I find that particularly egregious KK pronouncements in my files are underlined by thick red pencil strokes, presumably made by judges whose professionalism felt provoked by the legal blunders of the laymen.

I don't want to exaggerate the rule-of-law instincts of the Lüritz labor judges. Especially in the 1950s, the District Court would criticize the legal flaws of KK decisions but would not necessarily stand in the way of making employees pay for the financial losses caused by substandard Socialist accounting practices. In these years, it often happened that the court remanded faulty resolutions to the lay tribunals, ordered their correction, and—once repaired—enforced them anyway. In such cases, the court seemed more concerned for order than for law. But even a commitment to mere order can lead to more predictability of the law, more legal security, and, in the end, more justice. My judges' inclination to be finicky about the observation of legal rules, their attention to detail, their disrespect for allegations without proof, their willingness to listen to both sides of a story, over time turned them into people who defended not just a particular policy but also the rights of those whom it affected. A similar learning process happened in other labor courts of the GDR. It was a process in which East Germany's Supreme Court played a decisive role. It steered the initial insecurity of "people's judges" (who oscillated between solidarity with the defendant and wishes to protect the "people's" wealth) toward greater protectiveness of the defendant's rights. The first volume of the Supreme Court's labor law decisions contains among its fifty-five decisions thirteen cases dealing with balance deficits.

Perhaps one reason for the Supreme Court's interest in these issues was the justices' perception that the "material responsibility" case law of its district courts revealed some undercurrents of class division. It was so obvious that the Socialist trade functionaries who brought compensation suits against their staff were motivated by self-interest rather than a sense of responsibility for the public weal. As early as April 1954, the *Oberstes Gericht* admonished lower courts to "rule out any possibility of exploitation" when adjudicating employers' compensation claims for balance losses.[14] Those were strong words coming from a court that did not speak of Capitalist businessmen but of its own commercial functionaries. The years of charging workers for the accounting losses of Socialism's error-prone and inefficient consumer industry were indeed years of exploitation of overworked and helpless staff by their Socialist employers.

With the passage of the first East German Labor Code of 1961, the "material responsibility" issue was essentially defused. In cases of negligence, the new code limited an employee's liability for damage caused to his employer to one month's wages. The deficit cases in my Lüritz files decreased. In 1977, a second Labor Code reduced the liability for losses even by employees who had signed agreements to safeguard the specific funds or objects that went missing to at most three months of the defendant's pay. If a cashier now was sued for compensation, the worst he or she had to reckon with was a damage payment that amounted to no more than a fraction of the actual loss.

You might say that East German labor law had found a more convincing pedagogic voice. The law still wanted to impress upon a worker the need for orderliness and discipline. But its methods changed. The former compensation suits are now replaced by other ways of reminding negligent or shiftless workers of their duties: "educational proceedings," wage repayment claims for work that had been done badly or not done at all; "material responsibility" claims for damages other than balance deficits (that usually would result in penalties below a defendant's monthly wage); and, beginning in the 1980s, a growing number of dismissal suits brought against "asocial" employees who, in the view of their employers, were too set in their unproductive ways to be reformed.

The objects of the court's reeducation efforts also changed. In the earlier years, my Lüritz judges (just like bourgeois judges) had focused, quite conventionally, on the person whose individual responsibility for a particular calamity had to be determined. When in the 1960s, East German Socialism's hope for a "new man" revived, the law's educational goals became more ambitious and branched out. More is now at stake: not just the improvement of one individual defendant but also of the enterprise in which the violation of his duties has been allowed to happen; not just the compensation for a specific loss but also the political and personal relationships between all members of the work collective, and their responsibility to prevent similar conflicts in the future. The trial is now expected to throw light on just about everything and everyone who is connected to the case at hand. Everyone shall learn from the proceedings. On suitable occasions, the court moves its hearings from the courthouse to the enterprise in which the dispute arose and invites management, union representatives and staff to observe the legal morality-play in its authentic setting.

Admittedly, these edification spectacles cost time and money—and not just the courts'. Judges have difficulties rounding up enough participants for what are called "trials before an extended public"—if the hearing takes place during working hours, the management complains; if the hearing is scheduled in the evening, the spectators vanish. The court has to send around severely worded invitations to collect its audience. "We consider it essential that you attend this hearing," Frau Dankwarth, a no-nonsense Lüritz labor judge, informs the board of a *Konsum* store in a 1965 suit over unexplained cash deficits. A few weeks later, she tries to get an enterprise union organization to commandeer its members to attend a dismissal case: "Enterprise Union Secretary Hermann has to see to it that every member of the Union Leadership will be present at the trial." If in cases like these the file contains no data on the number of spectators attending the hearing, I can be pretty sure that most of the invited sent excuses. Large audiences usually are proudly registered in the protocol. I also doubt that the didactic messages for the "extended public" always fell on open ears. There is very little open criticism of the court's education efforts in my files. Political good manners required you to strive for collective betterment. But some of the reactions to my judges' admonitions sound so eager that I suspect some irony behind the protestations. This is how the manager of a bakery replies in 1965 to the court's detailed criticism of his enterprise's dismissal practice. He opens his letter with "the Court's first statement was particularly instructive ..."; continues " we drew an additional lesson from your remark ..."; and finishes "summing up, it can be said that the trial was for all of us an educational experience." Did the recipients of this letter believe what they read?

Initially, the practice of holding court hearings at the workplace of the parties had been driven by the hope that the collective might contribute to the reasonable resolution of a social conflict. But I can find no collegial deliberations on how to best resolve this conflict in the files. Rather, the contributions coming from the audience sound like the catcalls of (hostile or sympathetic) spectators commenting on a workmate pilloried by the law. "She's a slowpoke!" someone shouts from the audience in the 1965 hearing on the dismissal of a young worker from the enterprise. "She's slow but not cheeky," suggests somebody else. "She's not cheeky but pigheaded," claims a third. No wonder that in the 1970s and 1980s Lüritz judges seem to lose faith in the transformative powers of the collective. Instead of striving for the edification and instruction of their audience, they aim, again, for the resolution of a concrete and specific human crisis. Someone had been fired; he did not get the bonus to which he thought he was entitled; he was displeased with the work evaluation he had received from his employer. What could the law do for him? The court would still draw on a worker's enterprise or on his collective: for witnesses to testify to a defendant's working habits, for example, or for moral support to assist with someone's integration at the workplace. But the colleagues in these cases acted as supporting cast in a social drama, not as principals in a morality play. The court's attention was focused on the individual employee.

The closer the GDR drifts towards its eclipse, the more imaginative and flexible are the techniques by which my Lüritz labor judges try to protect individual rights and interests. Many problems are resolved by simple telephone calls. Somebody brings suit, for instance, because her enterprise reduced her wages by the number of days she stayed at home to care for a sick child. Frau Neuman, labor judge since 1978, calls the director and the chief accountant of the enterprise and explains the law. The missing sum is paid, the plaintiff's suit withdrawn. Slightly more than half of all labor suits in Lüritz end before their hearing because the judge talks one or the other side (and sometimes both) into concessions or surrender and the suit is dropped. In the 1980s, only about a quarter of all Lüritz labor law cases end with a judgment. Admittedly, if I just count who wins and loses, the judgments seem to side more often with the enterprise than with the worker. But that is true only for the *legal* outcomes of the cases. Deciding how to apply the sections of the Labor Code to a particular dispute is only part of a labor judge's work and not even that part, it appears, which is closest to her heart. Even if a legal claim has been rejected or withdrawn—indeed, even if the court denies its jurisdiction in the matter—the court often will address the problems that brought the employee before it in the first place. Here is an example. A truant, already fired because he missed too many work days, appeals a decision by his former enterprise's conflict commission under which he has to repay some of the wages which, supposedly, he did not earn. At the hearing, the enterprise produces evidence to show that the plaintiff had indeed been overpaid. He withdraws his appeal. But when the judge learns that the man is still without a job, she persuades the representative of the enterprise, right in the courtroom, to rehire his former employee. Not only the legal winner in this case has reason to be pleased about its outcome.

When a problem can't be solved right on the spot, the judges will write letters. Here is a 1988 instance in which such letter-writing helps an employee who—again, legally speaking—was defeated. A truck-driver with a list of previous convictions who in a fit of anger quit his job, later regretted his decision, sued his ex-employer to attack the validity of his own notice, and lost his suit. But the judge, Frau Walter, sends a letter to the Lüritz Interior Department: "In cooperation with the Labor Office it will be necessary to immediately instruct an enterprise to employ the plaintiff. Awaiting your response...." The answer comes within a week: the plaintiff has been rehired by the very firm which only recently asserted his dismissal by defeating him in court. Even in situations in which the court could perfectly legitimately reject a suit with formal arguments and save itself some work, it may not do so. A 1988 appeal against a KK decision, for example, complains about an enterprise's unjustified reduction of the plaintiff's annual bonus. But the plaintiff has missed the deadline for appeal; the defendant enterprise's representative, moreover, has appeared in court without his power of attorney. A West German labor judge would have rejected the suit as inadmissible, probably with pleasure would have made a mental note of the resulting gain in time, and would have proceeded to the next item on his list. But Frau Neuman does not send the parties home. She discusses with them the pros and cons of their disagreement, encourages them to settle out of court, orders a break to give the parties time for negotiations, when they achieve a compromise, records its terms, and, for the file, notes that the plaintiff has withdrawn his suit. "Closed," she writes on the folder and places it into her out-tray. Better than "closed": she has restored peace between the parties.

Was it really just solicitude for workers' interests that motivated Lüritz labor judges? I can think of other explanations for their strategies than human kindness. Work in the GDR was, after all, not only a right but also an obligation whose violation was called "asocial behavior" and punished as a criminal offense. The judges who so unbureaucratically saw to it that Lüritz citizens were not without a job and its rewards may, above all, have aimed for more efficient state supervision over outsiders and deviants and for their integration into more easily controllable collectives. If they did, their manifestations of concern were intended not to serve the individual but the state.

But this interpretation would concede less human warmth to Lüritz labor judges than, I think, a close reading of the records that they left behind would warrant. Here is an example: the correspondence between Frau Neuman and the brother-in-law of a down-and-out packer, already fired from his enterprise for drunkenness, known to Frau Neuman from some previous labor litigation. Since May 1986, both judge and brother-in-law have been trying to find employment for the shiftless man. In October, his in-law writes in a letter to Frau Neuman: "If we combine forces in our search for some suitable employment and if I, more than before, try to impress upon my relative the need for living up to one's obligations, we might find an acceptable long-term solution for him." In November, the allies are successful: their protegé finds work in one of the Lüritz fisheries. Frau Neuman asks him to come for a final admonitory pep-talk to the court-house and afterwards writes to his in-law: "H. gave me the impression of optimism. We left with the agreement that if he faces any unmanageable problems, he can contact me at any time. My hope is that this support will no longer be necessary." It is true: far more than in other societies, regular work, in the GDR, was a means of social education and control, and for my Lüritz judges this aspect of employment must have played an important role. But they also saw labor as a human right.

Obviously, the court was not the only social institution looking out for workers' rights. But the assistance from the enterprise, the work collective, or the union looked different from the support that an employee could hope for if he turned to the court for help. In most confrontations between a worker and his enterprise, the work collective, above all, a plaintiff's or defendant's brigade, could be counted on to back him up. But the collectives that I encounter in the case files—as character witnesses, social participants in disciplinary proceedings, and the like—in return for solidarity expect their colleague's adaptation to their rules. Collectives showed little sympathy for outsiders and loners. They did not like people who disturbed the warmth and cohesiveness of their little group. The plaintiff's actions "caused a lot of unrest in the work collective," says one social representative in a 1984 dismissal case. And in a similar case in 1989: many colleagues "no longer want to work together with the plaintiff because he stirs up so much unrest" among people.

Again, these quotes have to be taken with a grain of salt. In most instances, the files do not reveal *how* the collective came to formulate the views that its speaker represents in court. Sometimes, a fortuitous little note in the case file will reveal that only a few of the plaintiff's or defendant's colleagues were even present when the collective's standpoint was articulated and approved. Occasionally, a worker suing his employer over the re-wording of a reference will claim that it turned out too negative because the plaintiff's co-workers (who under East German labor law had to be consulted) did not want to stick their necks out by defending his performance. Admittedly, such accusations, too, confirm that collectives valued peace and quiet more than potentially confrontational discussions. "Collectives" were not "teams." Both groupings are held together by a common work project. But there was additional social glue that made the members of collectives stick together and dependent on each other: their striving for premiums and honorary titles ("Collective of Socialist Labor," for example) that could be endangered by one member's obstinacy and self-will. Work collectives were not only *inclusive* but also *exclusive*: those who could not adapt were outsiders who had no claim on the group's support. By the time a worker found himself in court, his comrades' patience, usually, had already been exhausted.

East German unions, too, did not like people who could not adapt and be integrated. It showed in the unions' legal work. In labor court proceedings, union functionaries could hold two different roles: they could be the "procedural representative" of the employee, that is, function essentially as his attorney, or they could be a "participant" in the proceedings, speaking not so much for the individual worker in court but for the union's general assessment of the issue under litigation. The role of "representative" was a familiar one: already in pre-Socialist days, union functionaries had served as worker advocates in court. The less well defined role of "participant" was new: it was introduced by the first East German Law on Court Organization of 1952 and required a union member to provide the court with information about the social circumstances of a legal dispute and to comment on the case from the perspective of the labor unions. The plural "unions" is misleading. In practice, despite the nominal existence of individual unions in East Germany, the one and only Free Federation of German Unions (*Freier Deutscher Gewerkschaftsbund*, or FDGB), the central union organization in the GDR, spoke for all. The tasks of a union "representative" and a "participant" thus differed in their philosophical perspectives: the first used law as a weapon for the defense of individual rights, the second as a means to advance social welfare. That both of these views existed side by side in East German labor law procedure suggested that both were considered legitimate objectives of the law.

At least in theory, that is. I do find litigation in the 1950s files in which a union "representative" with energy and passion argues the case of his worker client against the employer state. In 1956, for example, Klaus Kosewitz—who later would, for decades, serve as First Party Secretary in the district but who in the 1950s still was an ordinary union man—represented five stevedores in a suit against the Lüritz Port Authority to challenge a reduction in their wages due to an "unavoidable interruption of operations" during which the plaintiffs had been unable to perform their jobs. The Port claimed not to be responsible for their lengthy and unwelcome break: disturbances caused by the belated arrival of cargo or the breakdown of machinery were common in a port and outside the management's control. Although the defendants did not say so, they probably were right about their claim that in a rigid and tightly interwoven planned economy, failures in the performance of ancillary industries were harder to counteract than in the more flexible and more responsive Capitalist market. Very likely the defendant indeed was powerless to avoid the interruptions. But Herr Kosewitz will have none of it. To accept the port's excuses, he says, would mean "to cover up shortcomings in its labor management." Why does the port not sue the East German railroad for its belated delivery of goods? The costs of managerial failures should not have to be borne by employees. Well, maybe Herr Kosewitz was a little more discreet in what he said. But that is what his arguments boiled down to. He won his clients' case--and added, in a letter to the court, that the decision "naturally also must apply" to other stevedores' forced inactivity in similar situations in the future. A Socialist test case, as it where, won by a spunky union representative for his worker clients.

But soon the clear-cut frontlines from the early records—enterprises on the one side, workers on the other—are blurred by the union management itself. Beginning in 1958, the union functionaries participating in labor litigation in the Lüritz court increasingly argue not *for* the employee whose interests are at stake, but *against* him. Often, they try to persuade a worker not to bring suit in the first place, or, if he does, advise him to withdraw his claim. "I fully support the position of the enterprise," says a union man in a 1980 deficit suit against a salesman who accordingly is sentenced to compensate the state trade organization for the missing sum, but who on appeal--this time without the dubious assistance of the union--manages to achieve at least a settlement. In 1989, the union representative of an accountant who sues his enterprise for back pay declares in court: "It is the union's viewpoint that the plaintiff's claim is insupportable." I discover that it makes no difference whether a union member acts as an employee's "representative" (that is, supposedly, as his attorney) or as a mere "participant" (explaining the union's viewpoint to the court). In both incarnations, union officials are more likely to find fault with a worker's case than to support it. "You must realize that you are in the wrong," is what they usually tell their clients. Once, in a 1989 case, a union man admits to his ambivalent position. "As union functionaries, we stand between *Baum und Borke* [between a tree and its bark]" he says in a dismissal suit and approves of a worker's discharge that, in the end, the court declares illegal. Who needs enemies if he has friends like these? "I don't want any union representation," says someone accused of an "asocial life style" in 1980, knowing full well what to expect from the assistance of a union advocate. Sometimes, even people with a reputation for hard work complain that the union "has failed to represent their interests." Not surprisingly, more and more labor plaintiffs and defendants prefer representation by a regular lawyer rather than a union functionary. In 1975, I find the first professional lawyer making his

CHAPTER 5

appearance as counsel in a Lüritz labor case; in 1980, there are two; in 1985, nine; and by 1989, thirteen university-trained (and fee-charging) attorneys make their appearance in my labor files. The union representatives came for free.

Jurists were better placed to defend a worker's claims against his enterprise, or even against the priorities of the economy at large, because they analyzed a legal conflict not in terms of *interests* but in terms of *rights*. Legal formality depoliticizes an issue. It forces jurists to focus on the technical intricacies of a dispute rather than on its social implications. "Thinking like a lawyer" was a way of dealing with the world that mattered even more for judges and prosecutors (who besides possessing professional knowledge also exercised the power of the state) than for their colleagues of the Bar. The idiosyncratic features of the legal process—the different roles assigned to the participants in a trial; the predetermined sequence of their contributions to the hearing; the requirement to base all arguments on individually cited sections of a code; the need to preserve a written record of what happened in the courtroom; and all the other scripted twists and turns of procedural choreography—contributed to the social alienation of an issue and created distance between politics and law; distance, also, between the plaintiff or defendant and the work-collective of which he usually was part. Their professionalism protected the jurists in the courtroom against the bombardment with social and political demands to which all servants of the Socialist state were otherwise exposed.

The protection was far from perfect. After all, the judges, too, were children of the system. They, too, found themselves "between a tree and its bark," and it is undeniable that throughout the entire history of the GDR, its judges were torn between the letter of the law and their loyalty towards Socialism (or perhaps just the Party). Often, judges may not even have been aware of the conflicting value systems under which they operated. Here is an example. Six years after the *Wende*, I have a conversation with Frau Neumann about Herr Brügge, a Lüritz craftsman who under Socialism served for many years as union representative in labor trials, who in this capacity had often argued *against* the workers whose interests he supposedly represented, and whom I know in person as straightforward and as honest as can be. "A wonderful man; so nonpartisan!" Frau Neumann says of him. She, too, in retrospect, approves of siding with the totality of social interests rather than the individual; still clinging to the ideological big picture that in those days had guided her and her comrades at the court, and that, it seems, had also guided Herr Brügge in his work as union representative.

But when I read Frau Neumann's labor law decisions from the days of Socialism, I discover that, as a judge, she did not focus on the "nonpartisan" welfare of the whole but on the individuals in court. As far as I can see, she kept close to the specifications of the legal texts; to individual rights, including those of mavericks and misfits; to form and procedure; to *the law*. When it came to rendering judgment, the professional instincts of my labor judges seem to have outweighed their political convictions. Even the "people's judges" of the 1950s insisted on the observation of legal forms. In 1958, the Lüritz labor court annuls a dismissal because of what appears to be a minor formal flaw: all members of the enterprise's union council had consented, but not, as the law required, at a special union council session, but during a general assembly of the enterprise's staff. In 1960, the court excludes a union member from participation in a labor trial because his power of attorney identifies him as representative not of the defendant employee but of his employer. In 1985, the court rejects a compensation claim by the East German Railroad against one of its employees because he had not been included in the investigation of the accident that caused the damage. In 1989, the court reinstates an employee fired for truancy and work evasion because the enterprise's letter of dismissal had not included a reference number. Obviously, not all the court's labor law decisions are formally pristine. It happens that procedural rules are only halfheartedly observed; that conflicts of interests are overlooked; that participation rights are only superficially respected. Most violations of formality occur in politically sensitive disputes, which I will soon address. But in the majority of boiler-plate, run-of-the-mill labor law decisions it was the rule, not the exception, that my judges stuck close to the letter of the law.

Over the decades, Lüritz employers had to learn that the court cared more about the observation of legal rules than about the efficiency of the planned economy. In the early years, state-owned enterprises occasionally griped about labor court decisions that seemed to undercut the enterprise's fight for plan fulfillment. In 1952, the Lüritz Sugar Factory complained about a judgment assigning a factory-owned apartment to one of the enterprise's pensioners rather than to a recently recruited member of the workforce: "We cannot understand how the local court could decide this issue in such formalistic and un-dialectical manner." The judges were unmoved by the protestations. When in 1971, the selfsame Sugar *Kombinat* introduced reductions of the annual performance bonuses of "undisciplined" members of the workforce "in order to educationally impress upon the work collectives the need to maximize the enterprise's plan fulfillment," a Lüritz judge (I assume it was a judge) draws a big question mark next to the dubious argument and grants the suit of a *Kombinat* employee who protested against the cuts. If he has met the requirements for receiving a particular bonus, says the judgment, any worker, whether otherwise disciplined or not, has "an absolute legal claim" to it. In the final years of the GDR, Lüritz enterprises seem to have made their peace with the district court's insistence on procedural precision. "I have to accept that," says a department head of the VEB Fishing Industry whose "written reprimand" of four of his employees is overturned in court. They had been discovered in a Lüritz restaurant, at 10:30 in the morning, with empty beer glasses on the table, and had been ordered back to work. True, the four had refused to blow into a breathalyzer. But the reprimand had been issued *before*—and not, as the law required, *after*—a thorough conversation with the suspects about their alleged offense.

Can my picture of East German labor litigation possibly be right? I have described a court that resisted local pressures to increase performance; judges who respected the significance of legal formality; a labor case law that defended individual rights against the interests of the collective. Did the court not even make exceptions for politically touchy cases? Yes, in politically touchy cases other rules applied. But at least in Lüritz, these rules were more ambiguous, more complex, and could more easily be manipulated than I would have expected.

Given the structure of the East German legal system, the likelihood of a collision between labor law judges and state authority was slim. There was no judicial review of administrative decisions in the GDR, so neither the decisions of the planning bureaucracy (such as the determination of performance indicators for plan fulfillment) nor management decisions by the enterprise could be attacked in court. If an employee questioned the accuracy of the determination of a bonus, for example, the court had to exclude from its review all sovereign elements that went into the bonus' calculation. It could examine whether the statutory preconditions for the award's payment were fulfilled or whether (as the law required) the enterprise's union organization had been involved in its assessment. What it could not do was question the legitimacy of the underlying indicators for performance.

When exercising their ambition to protect a worker's interests, my Lüritz labor judges thus had to operate within a narrowly confined terrain. Depending on their frame of mind, they could show more or less respect for the official boundary between might and right. I discover that several of the "people's judges" of the 1950s and the early 1960s did not seem to be particularly worried whether they accidentally had overstepped the borders of the little realm assigned to them. In part, their insouciance can be explained by their very rudimentary legal training. But the early judges also drew confidence, I think, from feelings of solidarity with plaintiffs and defendants sharing their own class background and from the conviction that they were serving a good cause. As a result, some of the early labor law decisions seem more fearless than those of later, better trained, and more sophisticated judges.

The arguments my labor judges used to deal with problems that, by official standards, might have been outside their legal reach were plainly shaped by the results they tried to justify. In 1952, for instance, the Lüritz court awards 10% supplementary pay to the guard of a state-owned construction firm for night watches that according to the enterprise's lawyer had been included among the guard's contractual duties. The enterprise had paid the "night bonus" for several years but had discontinued the supplement when so advised by a "Directive of the Ministry of Reconstruction." The Lüritz labor judge, however, focuses on the language of the plaintiff's contract: "The Ministry's Directive cannot be considered a binding source of law but represents no more than an invitation to both parties to adapt their contract by mutual agreement to conform to statutory pay-scales." Six years later the court interprets a state-issued "Decree on Reimbursement for Travel Costs"—contrary to information provided by the Ministry for Food Supply—in favor of the plaintiff employee: "The Central Labor Division of the Ministry is in error if it claims in its submission that the plaintiff, in this case, is not entitled to a daily reimbursement." And in 1960 the court sides with three construction site managers who sue to enforce the continued payment of a "loyalty bonus" that even at the time it was—orally—agreed upon had not conformed to statutory regulations and whose termination had been ordered by the Ministry of Construction. To reach this outcome, the judge, Frau Dankwarth, decides not to rely on the parties' oral contract, which, as she herself admits, had been "illegal" at the time it was concluded. But since the enterprise paid the disputed bonus for a period of fourteen months, the plaintiffs gained what the judge seems to consider as a kind of vested Socialist right to its continuation. "It is a principle of the wage policy of the GDR that earnings may not fall below their previous level. A withdrawal of the bonus would reduce the plaintiffs' take-home pay and therefore is impermissible." Frau Rüstig once described Frau Dankwarth to me (a round and cheerful woman "who loved to dance") and I know her from her decisions as someone who faithfully believed in Socialism. So, true to her temperament and her convictions, she adds a postscript to her judgment that makes peace between the plaintiffs' rights and the improvement of society: she orders two of the plaintiffs, both still under forty years of age, to enroll in additional training courses that will help to raise their wages to the level conforming to the Ministry's official pay-scale. The third plaintiff is too old to be expected to submit to further education efforts—Socialism will pull him along the way he is. But the two others keep their promises to the court and apply for admission to the Lüritz Engineering College for the fall term in 1961.

A very similar case, decided just four years before the death of Socialism in the GDR, can illustrate how Lüritz labor judges, over the decades, became more professional, more formal, and politically more guarded than the generation of Frau Dankwarth was. The issue, again, is a reduction of the plaintiffs' take-home pay: this time caused not by an order of some ministry or other but by a change in the enterprise's own wage classification policy that led to the result that the ten plaintiffs—all radio mechanics with VEB Consumer Services—now receive less pay for the same amount of work they previously performed. As in Frau Dankwarth's case, the plaintiffs claim to be protected against pay cuts that are not warranted by their own misconduct. This time, their assertion of a vested right even appears to be supported by the language in §105 of the Labor Code of 1975: "If the enterprise revises its pay scales, it is obligated to insure that employees [the actual word is *Werktätige*, or "toilers"] do not receive less pay for the same performance." Under the new classification, even considerable extra efforts would not enable the plaintiffs to earn the same remuneration as before.

But the Lüritz labor judge of 1985 does not even address this argument. She dismisses the suit for lack of jurisdiction: the court can review only whether the enterprise was formally authorized to reach specific management decisions, she says, and may not second-guess the substantive legitimacy of its chosen pay scales. When the plaintiffs appeal their case to the Neuburg Regional Court, the appellate judges reject Frau Dankwarth's optimistic notion from the 1960s— that Socialism would not go back on previously achieved entitlements—as no more than a legislative program without any binding impact. Labor Code §105, para. I "does not provide a cause of action for an employee who wants to claim continuation of his previously achieved average pay," the judgment states. A Capitalist judge would have interpreted §105 no differently.

The 1985 case file, almost 200 pages long, reveals additional changes since Frau Dankwarth's days. Unlike their predecessors from the 1960s, the plaintiffs from the 1980s take care to properly organize their collective suit and elect a "group trustee" to speak for them. Instead of placing their faith in the labor union—"which did not represent their interests"—they hire an attorney to argue their case before the Regional Court. Not that they trust the court: their appeal complains of rumors that the District and Regional Courts allegedly had agreed on the legal strategies to disallow the plaintiffs' claim and voices opposition "to adjudication of this kind." The case file reeks of the plaintiffs' bitter discontent, and even their employer and the union representatives seem worried. After the plaintiffs lose their case before the Regional Court, the judgment is the subject of a "discussion" (the German word used is *Aussprache*, which suggests a trusting heart-to-heart) between the plaintiffs, fifteen management representatives, and several union people in the enterprise. The two-hour event is mentioned in my case file. "The debate covered a number of additional labor law issues and can be considered to have served its purposes," I read. Usually, reports on Socialist get-togethers sound more enthusiastic. I detect no echo of the insouciance and optimism that twenty-five years ago had colored Frau Dankwarth's case law.

Thus the official demarcation between judicial and political authority. But different rules applied in cases in which the court did not feel threatened by the demands of government and Party and knew itself to operate on its own territory. In situations in which the law unequivocally had assigned decision-making powers to the court and in which this power had not been curtailed by express and specific orders to the contrary, the judges felt safe enough to follow their own judicial inclinations: in most dismissal cases; most disputes over transfers;

and in all cases that I have seen that involved evaluations of an employee's performance. Admittedly, the boundaries of the judges' home-land, if we can call it that, were blurry. For example, in the mid-1980s, an internal Supreme Court directive had ordered all GDR district courts not to accept complaints by applicants for exit visas who had been fired for that very reason but to reject these suits under §29, para. II of the Code of Civil Procedure as "obviously without merit." As far as I can tell, all East German district courts, including the one in Lüritz, followed the order without visible signs of hesitation. But in many other labor law disputes that for whatever reasons had not attracted the attention of the powers above, Lüritz judges defended the rights even of political outsiders. My judges annulled the transfer of an accountant whom her employers had accused of political lethargy (1956); declared illegal a dismissal that had been instigated by the Party (1958); refused to count an employee's unwillingness to sign a proclamation of solidarity with the PLO as a "violation of labor discipline" (1985); held that if all legal prerequisites for an employee's end-of-year bonus had been met, it could not be reduced because of the recipient's political recalcitrance (1985); and came to the aid of an engineer who because of his mother's application for an exit visa had been transferred to another job (1986). Wisely, the plaintiff in the last case had not sued to regain his old position. But he objected to his employer's *job evaluation*, which had justified the transfer by accusing the plaintiff of a number of imaginary failings and of his—actual—decision to resign his Party membership. The court ordered the enterprise to issue a fair and objective reassessment of the plaintiff's work, and between the pages of the file I find his thank-you note, which gratefully acknowledged the judge's "help and support." If they could get away with it, my labor law judges liked to distinguish between law and politics and to side with the law.

In the event of border squabbles between right and might, they also occasionally managed to pull a conflict from the realm of politics onto the safer territory of the law. Here is a case from 1975 in which the judge successfully used labor law to trump criminal law and in this fashion prevented some youthful foolishness from being dramatized as a dangerous offense against the state. A young woman, nineteen years old and member of a "Youth Brigade" at the Lüritz Beverages Combine is sued by her employer under what East German law called "material responsibility" for having intentionally smashed three bottles during one of the brigade's regular night shifts. The broken glass had damaged the conveyer belt on which, from 8:15 at night to 5:30 in the morning, the defendant and her colleagues had to place recycled bottles for transfer to the enterprise's washing facilities. It took one-and-a-half hours for the conveyer belt to be repaired and for the brigade to resume its work. The enterprise's conflict commission (the in-house lay court that, as usual, decided the employer's suit against his employee) had ordered the culprit to repay the damage of 110.12 Marks and

CHAPTER 5

had reduced her "night bonus" for the date of the offense from 5.00 Marks to 3.50 Marks. A gentle judgment, one should think. But the young woman appeals the decision to the District Court: she hadn't been the only one from her brigade to raise Cain on the night in question. A risky move, for which the only explanation, it seems to me, is the rebelliousness of a nineteen-year-old.

The labor judge, Frau Dankwarth, decides to get to the bottom of the affair. She arranges not one but two hearings of the case: one in court, the second in the "Culture Room" of the Beverages Combine. Forty staff members attend. It turns out that the Youth Brigade hates its nocturnal work and often had discussed what could be done to interrupt its dreaded monotony. Brigade members agreed: "During the night shift, something must break down so we can get a reprieve from working all the time." In the night preceding the appellant's bottle-smashing, a drunken colleague of hers had also damaged the conveyor belt. The shift foreman took some time to report the incident to his superiors and chose not to mention it to the enterprise's Party Secretary. He, too, must have been concerned about the proper demarcation line between law and politics. As a result, the Party learned of the trouble only two weeks after it occurred. Now, the manager of the Beverages Combine speaks of "sabotage." The district prosecutor formally objects to the conflict commission's damage award: the matter was no labor law dispute but belonged in criminal court.

But no dire consequences follow. After her surprisingly unworried and outspoken hearing on the evidence, Frau Dankwarth confirms the judgment of the conflict commission: even unpleasant work does not entitle an employee to willfully destroy his tools. Two weeks later, the prosecutor withdraws his objection to the labor law decision. Somebody must have calmed the waves, and I wouldn't be surprised if it was Frau Dankwarth who had talked some sense into her nervous colleagues. Perhaps she said: "They're practically children! Let us deal reasonably with this matter." And manager and prosecutor allowed themselves to be persuaded.

Nine years after "Beverages Combine," "Orff vs. Phoenix Shipyard VEB" shows that East German labor law, over the years, did not lose its ability to shelter employees, even high-level employees, against the arbitrary disapproval of their bosses and the Party. I probably should say "somewhat shelter," because the protection was far from perfect. But labor law was influential enough to make it worthwhile for an employee to turn to the court for help against the whims of local politicians. In 1984, Herr Orff, a shipyard employee for 20 years and now head of a department, is suddenly dismissed: allegedly, he negligently failed to uncover the fraudulent accounting practices of one of the shipyard's innovator teams. He brings suit. The shipyard's reasons for the firing are indeed so threadbare that in the course of the proceedings it advances additional accusations to strengthen its case against Herr Orff: he is no longer tolerable in his post because on one occasion—fourteen years ago!—he had left classified materials openly about his office and because he currently is known to keep a little booklet with jokes about First Party Secretary Honecker in his desk. Not even the Lüritz Labor Office, which originally (as the law required) had approved of Herr Orff's immediate dismissal, sticks with this decision but recalls its consent as "not warranted under current conditions." The shipyard, willy-nilly, does the same with its dismissal notice. Herr Orff withdraws his suit.

But the real reasons why Herr Orff had to be removed so rudely continue to smolder. The files don't tell me what they are, and I can only guess. I do not think that politics lie at the bottom of this case: Herr Orff is a long-standing member of the Party and in his briefs does not present himself as a dissenter but as an insider whose feelings have been deeply hurt. Perhaps he doesn't get along with other members of the management. Perhaps he is a cantankerous curmudgeon. Perhaps somebody else is meant to get his job. It is obvious that not just the shipyard's leadership but that the Party, too, wants to get rid of him: the Party Secretariat already has confirmed Herr Orff's removal from the list of leading district cadres. In any case: three months after the original dismissal, the Phoenix Shipyard fires Herr Orff again, this time not with immediate effect but in line with the statutory period for giving notice. Again, Herr Orff brings suit against his enterprise. Herr Brügge, a member of the Federation of East German Labor Unions who is assigned to represent the Phoenix Shipyard union at the trial, is called into the Party District Bureau and is told that the enterprise will count on his support in court. Fifteen years later he describes to me how he was talked into defending the dismissal at the trial. It is the only incident in his long union career, he says, of which today he feels ashamed.

The court, asked to decide a dispute of which essential aspects never are articulated, does its best to navigate between the fronts. I assume that Frau Neumann, the presiding judge, has not remained ignorant of the fact that the Party, too, is interested in Herr Orff's dismissal. She sticks with the usual procedure in regular (that is: not for cause) dismissal cases and asks both parties to appear in court to work out what East German labor law called "an autonomous resolution of the conflict." Ordinarily, that would mean the employee's transfer to a loosely comparable position in the defendant enterprise. The parties' negotiations fail because the Phoenix Shipyard's pay offer for that new job stays 100 Marks below the monthly salary demanded by the plaintiff. When a settlement seems out of reach, Frau Neumann rejects Herr Orff's complaint. She agrees that the Honecker jokes in that desk drawer in the plaintiff's office are insufficient reason to dismiss him. But given his lax attempts to shed light on the accounting fraud that had been the initial cause of litigation, Herr Orff had shown a lack of "political vigilance" and thus had lost the trust of both the shipyard management and of its work collective.

CHAPTER 5

Peering back more than twenty years into a foreign past, it seems to me that Frau Neumann's decision was a compromise. She was willing to hold out a helping hand to someone dismissed for possibly dubious reasons but was not willing, when it was rejected, to get into potential trouble with the Party in order to save Herr Orff an additional 100 Marks a month. Again, I'm speculating. I have not been able to find out what the dispute really was about. Herr Orff, deeply offended by what he called the trial's "manipulation of the truth," appealed the Lüritz judgment and with the help of an attorney obtained a settlement in the Neuburg Regional Court that gave him a less influential post with Phoenix than he originally had occupied, but slightly better pay than the shipyard had offered him in Lüritz. The plaintiff "had prevailed in his essential purpose," Herr Orff's lawyer declared after the appellate ruling; at least, he and his client had saved face.

The story strikes me as significant because it shows how his engagement of the law ensured a much better outcome for Herr Orff's employment troubles than he would have obtained without the courts' assistance. Party, enterprise, and union leadership all wanted to get rid of him. True, the courts did not prevent injustice (if it was injustice) from occurring. But the appeal to the law, the use of courts as places in which a citizen legitimately could defend his personal interests, the procedures set into motion by Herr Orff's suit and appeal, nevertheless helped to mitigate and limit that (possible) injustice. Like Herr Böhnke's litigation over the Cooperative Hotel, which I described in the preceding chapter on property, Herr Orff's labor litigation, too, had helped to defend a citizen against authorities more powerful than he was.

"Orff vs. Phoenix Shipyards" also reveals that the Socialist state and Party did not necessarily present a monolithic front to be faced by a weak and lonely citizen. Yes, the enterprise's plan to dump Herr Orff had been supported, maybe even instigated, by the District Party leadership. But the Lüritz Labor Office (whose cooperation was needed for the plan's successful execution) after initial wavering refused to go along. The district prosecutor (who had brought the initial case for fraud against the innovator-group whose machinations had served to justify the anti-Orff campaign) refused to prosecute Herr Orff himself because of lack of evidence. The union (whose representative, Herr Brügge, had been enlisted by the Party to testify against Herr Orff at the labor trial) in this case was not supported by its membership: as the plaintiff's attorney revealed at the appellate stage, of sixty union members in Herr Orff's department at the shipyard, only twenty-five had been involved in the department's collective call for his dismissal. Referring to those Honecker jokes (which were supposed to justify the ouster), Herr Orff's attorney even risked a joke himself that seemed inspired by the sly and devious insolence of one of Bertholt Brecht's dramatic heroes. The jokes had neither "been read aloud in court during the evidentiary phase of the trial," the lawyer said, nor had they "been cited verbatim in the indictment." Neither the plaintiff nor the lay assessors had thus been able to address their offensiveness. They were inadmissible evidence.

But the year is 1984. The court is tired; at stake is not a criminal but a labor law case in which the jokes may truly not have played a role; and the attorney is Herr Arhuis, not a local man but from a neighboring town: a flamboyant and glittering outsider with the nimbleness and pugnacity of a terrier who by 1984 seems to enjoy something like a fool's freedom on the staid and boring legal scene in Lüritz. Five years before the Turnabout, the Socialist legal system is full of cracks and fissures in which, like ivy in a crumbling wall, doubt and dissent take root.

A 1988 letter by Frau Walter shows that even my Lüritz labor judges shared those doubts. She had rejected a collective suit by thirteen employees of the Lüritz shipyard for lack of jurisdiction: the plaintiffs wanted labor bonuses restored that had been reduced for reasons beyond their individual control, and Frau Walter restated the principle that we already have encountered—that "the court was not authorized to review performance norms set by the enterprise." But she is displeased by her own decision, and five days later says so in a letter to the shipyard management. Her judgment "must have appeared formalistic and unpersuasive" to the plaintiffs, writes Frau Walter. It is an "essential principle" of GDR labor law that employees must be given performance norms whose fulfillment or over-fulfillment they can control themselves by the amount of effort put into their work. At a minimum, the enterprise should have discussed the change of performance criteria with its workforce. Frau Walter "recommends" that the shipyard management do what she herself, as judge, had not felt authorized to do: that is, revise its own decision and restore the bonuses to their previous level. Frau Walter also sends a copy of her letter to the District Party Bureau.

I do not know what happened in the end. There is a little note attached to the case file—"Shipyard's reply in references folder"—and I cannot locate the "references folder" in the Lüritz archive. But I know what happened at the Lüritz District Court. In the last years of the GDR, the system's approaching fall is foreshadowed by its labor law statistics. Suits over terminations of employment rise: while in 1985, dismissal cases made up only 8.4% of the court's labor law caseload, by 1989, almost a third of all labor litigation deals with firings, mostly for cause. The majority of cases involve alcohol. My files reveal how much drinking goes on in Lüritz enterprises: terms like "breathalyzer" and "blood alcohol content" pop up with increasing frequency. Sometimes the plaintiff tries to defend himself with the assertion that "everyone in my collective drinks." In 1989, two deadly accidents at the Phoenix Shipyard are caused by alcohol consumption on the job.

CHAPTER 5

If possible, Lüritz labor judges try to preserve some stability in the rocky lives of alcohol-dependent workers by annulling their dismissals: in 1989, because the enterprise allegedly had not done enough for its employee's rehabilitation; in 1990, by copying West German principles of employment law and characterizing the enterprise's notice as "not socially justified." In June 1990, a last-minute decree of the GDR People's Chamber orders all East German personnel files to be purged of entries that denote disciplinary actions taken against employees—it is an attempt to cleanse what under Socialism were called "cadre files" of blemishes that a future Capitalist employer might hold against a worker from the (soon to be former) GDR. But the measure does not do much good. The law cannot hold back the avalanche of change. In the old days, East German judges had invalidated all dismissals to which the enterprise's union organization had not given its consent. In 1990, even before Germany's reunification on October 3, most of those union organizations have already been dissolved; new West German–style "works councils" have not yet been elected. State-owned enterprises are transformed into limited companies whose credit evaporates, whose orders disappear into thin air, and who must let go of much of their staff. In the last briefs by Socialist employers that I find in the Lüritz labor law files, the many titles and awards that enterprises used to boast of on their company stationery simply are x'ed out. At this point, Lüritz labor judges no longer quash dismissals: they have lost the power to keep the unemployable employed. Even the severance pay that the court occasionally orders for many enterprises is unaffordable. Sometimes, the employer and his former employee settle for installments. Law that once was helpless in collisions with the Party now must give way to the overwhelming force of the economy. In June 1990, Frau Neumann leaves her position on the Lüritz labor bench and accepts a job as legal counsel to the Phoenix Shipyard. That way, she will at least continue doing labor law.

CHAPTER 6

FAMILIES

In hard times, people rely on their families. The rule held true particularly for the first and last years of the GDR. When states collapse, one holds on to those with whom one shares older and tougher ties than government-produced and -sponsored commonalities. But even in the in-between years, when Socialism in East Germany seemed to grow stronger and to settle down for good, most citizens in the GDR must have depended on their families more than their neighbors in the Federal Republic did. In a state that does not recognize the contradictions and tensions between a private and a public realm, between *bourgeois* and *citoyen*, between self-interest and public-spiritedness, one needs a refuge to recover from the claims of the collective. In George Orwell's novel *1984* it is a little alcove in the hero's flat in which he tries to hide from the camera eyes of Big Brother. The GDR was a far less menacing place than Orwell's Oceania: more humane, more Prussian, not nearly as efficient a state as Orwell's dystopia, and instead of the omnipresent "Telescreen," only an occasional *Stasi* informant observed one's private life. Nevertheless, for many people in the GDR, the family must have been the most important niche in this society of niches.

It follows that the family law files in the Lüritz archive will provide a less reliable picture of daily family life in the GDR than, for example, the labor law files could draw of people's relationships at work. Court files, in any case, reflect only the *failures* in the lives of their protagonists: their misunderstandings, disputes, shipwrecks. In the GDR, happy families were all alike at least insofar as they could all withdraw into their niches. Unhappy family members were forced to leave their niche if they desired a legal resolution of their problems. But how typical were the relationships that litigation exposed to the light of day? In 1985, the roughly 80,000 inhabitants of Lüritz (city and district) brought 462 family disputes to court—not more than a tiny snippet from everyday family life in town. I do not know how most Lüritz family members interacted with each other and how they defined their relationship to the state. The F-files in the Lüritz archive tell me how the official Socialist image of the family changed over the life span of the system; what the disputants (and often: what members of their collectives who participated in the trial) expected from each other and the state; and under what political and practical conditions families lived their lives. But

CHAPTER 6

we must not forget that in the niche existence of most Lüritz families, things may have looked different from the way I will now describe them.

Most Lüritz family law records deal with divorces. Doctrinally, East German divorce law was ahead of its West German counterpart. In the Federal Republic, the Civil Code's traditional divorce law based on fault was only in 1976 replaced by a divorce law that no longer was fixated on the spouses' marital misconduct but instead tried to gauge the objective health of the relationship about to be dissolved. In the GDR, already a Decree of 1955 had introduced the breakdown of a marriage as the only legal ground for its resolution. The new East German Family Code of 1965 confirmed this approach and defined "breakdown" as "serious reasons" that caused a marriage "to have lost its meaning for the children, the spouses, and therefore also for society." The definition implies a close connection between individual and social welfare and explains why authoritarian legal systems prefer to base divorce on marital breakdown rather than on fault: because in their world view, a marriage serves not only the interests of its partners but also those of society, and its continued existence therefore should depend not only on the couple's mutual commitment but also on the marriage's capacity to serve its social functions. The Nazis introduced divorce based on breakdown in order to more easily replace childless marriages with marriages producing offspring. East German Socialists who talked about the "social functions" of a marriage were instead concerned about the welfare of the children if their parents separated. Since the "breakdown" of a marriage was defined as its factual collapse, each divorce required a thorough judicial investigation into the actual condition of the marriage. Again, this notion of objective marital health that may exist quite independent of the spouses' actual emotions explains the similarities between Nazi and Socialist divorce law: it required the court to carefully examine a marriage's condition and in this fashion gave it more control over divorces than a divorce law based on fault that can be (and has been) easily manipulated by the parties. In 1954, an East German family law article asserted that only a divorce law based on breakdown does justice "to the authority of our state."[15] The breakdown principle transforms a private personal relationship into a matter of public welfare.

So far, the theory. Practically, the question of "fault" or "breakdown" matters much less to couples splitting up than the moral climate in their country and the self-definition of the judges adjudicating their divorce. Today—under breakdown law—a marriage usually is considered beyond repair if only *one* of the spouses wants to get away from it. In the 1960s—under fault law—the West German Federal Court defended such a rigidly abstract concept of "marriage as an institution" that it found "misconduct" even in the loss of affection after years of involuntary separation during WWII, and so denied the "guilty" spouse the right to cut a bond that political upheavals had severed long ago. On both sides of the

Wall, authoritarian judges were for many years convinced of the unassailability of their positions, and on both sides, the pill, the sexual revolution, and the *Zeitgeist* caused divorce law to gradually relax in the 1970s and 1980s. In Lüritz, denials of divorces dropped from 7.5% of all divorce suits in 1960 to 3.5% in 1970, and in the 1980s disappeared altogether from the files. By the time the Wall came down, both Germanies—East and West—for all intents and purposes accepted divorce upon demand. Individual family members might be powerless in confrontations with the state. But in the end, even ruthless governments cannot successfully ignore the seismic shifts in the lifestyles and expectations of their citizens. Which is not to say that East German law, throughout the decades, did not attempt to coax and bully its citizens out of their private niches and to submerge them in society at large.

Still, the earliest family law decisions in the Lüritz Archive are practical and nonpolitical. The turmoil of the war and postwar years had disrupted many family relationships, and the judges and makeshift judges of this period did their best to bring some legal order into damaged and disjointed lives. In 1950, more than a quarter of all Lüritz divorces involve a spouse who is already in the West or whose location is listed as "unknown." The border between the Soviet and the Western Occupation Zones offers a chance to escape unwelcome obligations: husbands and wives who had been separated for too long have found new partners; fathers run away from child support; and sometimes a party or his or her attorney go West before litigation even is concluded. The family law files mirror the confusion and poverty of the postwar years. A divorce plaintiff asks the court to please divide the couple's "heating materials." Marriage certificates are often unproduceable because "all documents and personal papers have been lost." In the early 1950s, the aftershocks of the East German land reform reach the district court when some of the supposed winners in the gigantic land redistribution scheme—the "new farmers" or *Neubauern*—sue for divorce because their spouses are no longer willing to slave away on a couple's small allotment. At this early stage of East German legal history, the cooperation between East and West German family courts is matter-of-fact and nonpolitical. Both sides provide assistance to the colleagues across the border and are united in the goal to protect weak family members wherever they need protection. Divorces are quick and as painless as the law can make them. Although both sides still operate under the bourgeois fault rule that entitles only the "innocent and injured" spouse to obtain a divorce from the "guilty" party, the courts treat fault as merely a formal requirement that structures the proceedings. The plaintiff (usually the woman) claims that the defendant violated his marital obligations; the husband refuses to give evidence; the court imputes the correctness of the unopposed assertion—that is all. Witnesses are almost never called. It is the judge's task to process legal conflicts, not to improve the world.

CHAPTER 6

But all that changes soon. Already in 1950, five years before the introduction of breakdown divorce in the GDR, its brand-new Supreme Court declares that East German family law "also must promote the goals and ideals of society,"[16] and two years later the Court directs its family law judges not to ground divorces on the couple's evidence alone but to carefully investigate the actual state of the spouses' relationship with each other.[17] How else can a judge tell whether society is still interested in the preservation of the marriage? I get the impression that Socialist law in these years measures the quality of a marriage by its ability to carry out its daily tasks: as a housing-, work-, and educational arrangement that can serve useful purposes even if the parties to the arrangement no longer feel affection for each other. The court, accordingly, looks for the kind of evidence that can reveal whether the spouses still can function as an efficient team. Does the wife keep the household in good order? Do the children make it to school on time? Since not the emotional but the social condition of the marriage needs to be evaluated, the court calls witnesses who are in a position to judge the couple's family performance from up close: colleagues, neighbors, fellow tenants in the spouses' apartment block.

But since in all close and mingled human groupings gossip and rumors add welcome color and excitement to the monotony of daily life, the court's evidentiary hearings always veer back to the issues that had also been at the center of the old divorce proceedings based on fault: to the personal misconduct of the parties. Despite all rational intentions of the law, the public *interest* in the marriage tends to be crowded out by the public *curiosity* about the spouses' missteps and entanglements. The judges, too, cannot shake off their conventional outrage at immoral conduct. Their aggressiveness in getting to the bottom of the case diminishes the spouses' own control over their divorce. Divorce defendants who in the early years used to refuse to testify about their infidelities, by the end of the 1950s no longer assert their right to silence. In 1955, Frau Christiansen questions three witnesses on whether the wife exchanged kisses with another man; in 1960, Judge Kellner not only puts the wife's colleague (and suspected lover) on the witness stand but interrogates six other colleagues of hers, all teachers at the same Lüritz school, to find out whether any of them has ever seen the wife and alleged paramour together. "Yes, one afternoon at the railroad station," I read in the trial record and shake my head; "yes, once near the Policlinic," "my husband told me that Herr N. used to visit the defendant"—all this in a divorce case that is uncontested and that in the end leads to the dissolution of the marriage. I assume that one reason for Herr Kellner's thorough exploration of the evidence was the couple's own refusal to assist in the investigation of their love life. Herr Kellner—not someone to doubt his or the Socialist state's authority—may have felt entitled to quash this kind of passive opposition. Was it not his duty as a judge to uncover what Socialists called "the material truth"?

Labor collectives, too, were supposed to learn not to ignore their colleagues' personal problems but, as their brother's keeper, to help with criticism and advice to save endangered marriages. When Frau Rüstig learns in 1960 that a stevedore's fellow workers at the harbor consider his many dalliances and the resulting divorce suit of his wife to be the couple's "personal affair," she arranges a public discussion of "Socialist Morals and Ethics in Connection with the Divorce Suit Hauser vs. Hauser." Twenty-four dockworkers from the defendant's shift and two lay assessors attend. The record does not tell whether the one-hour admonition was a pedagogical success. Some of the participants appear reserved; others eagerly tell all they know about the new girlfriend of their colleague. As Frau Rüstig admits herself, the discussion "came too late" to save the marriage. But "in the future, workers at the VEB Sea-Port will pay more attention to budding love affairs amongst their colleagues."

The proud assertion appears not to have been an empty boast. I find many examples in the 1960s' files of work collectives trying to chastise, coax, dissuade, or otherwise use their combined moral weight to talk a colleague out of a planned divorce. Sometimes, they have been encouraged in their efforts by a superior or a judge; sometimes, they seem to act on their own initiative. "All representatives of the enterprises of both spouses encouraged them numerous times to look for a way out and to put some order back into their marriage," a couple's colleagues report in a divorce trial of 1965—the effort failed. In 1972, a father says in a custody dispute: "I wanted to divorce my wife but the entire collective was against it. They talked and talked until I finally gave up on the idea." In villages and enterprises, local Party secretaries may lean on comrades and admonish them to patch their troubled marriages. Sometimes, one of the spouses (mostly, it is the woman) comes to court to ask a judge to talk some reason into a straying husband or wife. Employers, too, may try their hand at marriage reconciliation. In 1958, the commanding officer of a policeman on the brink of divorce writes in a letter to his subordinate's wife: "In a few days, I will come up to Lüritz to talk about how to arrange your family affairs. I prefer personal conversations in such matters." Two years later, the Secretary of an enterprise's Free German Youth Organization (the East German junior organization of the Party) admits to having failed his obligations when he gives evidence at one member's divorce trial: "We should have gotten more involved in the plaintiff's family problems."

Looking at some of these divorces, especially those in one of the farming villages surrounding Lüritz, I can occasionally understand why a divorce might also be of interest to the parties' work collective. Take this example: the marriage of two agronomists on a collective farm is on the rocks, and the members of the cooperative are afraid of losing either one or the other valued specialist. So they arrange a public meeting in the "culture room" of the cooperative, at which a vote is taken to transfer the new girlfriend of the plaintiff husband to another village in order to eliminate the cause of trouble. I cannot tell what happened to the girlfriend in the end. But I find other cases in the files in which a work collective, or, indeed, a judge who is adjudicating the divorce suit, uses the same approach to save a marriage by suggesting the transfer of the new partner of one of the spouses to another job. It is a strategy that in a planned economy seems easier to realize than in a market economy and that in none of the Lüritz cases I have seen produced a visible success. Still, the method demonstrates the extraordinary trust in these years in the almighty power of the law to change behavior. The judge is seen as a player of marionettes who only has to pull the proper cords to make his figures move into the position that state and Socialist morals have assigned to him.

To do so, he needs and expects the help of the collective. In 1960, Judge Rüstig invites the cadre manager of the Engineering School to the divorce proceedings of one of his students in order to testify on "the efforts undertaken by the school to save the marriage" (barely any, as it turns out). Twenty years later, still the same ideological optimist, she proposes that the director of a Lüritz laboratory foil the divorce plans of two of his employees by transferring the husband's rival for the affections of his wife, also a laboratory worker, to an "isolated workplace" at the institute. But now, in 1980, the director no longer feels the pressure to cooperate. His polite rejection of Frau Rüstig's plans is not signed with the "Socialist greetings" customary between correspondents who are both Party members, but with the old-fashioned, bourgeois "yours sincerely." Many years later the director tells me why he chose that wording: because he wanted to distance himself from the court's manipulation of other people's personal affairs. To call the undertaking illegitimate even in 1980 required more political spirit than he was willing to invest in the matter.

That was Frau Rüstig's last year on the bench. In May 1980 she retires; the last Lüritz member of the generation of "people's judges" who are respected by the younger judges at the court, but whose naïve and eager efforts to improve the world are also, occasionally, smiled upon. By now, the uninhibited involvement of collectives in the resolution of family disputes had become something of an embarrassment to the East German administration of justice. Former Supreme Court judge and Minister of Justice Hilde Benjamin admitted in 1982: "We overrated the participation of collective representatives."[18] Indeed, the testimony of those whom I encounter in divorce files from the 1950s and 1960s seems motivated less by feelings of proletarian solidarity with the divorcing couple than by the pride of playing an important role in an entertaining scandal. Housemates and neighbors of the spouses rarely show restraint. Maybe the forced proximity of daily interactions in close space dulled people's sense of separation between their own and others' lives. "The walls are thin and if someone talks a little louder, we can hear everything," a neighbor says in 1960. "Often, we could hear arguments already early in the morning," a fellow tenant says in another case and adds in a hurt tone: "The parties did not speak to me about the reasons for their fights." Some testimony reflects the suffocating supervision by one's neighbors in a life at close quarters. "The plaintiff, as a rule, comes home around 5 PM," somebody tells the court. "Then she changes clothes and leaves again. She returns either with the last bus or early in the morning." Many witnesses report no more than rumors and neither the judge nor the officers from the Lüritz Youth Agency (who participate in custody disputes) seem to find fault with third-hand evidence.

Divorces that involve representatives from the spouses' work collective look a little different. Their evidence tends to be more reserved and more concerned about a comrade's welfare. The familiarity of people sharing the same workplace is more constructive and more positive than that of tenants brought together only by a housing shortage. In 1970, a department manager who (together with five other notables from the couple's enterprise) tries to talk the spouses out of their intended separation, says at the outset of the reconciliation meeting: "It is the purpose of this discussion to understand Colleague F.'s motives for his decision without invading the privacy of his marriage." But to my Western eyes, what follows in the record of the meeting looks so intensely private that tactful reticence appears to be a hopeless undertaking. Still, the participants must have done a better job than I thought possible: as I learn more than thirty years after the event from the "Register of Lüritz Inhabitants," both spouses still live together at the same address.

But work collectives also get annoyed if one of theirs is unwilling to listen to advice. "It is impossible to talk with the defendant about his marital problems," I read in a divorce file from 1980. "He is a complete loner who only wants to do his job." Up to the last days of the GDR, fellow workers remain surprisingly convinced of their ability to judge the health of their colleagues' marriage. Here is a quote from the assessment of the reconciliation chances of a couple with long-standing problems: "The collective is convinced that this marriage can be saved. But the defendant must reign in some of his weaker traits. The plaintiff should not only focus on the defendant's negative characteristics." In this particular case the colleagues are mistaken. Six years later, the marriage is divorced—at a time when both spouses, now in their sixties, probably have less strength to build their separate lives than they had at the time of the initial litigation. There is no denying the good will and comradely concern that are reflected in some collective interventions. They may explain why, since the 1970s, I occasionally encounter cases in which the colleagues do not speak against, but *in support* of a divorce or in which they keep a close eye on a fellow worker even *after* his marriage has been terminated. Here is a citation from 1980 that shows a work collective at its best: "In the last couple of years, we often had to argue with the defendant because of his heavy drinking. In the last five weeks, he has not had a single drink at work. We think that the parties' marriage definitely should be dissolved, both in the interest of the plaintiff wife and of the children. On the other hand, we obviously fear that the defendant will lose yet another hold on life when he gets divorced. Knowing all this, we will do our best to take care of him in the future. We do expect, though, that he does at least a little bit to help us."

I cannot tell whether this kind of brotherly support was common among East German work collectives. I do know, though, that at least the courts began to doubt the benefits of collective marriage therapy. The participation of collective representatives in divorce proceedings sank from 15.3% of all cases in 1976 to 5.5% in 1989. Moreover, the way in which the Lüritz court *used* the collective input changed. While earlier, the spouses' workmates had been asked to comment on the inevitability of divorce itself, they were in later years more often questioned over custody issues. But since even in contested cases, custody in the GDR almost always was awarded to the mother, the colleagues' view of the mother's suitability had little weight. By the 1980s, the Youth Authority played the most important role in custody decisions. The human insights (or prejudices) of the couple's colleagues were replaced by the professional influence of social workers. In 1989, five times more functionaries from the Youth Authority than representatives of work collectives participated in East Germany's divorce proceedings.

That does not mean that Lüritz judges had renounced their claim to often have a better understanding of the divorcing couple's needs than the spouses had themselves. Judicial marriage management seemed to come naturally to them. Besides the outright denial of divorce, the judge had other means to assert authority over the spouses' life plans—primarily by suspending the trial (for up to a year) in order to give the parties time and opportunity to mend their marriage. If spouses objected to suspensions, the court, supposedly, was to override them only to protect the interest of children. In practice, judges were less hesitant. The early people's judges in particular, who liked to resolutely use their powers to improve the world, seem to have seen it almost as an obligation to step in if the couple's own attempts at reconciliation faltered. "In the interest of marriage preservation, it cannot be left to chance whether a couple has the willpower and energy to overcome their problems," I read in a 1973 divorce file. In 1968, Frau Dankwarth (who decides family law as well as labor law disputes) suspends for six months the divorce suit of a woman against the violent and alcohol-dependent father of her child because she believes that an alcohol rehabilitation program for the husband might preserve the marriage. "The court alerted the spouses to a realistic possibility to save their relationship," she writes. Lüritz judges also like to suspend divorce proceedings in situations in which a couple has just been assigned a much desired space in one of the GDR's state-run holiday resorts: "Here is an opportunity to overcome their conflict of which the parties absolutely must be made aware."

My judges' marriage philosophy is superficial, practical, and stern: just try a little harder and you'll see that things are not as bad as you suggest. "It must be expected of the marriage partners…" is a standard formula in many court decisions. What the court expects are self-denial and discipline. Marital loyalty as a civic duty? Maybe that is the reason why Frau Dankwarth (whose reasonable and instructive resolution of labor law disputes I just admired in the preceding chapter on labor law) issued particularly harsh decisions to adjourn divorces. The mere promise of a hitherto brutal husband to reform is good enough for her to delay the wife's divorce suit: because Socialism will always accept repentant sinners back into the fold and because, again like a real Socialist, Frau Dankwarth does not distinguish between a person's public and his private self and therefore sees his violation of marital duties as not essentially different from the violation of his labor obligations. Both are owed society just as much as they are owed one's family and oneself. It does not seem to occur to Frau Dankwarth that the loss of trust within a marriage is weightier than the loss of trust in socially more distant relationships.

It is quite possible, of course, that at least on some occasions, a judge's suspension of divorce proceedings was simply meant to demonstrate her own authority and to insist that her judicial diagnosis of the marriage trouble was correct. I find a few cases in the files in which *consecutive* divorce suits of the same couple were *both* suspended: as if to reassert the reasonableness of the judge's initial ruling. "I almost always could tell whether a marriage could be saved or not," Frau Rüstig told me, looking back upon her days as judge, and for corroboration, proudly mentioned the bunch of roses that a happy couple once had brought her after reconciling in her courtroom. And did the peace last? Well, no, Frau Rüstig admitted. As she later learned, the couple did eventually divorce. "But that was after my time," meaning: that was after Frau Rüstig had passed on the responsibility for the spouses' welfare to younger colleagues at the Lüritz court. In the spring of 1980, the Regional Court in Neuburg overrules one of her last decrees suspending a divorce. Frau Rüstig's efforts to save the marriage had been "praiseworthy," the appellate judges say. But reconciliation at this point was "hopeless."

I have tried follow-up on the fate of some of the Lüritz couples whose divorce plans were derailed by the suspension of their suits. Given the limits of my time and sources, the results were spotty. The post-reunification register of the inhabitants of Lüritz (my copy dates from 2001) sometimes can tell me whether spouses who once felt that their marriage was beyond repair many years later still live together at the same address. Sometimes a collection of index cards in the Lüritz archive containing the name of every litigant at the Lüritz District Court reveals that a spouse has brought more than one divorce suit against the same wife or husband. But my data are unreliable: I do not know whether spouses moved away or died and my impressions of the success or failure of my court's reconciliation policy remain anecdotal. As far as I can tell, the most implausible suspensions always failed: at least upon appeal, violent marriages regularly were divorced. But even a number of more hopeful-looking cases in the end resulted in divorce. Over the years, the court's peace-making efforts tired. Suspensions dropped from 13.8% of Lüritz divorce proceedings in 1965 to roughly 6% in 1985. By 1989, only 4% of all divorce suits in the entire GDR were adjourned to facilitate the couple's reconciliation.

In part, the sinking figures probably reflect the growing workload and the weariness of judges who were increasingly reluctant to exert themselves in the pursuit of doubtful ideological successes. My judges did not seem to lose their authoritarian demeanor, though. Perhaps the conviction of being always in the right is a professional disease of family court judges everywhere. If it is your daily job to realign lives that are out of kilter, you may be tempted to treat the clients of your court as patients rather than as autonomous adults. Most divorce plaintiffs were women (more dependent than men); most suits affected children (even more dependent); many defendants in family law disputes had money or drinking problems (again, a sign of social weakness), and the adjudication of their problems took place within a legal system in which the gradient of authority from state to citizen was steeper than in a Capitalist democracy. As a result, the attitude of Lüritz judges toward the parties in a family law dispute seemed even more parental than in other civil litigation. Occasionally, the self-righteousness of a legal system that knew all the answers could be crushing.

Take Lüritz case law on the termination of parental rights. Under the GDR Family Code of 1965, termination required "the grave and knowing violation of parental obligations by the person entitled to custody" and had to be ordered by the district court upon application by the Youth Authority. Parents who lost their child by way of termination could sue to have their rights restored if they could convince the court that they had overcome their previous failings. Here, too, the rule applied (at least in theory) that Socialism was always willing to reintegrate repentant sinners. Practically, termination decisions could be rescinded only if the child had not yet been adopted, which meant that the rule affected mostly older children who were difficult to place. Temporary interventions in parental rights that were intended to protect the child, but not to permanently sever family ties (such as provisional placements in state institutions or with foster parents) did not require any court involvement but could be ordered by the Youth Authority on its own. The parents could not challenge such orders in court but could only lodge informal complaints that were decided by the Youth Authority itself.

There were not many terminations in the GDR; in 1982, only 524 cases in the entire country. Lüritz fit into the national pattern. If we forget about the transfer of custody from one unsatisfactory parent to the other, more suitable parent (which left the child within his family), there were not more than two or three court decisions a year by which my judges permanently severed a child's legal ties to his parents and placed him under the authority of the state. At least as far as Lüritz is concerned, the many horror stories that spread through the German press after the collapse of Socialism—that children of dissidents were torn from their parents by what the newspapers called "forced adoptions"—were definitely false. Searching through all terminations of parental rights that happened in my town between 1965 and 1989, I have not found a single case in which a child's removal from his parents' care could be explained by the parents' hostility towards Socialism. And yet, I would not call the Lüritz termination case law "unpolitical." The Youth Authority's suits to remove a child were not triggered by the wish to restrain a parent's political unruliness and to limit his or her pernicious ideological influence over a future citizen. Nevertheless, the judges' and the social workers' notions of proper parenting; their attitudes toward work, toward women, toward social outsiders; their views of the importance of legal formality were saturated with the ideology of Socialism like a sponge with water.

Usually, it all began with the court's question as to whether a parent's unsatisfactory work performance or, worse, the lack of any suitable employment, indicated serious parental failure. The question applied to mothers as well as fathers. Already in 1950, the GDR Supreme Court had held that marriage was not a legal institution meant to insure a woman's livelihood. In the GDR, "everyone, including every woman, is obligated to put his or her labor power at the disposal of the Socialist economy."[19] As far as I can see, almost all East German women accepted the idea that they could not expect to be supported by their husbands if their marriage failed. In 1988 in Lüritz, only 1.9% of all divorces included the award of a short-term transitional allowance to the wife. Life-long alimony was unheard of. Since almost all women in the GDR held down a job (toward the end, 91% of all East German women worked outside their homes, compared to 44.1% of women in the Federal Republic),[20] they would be able after a divorce to stand on their own two feet. So far, the theory on which both judges and women in the GDR seemed to agree.

If a mother did not live up to this expectation of autonomy, it was considered her own fault. Judges refused to see that a woman's cherished independence might well begin to totter when after a divorce she suddenly was expected to handle on her own all those duties that before the break at least had partially been shared: children, job, and household. Nor could unmarried mothers count

CHAPTER 6

on the court's lenience if, without the support of their child's father and overwhelmed by work and household duties, they began to neglect either their children or their job. Not showing up for work might lead to a prosecution for "asocial behavior." Neglecting the children would provoke, first, supervising measures by the Youth Authority and then, eventually, a suit by the Agency for termination of parental rights. In the Federal Republic, a single mother overwhelmed by childcare obligations could have stayed at home and lived on welfare payments. In the GDR, it was expected that she place her children in a state-run nursery and thus would be in the position to manage both her tasks: work *and* childcare.

Not even East German mothers themselves raised the objection that children need time and attention even *after* they come home from daycare and the mother returns from work. "She had no explanation for her inability to cope," an unmarried mother with a full-time job and five children aged between two and twelve said in a termination case in 1969. When judging how much mothers should be able to achieve in the course of an ordinary work day, both the court and the Youth Authority seem merciless. In 1976, a mother loses her parental rights over her five children because they were inadequately taken care of "despite the fact" that the woman's employer (ostensibly to ease her lot) had moved her to the early morning shift (which meant that she had to leave the house before 5 AM). Since she now came home in the afternoon, she should have been able "to properly occupy and supervise the children after their return from daycare," ruled the court. Three years later, a twenty-seven-year-old divorced mother loses her three children, aged between three and eight, because her housekeeping had not improved even after her enterprise "as a favor" had reduced her workload. By how much? Instead of eight hours, the mother now had to spend seven-and-one-quarter hours daily cleaning equipment at her factory and had paid for the relief by waiving her right to a "household day" (the monthly day East German women employees were allowed to stay away from work in order to take care of household duties) and by accepting lower wages. It is true: her children had been badly neglected. But the file contains no accusations of abuse and nothing about alcohol, questionable visits by unknown men, too many nights out on the town while the children were asleep, etc. The mother's only crime had been exhaustion.

I am amazed to see that even the women judges of my district court (most of whom, too, had to juggle work, household, and childcare duties all at once) never seemed to notice how differently their custody decisions treated the childcare obligations of men and women. In theory, East German family law unequivocally insisted on gender equality. Already the Family Code of 1965 had ceased to differentiate between the rights of men and women. That was to be expected from a country that counted Friedrich Engels and August Bebel among its ideological ancestors. When over the decades it became obvious that formal legal equality alone was not enough to put men and women on an equal footing, East German legislation and case law introduced a number of privileges for women, designed to make it easier for them to combine an outside job with childcare: the monthly "household day" (not available to men); the "baby year" (allowing mothers, on state pay, to stay home to care for their newborn during the baby's first year of life); the preference for working mothers over fathers if divorcing parents could not agree on custody. GDR family politicians knew how difficult it is to change behavior with the help of law, and therefore carefully kept watch on whether their law succeeded in assimilating the lot of men and women. At every divorce, each partner had to fill in a questionnaire that was meant to track the state of family life in the GDR. Question No. 4 asked both divorcing parties independently of each other: "Did you have problems realizing gender equality in your marriage?"

The answers to question No. 4 reveal that many marriages did indeed have problems, but that most spouses (including wives!) considered those problems as quite normal and therefore did not think of them as something that was amenable to change. "No problems. I sometimes, for my part, did not live up to my family obligations," is the typical answer of a husband in 1980, and in 1983, another husband writes: "One cannot really speak of problems of gender equality in our marriage. But the main household burden was shouldered by my wife." The women's view of the situation was the same. "No problems," a plaintiff wife writes on one occasion. "But the child was mainly taken care of by the mother and by Grandma. My husband did not feel responsible for the household." The termination cases in the Lüritz archive show that judges and youth functionaries, too, saw childcare and housework primarily as women's work. Virtually all suits for termination are directed against mothers, and in virtually all these cases, fathers are invisible. By the time of the termination suit, most fathers have lost contact with their children long ago. If they once had been married to their children's mother, they may have disappeared soon after the divorce. Under East German law, both parents, even after losing their parental rights, continued to be responsible for child support unless their child had been successfully adopted. But the Lüritz termination files virtually never tell us where the fathers are nor why they do not care for the child themselves or pay support.

Instead, court and youth functionaries aim their reproaches for the child's neglect entirely at the mother, who has stayed around to take the blame. The kind of flaws and failures of which mothers are accused are specifically feminine and never would have been held against a man: a baby's diapers "were gray and scratchy" (1969), the apartment was "uncomfortable and incompletely furnished (1968)," "dirty or un-ironed laundry was littering the room" (1976). The criticisms resemble the reproofs that divorce-seeking husbands liked to raise against their wives: "The beds weren't always made" (1960), "dirty dishes were standing around for days" (1970), "I was very much neglected in my marriage" (1980). At least as far as my termination files are concerned, the burdens of gender equality had to be borne by the women alone. Only very rarely do I come across a case in which a parent is accused of physical abuse. On the contrary, at least some of the children seem to do reasonably well despite their obvious neglect: "All in all, the children's condition is acceptable," one judgment states, and in another one I read: "The children have not yet suffered visible harm." The termination orders of the Lüritz District Court protected children primarily against dirt, disorder, and an unstructured and undisciplined lifestyle.

In other words: most of the Youth Authority's termination suits were directed against women who had been registered as "in danger of succumbing to asocial tendencies," against whom the prosecutor had launched an investigation for "asocial behavior" under §249 of the Criminal Code, or who already were arrested for what in other Socialist countries was, more aggressively, called "parasitism." Criminal law and family law worked hand in hand to exclude these women from society. The harshest accusation raised against them was that they refused to take advice, to learn lessons, to bring some order into their messy lives. Hence the law's willingness to reaccept those who saw the errors of their ways, admitted their need for education, and threw themselves into the arms of the collective: they could regain their children or, if their repentance came soon enough, could altogether avoid the termination of their parental rights. In 1971, a mother regains her three children, whom she had lost thirteen years earlier, because she finally has learned to adjust to Socialist expectations: "She [now] always signs up for special shifts and participates in meetings and demonstrations." Two years later, a mother of questionable morals avoids losing her child by signing an agreement with the Interior Department in which she promises to change her life "so as not to cause educational trouble for state authorities and for her enterprise." Note: it is not just the children's but also their mothers' education that the court seeks to ensure.

Those mothers unwilling to submit to collective pedagogy are treated as outsiders to whom ordinary procedural restraints do not apply. Usually, I can tell already by the thickness of a termination record whether the mother whose parental rights it deals with did or did not hold down a proper job. If the defendant mother happened to be an industrious and steady worker, the court record is bulky and the court's investigation of her alleged neglect is thorough and precise. By contrast, the files of *Assi* mothers losing children are thin and skimpy. If an "asocial" mother already is in prison, service of process often will arrive so late that she no longer can participate in the trial, and the court will render its termination verdict in her absence. Often, the mother's criminal case file proving her conviction under §248 of the Criminal Code is the Youth Agency's sole "evidence" for a mother's "grave and knowing violation of parental duties." If *Assi* mothers name witnesses who could describe their close and loving relationship with their children, the court will often fail to call for their testimony. In theory, the Agency, which sues for termination of parental rights and is a party at the trial, should be governed by the same legal rules that apply to the defendant mother. But practically, judge and youth administrators act as allies pursuing the same goal (namely: to remove the child from the control of an undisciplined and shiftless parent), and the Agency is rarely asked to prove its case. Especially in trials involving young and healthy children who are easily adoptable and whom the state prefers to be raised by more orderly and integrated parents, the court makes light of the procedural rights of asocial mothers. In such situations, the Youth Agency may undermine the mother's case even before it is brought to trial by prematurely removing allegedly neglected children from their homes and, in this fashion, weaken the emotional bonds that a court otherwise might hesitate to sever.

As a result, some of the Lüritz termination cases look as if judge and social workers joined forces in an unholy alliance to deprive a despised, uncooperative, and helpless mother of her children. In those cases, the most negative features of the system come together: the court's reluctance to question the authority of a state agency; the self-righteousness of judges who feel empowered by the pedagogic ambitions of their ideology; their didactic outrage at people unwilling to accept advice; the rejection of misfits in a society defined as a work collective; the conviction that it is a civic duty to conform to public expectations. Some of these judgments (only some, I am relieved to say) strike me as so cruel and unjust that I am shocked more deeply by them than by many of the appalling criminal sentences from the Cold War years.

Maybe this is the occasion to admit what some readers may have suspected all along: that my reaction to these (and many other) Lüritz court decisions demonstrates how difficult it is for even a well-intentioned observer to keep herself out of the story that she is investigating. Because I lived and worked for more than half my life in the United States, the closeness and the obtrusive solicitude of East German law appear to me more threatening than many transgressions of the Party. Because to all governments, labeling certain acts as deviant must be a tempting strategy of political discrimination and repression, I expected East Germany's criminal law to be more easily corrupted than its more emancipated and progressive family law. Because I have children myself and would have rather gone to prison than lose them, I am more outraged at some of the Lüritz court's termination decisions than at many of its sentences punishing "flight from the Republic." What follows is a description of the—in my view—most brutal judgment that I have found in the Lüritz archive. It is not representative

CHAPTER 6

of my court's judicial output: most of its case law is more or less reasonable or at least defensible. But it is a typical example of how Socialist injustice, when it happened, reflected the mind-set and the limitations of the Socialist judiciary. I read the case file almost in a daze, turning the pages with a shaky hand, waiting and hoping for a voice to call a halt to the injustice. It did not come. Here is the story:

On New Year's eve of 1967, a young woman with a somewhat messy lifestyle and three children between eighteen months and five years old is beaten up so badly by her husband that she suffers a concussion of the brain and is taken to hospital. The same night, the Lüritz Youth Agency transfers the children to a children's home and only a few weeks later, in January 1968, places the youngest with a foster family, who wants to adopt the child. In February 1968, the Agency establishes contact with two other families eager to adopt, and in July 1968 brings suit to terminate both spouses' parental rights over all three children. On August 1, 1968, Frau Dankwarth without much ado grants the request.

I do not know how long the mother had to remain in hospital. But by November 1968, she is divorced from her abusive husband, has married again, and, with the help of an attorney, sues for the repeal of the termination order and for the restoration of her parental rights. Her lawyer asks the Youth Agency to wait with the planned adoptions until the court has had occasion to adjudicate the mother's suit. On December 20, 1968, the Agency, in the midst of negotiations with the children's prospective new parents, states in its brief responding to the mother's suit: "There is no evidence that the mother's relationship with her children has taken a positive turn. By 'positive' we mean the mother's willingness to accept that the Youth Agency's decisions are taken solely in the interest of the children. She is not ready to do so. On the contrary: Frau K. tried to arrange interactions with her children without the Agency's consent thus jeopardizing, once again, the educational intentions of the Agency."

The District Court takes almost five months before it rules on the mother's suit—longer than in most Lüritz divorce cases. Does it intend to give the children time to become imbedded in their new families? When the case is finally argued on April 28, 1969, some astonishing evidence comes to light. The Youth Agency, which at the termination trial in August 1968 had accused the mother of having failed to supervise her children, already on New Year's eve had learned from neighbors what had really happened but had kept this information from the court. As long as she had been healthy, the mother had taken loving care of the children. Her new husband is willing to accept them into the couple's home and gives a moving description of the mother's devastation by the children's loss: "I see it everyday how she grieves their absence; she is crying all the time." Since Frau K. had been released from hospital, she had done everything in her power to remain close to her children: had regularly paid the state for child support; had visited the two older ones (on some occasions, in violation of the Youth Agency's prohibition of any contacts) in their children's homes; for Christmas 1968, had tried to bring them oranges and bananas (precious gifts in the GDR that took a lot of time and effort to get hold of) only to be told that the children, unbeknownst to her, had secretly been transferred to another children's home outside of Lüritz. Still, Frau K. continued to search for ways to reach her children until she was warned by the police no longer to contravene the orders of the Youth Authority.

Herr Taddäus, who presides at the new trial (why he? why the director of the District Court himself?), takes no visible note of any of this evidence. I cannot tell how far he even listens to the mother or her lawyer. According to the minutes of the hearing, Frau K., at one point, "loudly swearing leaves the court room"— perhaps she got so agitated that Herr Taddäus threw her out. The files convey the image of an impulsive, warm-hearted, and undisciplined woman; a maverick. At the original termination hearing, one of her neighbors had accused her of "never coming to the house assemblies" (which under Socialism were more or less obligatory). In any case: Herr Thaddäus dismisses the mother's suit to regain custody of her children. Here are his stated reasons:

> In the course of the proceedings, the plaintiff has on several occasions expressed her unwillingness to accept any outside help and support and has rejected the notion that other people should get involved in her family problems. The plaintiff's positions show that she fails to understand both the humanitarian character of our Socialist state and its goal to create a Socialist community of men. She therefore is incapable of raising her children to be healthy, happy, capable, and well-rounded human beings. She cannot bring them up to be active builders of Socialism.

In September 1969, the Regional Court in Neuburg rejects the mother's appeal. I seem to detect a faint undertone of regret in the appellate decision: the Neuburg court does not base its judgment on the mother's refusal to conform but on the welfare of the children, who at this point in time have been removed for twenty months from the parental home and who for the last nine months have had no contact with their mother. Since, under §51, para. 3 of the East German Family Code, the *restoration* of parental rights after their termination requires not only that the parent has mended his or her old ways but that the child's return advances its "best interests," that clause could serve to calm whatever pangs of conscience the appellate judges may have felt. Whatever their state of mind, they, too, chose to ignore the fact that, under §51, para. 2 of the Family Code, the *initial* termination of Frau K.'s rights in August 1968 presupposed the "grave

CHAPTER 6

and culpable violation of parental obligations," that absolutely no such violation had been shown, and that the Youth Authority had used misrepresentation and deceit to steal a mother's children.

I find the case so incomprehensible that I decide to speak with Frau K. myself. Armed with a letter of introduction by the current Lüritz court director to the local registration office (attesting to my bona fide research goals), I obtain her address. Frau K. lives in one of those large pre-fab apartment houses on the outskirts of town; the sidewalks are not yet paved, and, as I search for the right street, sand trickles into my shoes. But I am on the wrong track: the woman who in the end answers my bell is much too young; it is purely by accident that she shares Frau K.'s name. Back to the registration office, where the friendly official at the desk will check once more among the old index cards in the basement. She returns with a sober look: Frau K. died in 1973. She was thirty-two years old.

What does one die of at the age of thirty-two? The woman from the registration office, who notices how much I take the case to heart, has a suggestion: she knows someone in the village where Frau K. lived in the end and will make inquiries; why don't I telephone her tomorrow morning. Next day I learn that four years after losing the fight for her children, Frau K. committed suicide. She and her new husband had another baby together but it had not been enough to make her want to hold onto life. That's how things look to me, who from seventy-six pages of a court file cobbled together the story of a victim. Maybe I was too hasty in my judgment; too suspicious; too credulous. Maybe nobody in this world could have helped Frau K., and the courts were right to give the children of so fragile and undisciplined a mother to more responsible and solid parents. Maybe the new adoptive parents of the children were important people in town, and the Court and Youth Authority had eagerly placed themselves at their service. I only know for sure that the Youth Officials lied; that the judges did not challenge the lies; that Frau K.'s rights to her children were not respected, but trampled underfoot; and that the law served as an instrument to enforce conformity with a self-righteous state.

Lüritz family judges continued to believe until the 1980s that only docile citizens could make good parents. As late as in 1979, an *Assi* mother looses custody of her two-year-old child because she does not have a steady job, is 5000 Marks in debt, keeps a "totally unsatisfactory supply of baby food" in her kitchen, and because—"without good reasons"—she chose to have her child cared for "by a family of her acquaintance" rather than "by the state's childcare center that offered her a place." Another "asocial" mother, also unwilling to place her child in a state-run nursery school, loses it as well: "The full measure of her guilt is demonstrated by the fact that Frau M. rejected the state's offer to help her return to an orderly way of life." But then, in November 1984, a judgment of the Neuburg Regional Court introduces a radical course change. A Lüritz mother, supposedly "asocial" and with a one-year prison sentence for theft in her past, loses her four-year-old son in one of the Lüritz court's usual quick and dirty termination trials. She is accused of barely taking any interest in her son, who spent the last three years in a state children's home. Both the court and the Youth Agency are particularly affronted by the mother's frequent moves between Lüritz and two neighboring towns, which made it impossible in recent years "to exercise continuous state and social influence on her behavior." Although both the mother and her lawyer are present at the trial, her witnesses are not called to give evidence.

But the mother had chosen the right attorney to assist her in her fight: Herr Mohr, a product of the new, more insecure and disbelieving GDR, who as a student at Berlin's Humboldt University had decided to become a lawyer because he was ashamed of the forced exile of East Germany's most rebellious and most famous singer, Wolf Biermann; who was convinced that law must also protect the interests of outsiders; and whom I often have encountered in the court records of the 1980s as an optimistic and aggressive warrior for his clients' rights. Herr Mohr appeals the termination verdict for lack of guilt required by §51 of the Family Code. Miraculously, the Regional Court agrees and returns the case for further investigation to my district court: the Lüritz judges had failed to question the statements of the Youth Authority, which as a party to the dispute had to prove its case, and had "for no evident reason" refused to call the mother's witnesses. And then the most amazing sentence of the Neuburg judgment: "Neither the defendant's criminal record nor her apparent lack of punctuality and labor discipline represent, on their own, violations of her parental obligations." In other words: *Assis* can be good parents. Worker and mother, citizen and individual human being, are not identical. The Regional Court reacknowledges the invisible boundary between state and family, between public and private life.

At the new termination hearing back in Lüritz at which, this time, the mother's witnesses are given a chance to speak, their evidence reveals how determinedly and (I am looking for the strongest word that comes to mind) how dastardly the Youth Authority pursued its goal of separating mother and child. To demonstrate its power? To remove a child who should be raised to become an industrious and committed Socialist from the pernicious influence of a warm, undisciplined, and spontaneous mother? As it turns out, the youth officials had forbidden mother and grandmother (who often cared for the child) to visit it at the children's home and—when the women disregarded the prohibition—had moved the little boy to another home to prevent future contacts. The grandmother had managed to secretly visit her grandchild in the new home, too, and had brought him photographs of his mother. The mother had sent lovingly assembled parcels. Now Frau Neuman, who again presides over the termination hearing, has no choice but to dismiss the Youth Agency's suit. To save at least

CHAPTER 6

a little bit of the court's face (or so it seems to me), she splits the court costs between the parties. But Herr Mohr appeals this decision, too, and again the Regional Court sides with the defendant: because the Youth Authority lost its suit, the court costs must be borne by the state alone.

It would be too much to claim that from now on, my Lüritz court handled termination suits against asocial parents with the same care and solicitude as those directed against defendants of whose work-morality the court approved. Yes, in cases involving slackers and other misfits, the judges do pay a little more attention to procedural details than they did before. But their (and the Youth Agency's) deep irritation in the face of unstructured lives "without perspectives," and their annoyance at many *Assis'* talent for evading all educational efforts by the state, are still quite obvious. My judges felt responsible for maintaining order and security in town. They were part and parcel of an authoritarian system of government and viewed their pedagogic tasks in a more narrow and less imaginative fashion than the East German Family Code, with its decidedly emancipatory undertones, suggested. The Code, for instance, defined marriage as a union "based on mutual love, respect, and loyalty," and one who reads the section might be surprised to encounter such an emotionally loaded word as "love" in a code of law. But the Lüritz judges (at least in their court decisions) defined "love" not internally, as attraction and attachment, but externally, as regularity and order. Passions, obsessions, and any other lack of self-control did not fit in with their ideal of marriage. When, in 1960, the director of a Lüritz enterprise leaves job and family to follow a new woman to a new town in which the only work that he can find is a place on an assembly line, the Lüritz judge is just as outraged by the man's professional as by his personal desertion. "He treated his family and his enterprise with the same frivolity," she writes. Both breaches of faith were violations of the runaway's obligation to society. An order to suspend the divorce suit of another couple, again in 1960, outlines the court's idea of a good marriage: "The defendant reports that the plaintiff is a good housekeeper and keeps his clothes in exemplary order. That means that all prerequisites are met to allow the parties to lead a harmonious marriage." Twenty years later, a divorce judgment explains: "Because of existing weaknesses of character, the plaintiff was unable to bear the necessary love and respect for the defendant." Even in the 1980s, marital loyalty appears to be a civic obligation. No wonder that, in the same vein, my Lüritz termination judgments are more likely to be filled with talk about dirty laundry than about the lack of parental warmth, and that up to the very end, Lüritz judges seem to find it difficult to see human relationships not only as social but also as emotional affiliations.

My judges' skepticism and unease about the irrational and uncontrollable world of feelings also may explain the court's ambivalent attitude toward the

East German Marriage and Family Counseling Service, which was introduced by law in 1966 and established in Lüritz in 1971. According to the statutory language, the counseling offices were intended "to help citizens lead their lives and educate their children guided by Socialist law and Socialist morality." That sounded like a state attempt to push family morality as a public duty. But the law also recognized the very personal nature of marriage and family relationships. Someone in need of help could turn to an office in another town for counseling, the law allowed anonymous requests for help, and the counseling staff was pledged to secrecy. These rules recognized maybe not a right to privacy but at least a need for it. Because both the court and the counseling office served as points of first contact for people with family problems, they were expected to cooperate by way of references and the exchange of information. The Lüritz court director had to compose annual reports on this cooperation for the Regional Court in Neuburg, of which a folder full of carbon copies has survived among the treasures of the wood cellar.

Not that there appeared to be much to report. The Lüritz counseling office often was closed for months because its director, a social pedagogue, was in ill health. And there were barely any clients. In 1976, eighty citizens came for advice; by 1982, the number was down to thirty, most of them women complaining about abusive husbands or unpaid child support. Nevertheless, Herr Taddäus, year in, year out, submitted almost identical Socialist messages of success to the Appellate Court in Neuburg: praised the "close contacts" between his court and the Counseling Service; described how divorce judges regularly referred parties to the Service for advice; asserted (without giving figures) that "many" marriages in this fashion had been saved; and more likely than not concluded his report with a formula like "it can safely be stated that the Counseling Service enjoys the confidence of our population. With Socialist greetings...."

But the tone and content of the reports begin to change in 1985, when a psychologist takes over as director of the Counseling Service. The number of clients shoots up: in 1988, 250 people come to the Service for help. But the cooperation between court and Counseling Office deteriorates. In 1988, the new director of the District Court, Frau Walter, complains in a letter to the Regional Court that the Counseling Service now obtains most of its clients by way of medical referrals; that unlike the court, the Service "offers no advice to spouses trying to resolve their marriage problems," and that its new director does not consider the input of judges to be particularly useful to his agency's concerns. Frau Walter's letter sounds not only critical, but hurt. She is upset to find that the court's approach to marriage troubles is no longer shared by others in the field. The family law judge seems to fear that her own work might be threatened by the Counseling Service's unabashed attention to the emotional and (I assume) sexual needs of individual marriage partners. "He is entirely preoccupied by medical issues," she complains about the Service's director, and she means: "He disregards the social aspects of marriage and family."

Frau Walter criticized a development to which her own court had contributed. The increasing ease of divorces over time, the growing reluctance of the court to include collective representatives in divorce proceedings, the drop in suspension orders, the greater attention paid to procedural precision in termination cases—they all were symptoms of the same ideological climate change that affected the court no less than the Lüritz Family Counseling Service. Both institutions' work could not escape the (occasionally reluctant) insight that even under Socialism real differences and tensions existed between people's public and private lives. Even before Frau Walter raised alarm about the family counselors' regrettable attention to their clients' inner feelings, I had encountered signs of protest in the family law files of litigants complaining about state invasions into personal affairs. Admittedly, for many Lüritz citizens the court remained a source of parental help and guidance almost to the end. There's no denying that the pedagogic efforts of the system looked attractive to some people at loose ends. As late as the mid-1980s, Lüritz spouses came to enquire from the court what they might do to save their crumbling marriages. "I was in court more than once to ask what I could do to win back my wife," the defendant husband said in a 1985 divorce case. As to be expected, the judges' answers to such questions remained resolutely on the surface. "Flowers and chocolates," was a typical bit of advice. Flowers and chocolate had not helped the husband in the case just cited: his wife, with a full-time job, had long lost patience with her husband's expectations to be served and pampered.

Still, I find fewer people turning to the court for help and guidance in my files than I find people who resent the state's attempt to meddle with their personal affairs. In the 1970s, objections to the collectivization of divorce are usually presented as the mere personal preference of a litigant. "The parties did not consult the Family Counseling Service and did not ask for collective help because the plaintiff wife did not want anyone to know about her troubled marriage," I read in a divorce petition from 1970 and Frau Dankwarth, to her credit, makes do with the parties' own testimony to establish that the marriage is beyond repair. By the 1980s, the parties' opposition to the participation of collective representatives in divorce proceedings sounds more impatient. Responses to item no. 10 on the questionnaire for divorcing spouses—"Have you or others tried to engage collective help to overcome your marital troubles?"—are short and to the point: "No! I consider that useless" (1980), for example, or "I don't want to wash dirty laundry. I only want to get divorced" (1985). Respondents do not just object to the invasion of their privacy but question the legitimacy of the invasion. In a contested custody case of 1980, a father writes in his brief: "I am of the opinion that the comrades from the Party District Bureau are in no position to properly evaluate this conflict." "Why would strangers have anything to say about the education of my children?" a divorcing mother complains in 1981 whose work collective, at the trial, had advocated that not she but the children's father should get custody. In 1985, a defendant husband states: "I do not think that my divorce is a proper topic of discussion for my enterprise." In the very last years of the GDR, in most divorce questionnaires, the room for entries under item No. 10 is left blank. The question seems no longer relevant.

And when the Wall collapses, Lüritz judges have come around to share this view. It is so obvious that in these uncertain times people need a niche in which they can find that warmth and support that the Socialist state can no longer give them, and probably never could. "Don't get divorced," a Lüritz judge counsels a couple in the spring of 1990, well aware of the fact that she herself will remain in office only for a few more months. "Marriage is such a safe hinterland." Who knows how difficult it will be to build a new life under Capitalism. Things will be easier together. The divorce suit is withdrawn.

CHAPTER 7

PUNISHMENTS

With between 400 and 500 defendants a year, criminal law made up about a third of the caseload of the Lüritz District Court. None of the judges of my court could totally avoid it. Some of them specialized in criminal adjudication. But civil judges, too, at least on weekends, had to take their turn confirming arrest warrants issued by the police or the prosecutor's office. Criminal law was more politically charged than other areas of the law: besides the law, the interests of society, the rights of the defendants, and their own judicial conscience, judges also had to bear in mind the ever-changing goals and worries of the Party. Moreover, criminal law is that area of law in which this report most easily can miss its mark. My criminal law files are less complete than my other Lüritz records. Given the paranoia of this legal system, even those files I do have may have left out or have distorted important details of a story. Can I trust the court records of a legal system that had political crimes investigated not by the regular police but by the *Stasi*; that adjudicated those crimes not in Lüritz, where they were committed, but at a safe distance from the local population by the Regional Court (or, in less serious cases, by another district court) in Neuburg; that adjudicated even many ordinary Lüritz crimes behind closed doors; and that in precarious cases did not provide someone convicted with a copy of his judgment but only allowed him to read and then return it before being led out the court room?

At least the secretiveness of these arrangements suggests that what they hid may have been closer to the truth than had it not been swaddled in protective layers of concealment. I have no choice: I must rely on all the information about criminal law in Lüritz that I can collect. What is that? The Lüritz archive holds the criminal *judgments* of the District Court since 1952 but not the *case files* (which contain the briefs of prosecution and defense, the protocols of hearings and the like) because in the GDR criminal case files were not stored in court but in the prosecutor's archive in Neuburg. That's where they still are kept today. After lengthy negotiations with officials from the Ministry of Justice and the State's Ombudsman for Data Protection, I am allowed to view the files in Neuburg and discover that they go back only as far as 1968. So much for the *ordinary* criminal case files. Today, the *political* criminal trial records are held by the Archive for the Documents of the Former Ministry for State Security (also called Birthler Archive, for its current director, or *Stasi* Archive, for that infamous ministry's abbreviated name), which, luckily for me, operates a regional branch in Neuburg. New applications to gain access; new negotiations with officials. I am told that I want to see way too many records. Under *Stasi* Archive rules, the names of all defendants (which I already know from a box of index cards in the prosecutor's office) have to be blackened out to preserve their anonymity, and the Archive does not have enough staff to do the job. Data protection! In the end, I get to see a tolerable portion of the records on my list, but the *Stasi* files on Lüritz subjects, too, do not date further back than 1969.

But the stacks of arrest warrants that I discovered in the wood cellar go back to 1953 and contain useful biographical information on their protagonists (age, gender, occupation, and alleged transgression) and, equally intriguing, personal statements of the apprehended culprits when they were brought before the judge —who almost always would approve of the arrest. Another wood-cellar treasure: a bundle of judicial approvals of police searches and seizures (again, not without gaps) that illustrate what kind of contraband the guardians of law and order were interested in (mostly items used to flee the country: maps, flashlights, rubber dinghies) and how diligently they observed procedural rules when they undertook their searches. And then there are the copies of weekly reports that the Regional Court in Neuburg had to submit to the Ministry of Justice and the Supreme Court (now held by the Federal Archive in Berlin) of which many deal with offenses that took place, or were rumored to be imminent, in Lüritz. But these reports, too, did not consistently find their way into the wood cellar (were some shredded?) and thus do not completely cover the entire lifespan of my court. To fill in the blank spots in my picture of crime in Lüritz, I may have to fall back on my *pièce de résistance*, the *Lüritz Sentinel*, in the city archive.

One ray of encouragement among my often cloudy sources: I learn from the index of defendants kept at the Neuburg prosecutor's office that, at least since 1968, not more than 1% to 2% of all Lüritz miscreants were classified as "political" offenders whose crimes were not adjudicated by my district court but by the Regional Court in Neuburg (or, in less touchy cases, transferred by the Regional Court to the Neuburg District Court). These are the "Ia-cases," named after "Chamber Ia" of the regional court, which dealt with all offenses investigated by the *Stasi*. Studying these cases in the Birthler Archive branch office in Neuburg, I make a second discovery: that my idea of what might make a case "political" is not necessarily identical with the definition of East German law enforcement and the Party. To them, "political" would often simply mean "potentially embarrassing." Whether a delinquent would be put on trial in the town where he lived and worked or (out of the sight of neighbors and colleagues) in the regional capital depended primarily on whether his offense might "unsettle" the local population or whether, if news of the trial spread, it might damage the GDR's reputation in the West. But the assessments of what type of court reports or

CHAPTER 7

rumors might give rise to Western scorn were shaped by political phobia and by the (rather bourgeois-looking) fear of fouling one's own nest. As a result, the characterization of offenses as "political" seemed to be driven mainly by concerns for reputation. "Asocial" citizens or "*Assis*," for example, whose absenteeism, drunkenness, or sleeping-on-the-rough often was punished with lengthy prison sentences, were almost always put on trial in their hometown. I would call compulsory work and the educational obsession that fueled Socialism's prosecution of bums and loiterers "political." Ordinary citizens who tried to flee the GDR usually were indicted in Lüritz; people of higher social or political rank (such as high-school teachers or department heads) probably would have to face the Regional Court in Neuburg. For me, all "flights from the Republic" were "political." In 1982, the Regional Court returned a case of "public defamation" (in other words, someone had gotten into a swearing match with an official) to my Lüritz court because the offense had wrongly been classified as "political": the defendant's railings had, indeed, contained neo-Fascist slogans but had not, as initially feared, been motivated by a general attitude of political opposition to the GDR. I am relieved to find that in my search for daily legal life under Socialism, I very likely will encounter enough "political" offenses among my Lüritz files not to have to worry about obtaining too idyllic an impression of my subject.

Still, until 1952 (the year of the first Lüritz criminal judgment on the archive's shelves) the picture remains blurry. My files say next to nothing of the *Russian* use of criminal law in the immediate postwar years. Occasionally, I find a little accidental morsel of evidence that like a momentary flash of light illuminates the Occupation Power's exercise of its capacity to punish: when a defendant's previous criminal record includes the entry "Soviet Military Tribunal; espionage; 25 years," for instance (apparently, he was released soon enough to get into new trouble with the authorities), or when in December 1945 a letter of the Central German Administration of Justice (which under the supervision of the Occupation Power controlled the East German judicial apparatus) orders East German criminal courts to submit "regular reports on all events of special significance, especially those affecting the interests of the Occupation Forces." Not a single word in all the pages that even hints at Soviet crimes committed *against* Germans: the rape wave terrorizing German women; the marauders among the Soviet liberators who caused such fear among the population that even in February 1948, many Lüritzers refused to take up jobs from which they could not return home before the fall of darkness.[21] East German courts had no jurisdiction over Soviet soldiers and no authority to even take note of Soviet crimes. Their dealings with their own state were precarious enough. In January 1946, the courts are ordered to submit bi-weekly reports on all incidents of "sabotage" within their district to the "Central Justice Administration." Two months later, another letter from the "Justice Administration" requires trial courts to list all prison inmates by party affiliation.

Such bits of data show how quickly the legal climate in my town is becoming dominated by politics. In October 1948, the *Sentinel* reports on a parliamentary debate in Gram (then still the capital of the provincial government) on whether the leading judges and prosecutors in the province should be required to have earned university law degrees. "We need men who are professionally qualified," says a speaker from the Christian Democratic Party. "Their faces must be scarred from their dueling days in university!" shouts a member of the SED. General laughter in the House. A motion supported by the Christian and the Liberal Democratic Party suggesting that at least the highest legal offices in the province should be staffed with professional lawyers is voted down by a slim margin. In 1949, the last university-trained judge leaves the Appellate Court in Gram (and presumably goes West): as rumor has it, because he objected to the placement of a bust of Stalin in the court's entrance hall.

During these years in Lüritz, Herr Curtius, an ex-attorney with a proper law degree, takes care of the court's *civil* case load, but *criminal* adjudication is handled almost exclusively by "people's judges": Herr Teubner (who under Hitler spent several years in prison), Herr Kellner (also a victim of Nazi persecution), and Herr Arlt, about whom I know very little and who does not stay on the Lüritz bench for long. Back in Berlin, the Central Justice Administration frets over the insufficient numbers and the poor quality of judges in the Soviet Occupation Zone, but I find no complaints about the Lüritz court. In the eyes of their superiors and the Party, the Lüritz judges appear to do at least an unobjectionable job. The bits of criminal case law I discover here or there would not seem out of place in a more bourgeois past. In 1949, the *Sentinel* reports on lenient sentences for small-time sinners and on tough verdicts for offenses against property rights or public morals: one-and-a-half years in prison for bigamy, five years for a swindler extracting gifts or money from various women to whom he promised marriage, two-and-a-half years of hard labor for the chairman of the workers' council at the Lüritz harbor who had embezzled vacation funds (though it must be said that the prosecutor had asked for five years).

Criminal justice in the immediate postwar years in Lüritz reflects the problems of a country gripped by fundamental change. Civic disorder and scarcity collide with the freshly minted institutions of a new society such as land reform or economic planning. Police and prosecutors battle black-market deals, sabotage, and the many efforts to squirrel goods away from the state's grasp or to line one's pockets that often were necessary for survival in the midst of economic chaos. By September 1947, the radical expropriation of all large-scale agrarian landholders—the "Land Reform"—has been carried out: in the vicinity of Lüritz, 670 "new farmers" try their best to keep their tiny farms afloat. Refugees from

CHAPTER 7

the Eastern parts of Germany and local residents crowd towns and villages and must learn to get along. Everything is in short supply: housing, food, clothing, all daily essentials. The border to the Western half of Germany is not yet closed. Criminal law must help to control and steer the general disorder.

In Lüritz, caseloads seem to be too heavy to be handled by my court alone. Besides the *Amtsgericht* (magistrate court)—which will keep this name until the Justice Reform of 1952—a number of "emergency courts" of uncertain provenance sit late into the night to process the many trials. Petty speculation and black-market deals usually are punished by short prison terms or fines; perhaps because the judges, too, can sympathize with someone's yearning for American cigarettes or proper coffee beans. Occasionally, defendants even are acquitted. By comparison, "economic crimes"—such as the failure to meet state-set quotas for grain or milk—are harshly punished and often lead to the expropriation of a delinquent farmer's land. "We can't afford to tolerate the mismanagement of land that the Land Reform bestowed upon new title holders to be cherished as their very own," the *Lüritz Sentinel* pronounced in its account of one such trial. Another *Sentinel* crime report from 1949 lauds heavy penalties for "big-time racketeers" and other speculators: "The people must be shown that energetic action will be taken to ensure that all saboteurs of the new democratic order will meet the punishment that they deserve."

But people in Lüritz rather look the other way. Although the number of *civil* lawsuits (enforcing ordinary private claims) is on a steady rise, the public shows little interest in the state's *criminal* admonishments. A short-lived series of public meetings at the Lüritz courthouse at which the judges talk primarily about their criminal case work suffers from low attendance and a shortage of people willing to speak up. "The discussion was quite listless," the *Sentinel* reports on the first meeting in October 1948, and, nine months later, describes the third public discussion at the court as "meager." The article complains that the few questions coming from the audience "dealt only with the questioner's personal interests." These days, the *Sentinel* publishes a comic strip whose antihero is called "Me First!" and who thinks only of his own advantage, does not pull his weight, sponges off other people's work, etc. until some muscular men in work clothes kick him out of the enterprise/the building site/the farm yard and send him on his way. A courtroom is the natural habitat of anyone who, like "Me First!" insists on the protection of his rights. Even the Lüritz "people's judges" took a while to learn that criminal adjudication should no longer balance the individual's rights against society's need for protection but should resolutely focus on the interests of the state.

The turning year is 1952. Back in the "Property" chapter we already saw how, in the course of a single year, the pressure of the new decrees on economic crimes persuaded Lüritz civil judges to repress their inclination to make occasional allowances for human frailty. The same is true for criminal law judges. True, there is evidence suggesting that they did not enjoy their role as punishers. Checking through all the 1952 convictions of store managers and cashiers for losing money due to inaccurate accounting, for instance, I discover that the heaviest penalties were meted out to those who already had fled West and thus were safely out of reach. It also occasionally happens in these years that Lüritz judges sign arrest warrants several days *after* the suspect's interrogation by the police, thus giving him the chance to escape across the (still open) border. Twice this year—in January and in June 1952—the Appellate Court in Gram finds it necessary to hold criminal trials in the Lüritz courthouse to demonstrate to local judges how they should deal with enemies of the new order. The *Sentinel,* reporting on the shows, speaks of "severe but just" sentences for black-market deals and for the embezzlement of state-owned merchandise. In mid-November 1952, another *Sentinel* article must have given the Lüritz criminal law judges (Herr Teubner and Herr Kellner) additional cause for worry. It rails against the much too lenient sentences for two former workers at the shipyard convicted of "disturbance of the peace" (a political scuffle?). "I don't understand the court," a former colleague of the culprits says, whose name and full address, together with the names and addresses of three other critics of the verdict, is listed in the paper. The article's most poisonous line: "The District leadership at the Lüritz Party Bureau also disapproves of this judgment and calls for an immediate appeal."

I do not know whether the prosecutor did appeal the case and how the story ended. But I can tell that subsequent criminal judgments of the District Court became increasingly draconian. "Evil act meets just deserts," the *Sentinel* writes on December 8, 1952, praising the court for punishing a young man's robbery of a woman's purse with six years of hard labor. A day later, the paper lauds "severe penalties for violations of state property." It took my Lüritz judges until the end of 1952 before they fully accepted (or at least obeyed) First Secretary Walter Ulbricht's claim that every criminal conviction should also count as "a political act." Loyalty toward the Party did not always translate into harsher punishments. The severity of criminal law in Lüritz (and elsewhere in the GDR) did not remain constant. It rose or sank depending on the Party's current hopes and fears, lost some of its intensity and terror in the course of the country's gradual consolidation, and only in the very last years of East German Socialism shot up again to reach new hights of panic as the system was unraveling. What stayed unchanged throughout East German legal history, however, were the Party's claims to the political loyalty of its judges and the judges' own acquiescence to this claim.

Is there a progression or something like a plot line running through criminal law developments in Lüritz that might give meaning and historical direction to my story? I think I can discover such a line—a fault line in a quarry, so to

CHAPTER 7

speak—among the bundles of arrest warrants dug out from the wood cellar. Arrest warrants offer a different vantage point from which to analyze a legal system than its criminal judgments do. States punish those acts that contravene their plans and interests, and criminal trials have the purpose of uncovering whether and to what extent the defendant's actions have indeed violated state-protected goods. But at the time a judge approves of an arrest, nobody knows for sure what really happened. Arrest warrants reflect the *fears* of a legal system, not the actual *damage* it incurred through the commission of a crime. Usually, a connection exists between fear and damage: alleged murderers are more likely to be arrested than alleged pickpockets. But in a legal system driven by insecurity and paranoia, like that of the GDR, the nexus between fear and damage is weaker than under the rule of law, where even the law's immediate reactions to surprise and shock are more meticulously structured by legal rules than they were under Socialism.

The trial records proper in the Lüritz archive reflect (with many interruptions) the gradual rationalization and calming down of criminal case law in the GDR. As the years wear on, "political" crimes lose in importance; "ordinary" crimes like property offenses or traffic violations move into the foreground. By contrast, the arrest warrants reveal the system's most immediate and uncontrolled anxieties in the face of unpleasant surprises. They are not yet checked against a rational evaluation of the facts. They trace the system's raw and unarticulated fears of hidden dangers. What and whom Socialism was afraid of changed over time, and these changes can serve to draw a plot line for my legal story. In the years up to the construction of the Berlin Wall, most arrest warrants dealt with alleged attacks on Socialism as a political and economic system by Capitalist or Capitalist-inspired enemies such as spies, saboteurs, and racketeers. After the Wall was built and the survival of the GDR no longer seemed in question, the law turned its attention onto deviants who threatened Socialism from within. In the 1960s, the most likely candidates for arrest were potential fugitives (who refused loyalty to the state and Party) and thieves or embezzlers of "people's property" (who refused to respect the state as lord of the economy). In the 1970s, the consolidation of East German Socialism went hand in hand with increasing worries about deviants who still refused to join its blessings. Now the majority of warrants were directed against the *Asoziale*: maladjusted bums and idlers who withdrew from the demands of the collective into a private world of drink and drifting. And in the final decade of the GDR, Lüritz arrest warrants chased after new and even more alarming groups of outsiders: *applicants* (what they applied for—namely exit visas—required no articulation), who tried to force the state to let them go by ever more inventive protest actions and appeals to Western media and dignitaries, and so-called *non-returners*, who had made use of short-term travel permits to the West by staying there for good and whose unlikely apprehension was sought by the police and ordered (symbolically, I suppose) by a warrant of the court. Four decades; four sets of shifting fears and apprehensions. Of course, the different phobias overlapped in part: periodizations never are exact. But the overall line of development, I think, is right: a line tracing the hopes and disappointments of a legal system that starts out single-mindedly and ruthlessly, rises with growing confidence and optimism, falls as the people's faith and energy are wearing thin, and that, throughout the decades, depends upon the grudging and fragile loyalty of its citizens.

From 1952 to 1961—that is, from the official announcement of "the construction of Socialism" in the GDR to the building of the Berlin Wall—criminal justice in Lüritz was concentrated on the self-preservation of the system. The term "flight from the Republic" already was part of the political vocabulary. But it was not particularly difficult to make one's way into the Federal Republic. When in the spring of 1953 two employees of the district court go West, they escape in such orderly fashion as to first complete their current work and clear their desks. Why didn't colleagues raise alarm? an angry letter from the Regional Court inquires. But how could one keep them back? The border is essentially open, and human traffic between the GDR and the Federal Republic does not move just in one direction. The labor market stretches across the border: West German citizens occasionally move East in their search for a better job or cheaper housing, and some unsteady people shuttle back and forth. In 1958, 13.4% of the criminal defendants at "Lüritz/District" (one of the two departments of the court) were so-called returnees who had come back to the GDR after an unsatisfying move to the Federal Republic, and a 1959 criminal case file mentions a "West-refugee camp" in the vicinity of Lüritz.

Without an authoritative Western border, the new Socialist state is in danger of losing control over its citizens. East German criminal law is undermined by the ease of escaping its reach. Many arrest warrants issued in these years reveal that the accused already had found safety in the Federal Republic. In 1955, forty skilled workers from the Lüritz shipyard abscond to West Germany; the next year, Phoenix VEB loses so many welders that the shipyard has to run special welding classes to replace the runaways. A report by inspectors from the Neuburg Appellate Court to the Ministry of Justice mentions a former Lüritz industrialist, long gone West, who had returned to Lüritz to hire workers for his enterprise in the Federal Republic. The law had not prevented his recruitment trip.

In December 1957, an amendment to the GDR Statute on Passports for the first time prohibits the unauthorized "entry" into or "departure" from the GDR; the maximum penalty is three years in prison. The first "flight-from-the-Republic" cases begin to show up in my Lüritz case files. At this point, most prison terms for fugitives are measured in months rather than years; Socialism still seems embarrassed about the new heavy-handed measures. Shouldn't a state that claims to follow more humane goals than its Capitalist counterpart manage to keep its citizens at home without draconian threats? In the fall of 1958, the East German Ministry of Justice orders its trial court inspectors to recommend more lenient penalties for infringements of the "Passport Statute," especially for fugitives illegally *returning* to the GDR. Close relatives of people who have fled are to be invited to "conversations" at the courthouse in which a judge discreetly should inform them that their loved one will not face punishment should he or she return. And, please, no more dramatic police searches or "Wanted" posters going after fugitives!

But all these efforts to de-escalate the problem seem like attempts to fix a broken dike with plastic sheets. On both sides of the German border, the Cold War has fueled fear, aggression, and political self-righteousness. My court files offer only accidental glimpses of the actual war maneuvers: for instance, when a Neuburg report to the Ministry of Justice mentions "enemy activities within the territory" (a number of judges and prosecutors in the region had received "smear leaflets" in the mail), or when, in 1957, an arrest warrant for "defamation of the state" names as the culprit someone who had picked up a bunch of flyers issued by West Berlin's Social Democratic Party ("Free Elections!") and had then dropped the missives, one by one, supposedly to increase their impact. But the chill of the Cold War has also reached the courtroom. The Lüritz criminal judgments from the 1950s reflect a Manichaean division of the world. The German-German border marks the separation of light from darkness. The GDR represents the "Peace Camp"; the Federal Republic the camp of "war-mongerers and NATO revanchists." Socialism is always in the right. In March 1952, Judge Teubner, adjudicating the legal fall-out of a violent village brawl, had still conceded in his judgment that the victim of the fight, the village mayor, was publicly known as someone "whose stewardship left a lot to be desired." Now, in 1958, the Regional Court affirms a judgment in a similar case, this time involving only verbal, not physical, aggression against a local mayor ("an idiot!"), by emphasizing the unquestionable dignity of Socialist office-holders: "In our workers' and farmers' state, only those functionaries are chosen to be mayor who truly represent the interests of the electorate." A verdict of the Lüritz trial court, again in a case of "defamation of the state," calls local police representatives—as it were, *ex officio*—"the most circumspect and responsible members of the People's Police." And it is not just Socialist law and order that my files depict in the most favorable light. In every way, East German society is superior to its counterpart across the border. "The physical punishment of children that is the rule in Capitalist societies rightfully is frowned upon by the workers of our republic," a conviction for child abuse claims in 1960. Many judgments paint the GDR as a state in which young people can look forward to their future. In February 1958, Frau Christiansen punishes four young people caught on their way to West Berlin for "violations of the Passport Statute" with prison terms of between six and eight months. They "must understand that young people, upon their arrival in West Germany, will be pressured to join NATO and mercenary troops." Nine months later, Herr Kellner writes, again in a flight case: the judgment must demonstrate to the young defendants that fleeing to West Germany "entails the risk of sharing the fate of hundreds of thousands who cannot find work and miserably end on the street or in the Foreign Legion."

I encounter the same fantasies, viewed from the other side, in some arrest warrants for young runaways who, brought before a judge, explain their attempted flight with their intended goal to join the Foreign Legion. The Legion is one of the avatars of the Cold War. The image of mercenaries making money by waging war in desert states fits well into the judges' image of Capitalism's brutal venality. For the young men eager to shake off Socialism's petty utopianism, the Foreign Legion represents unlimited freedom and adventure. Neither of the two images comes close to depicting reality in the Federal Republic. But both reflect the ideological intensity of criminal adjudication in these years. More is at stake than just the individual defendant. Each crime is also a collision between two political worlds. Each criminal judgment must take sides in this collision. Even seemingly banal and paltry local conflicts must be understood in their worldwide context. These years, the Neuburg Court's bi-annual update for the Ministry of Justice that summarizes the state of law within the region begins with a global political weather report. Here is an example: "The Warsaw Treaty, concluded at the beginning of the year, is of great international importance." And another one: "During the second half of the year, significant political developments contributed to the consolidation of the GDR. One event deserving particular mention was the Conference of Foreign Ministers in Geneva." Shouldn't the authorities in Berlin know more about what happened in Geneva than the judges of the Neuburg Appellate Court? But these grand political assertions (that often could be substituted for each other without the risk of losing meaning) are not intended to convey concrete and factual information. Rather, they are supposed to demonstrate that the Regional Court in Neuburg is well aware of its historic role in the fight between good and evil. In October 1968, Frau Christiansen writes in a conviction for the illegal possession of a weapon: "One has to take account of the specific point in time at which the defendant acquired the gun. The counterrevolution in Hungary had just been quashed." In the world battle of political systems, there are no quiet wind-shelters in which a criminal can break the law in private, so to speak.

Crimes are also dangerous because they undermine the people's faith in Socialism. Again Frau Christiansen, in a judgment that punishes the embezzlement of 5000 Marks by the manager of a state cooperative with two-and-a-half years of hard labor: "The offense has the potential consequence of causing some

CHAPTER 7

members of the cooperative to doubt whether coop stores are adequately supervised." As we saw in the chapter on labor law, such doubts would have been well-founded. But Socialism has no room for dissonance and reservations. As Herr Steinmetz put it in a 1959 conviction of several young men contributing to a village brawl: "Every attack on the unanimity of the collective leads to disagreement and to the lessening of labor productivity." The same year, four petty offenders receive for the collective theft of seven bottles of wine a "public censure" and the same admonishment to strive for unity: "The defendants must understand that the standard of living can only rise as the people's property increases. It is their duty to commit all their strength to the cause of Socialism." Everyone must close ranks!

It comes as no surprise that the authors of such judgments like to use the word "we" in their decisions—"in our Republic," "with us," "we in the GDR"—and that they are fearful of unauthorized intruders into the collective unity that they so eagerly promote. In a 1958 prosecution of a man who despite months-long stays in Lüritz had never registered with the police, Herr Kellner praises the wisdom of the GDR Registration Decree of 1951: "It guarantees that no dark elements can sneak into our country." Lüritz criminal case law of these years focuses on the actor rather than the act. "Friend or foe?" is the court's first question in each trial. Judgments begin with a short political profile of the perpetrator. Here is an example: "The defendant is a member of the Free German Labor Union and the Democratic Women's League. She has not joined a political party. Last year she vacationed in the Federal Republic. Her daughter has fled to West Germany." That about says it all. The forms for arrest warrants in these years contain a space where the interrogating judge can enter a suspect's "financial circumstances" to reveal his class association. The entries for "occupation" at the beginning of each warrant also indicate what kind of person stands before the judge. Many of those detained are listed as *Grossbauern* (large-scale farmers) and it does not take much to fit that definition: forty-four hectares in one case, just nineteen hectares in another. Once, in 1959, an accused qualifies as a *Grossbauer* with twelve hectares to his name, just four hectares more than the "new farmers" created by the Land Reform, who plow their little lots of about eight hectares with the state's approval. There are other verbal shadings of distrust. One defendant "for some time now has played with the idea of leaving for West Germany"—friends or neighbors must have told the court about some conversations. In 1958, a prosecutor describes the accused as "having been born into a *Grossbauer* family." Somebody else, not quite so worthy of suspicion, is the son of a *Mittelbauer* (a farmer with midsize holdings).

Knowing the class background of the defendant was meant to help the judge to properly assess his dangerousness. Above all, Socialism feared for its economy and for the authority of government and Party. Most crimes against the state (in these and later years) were prosecuted not at the local level but before the Regional Court in Neuburg, and since the Neuburg records do not reach back into the 1950s, I know of the worst Lüritz cases only from occasional articles in the *Sentinel*. In May 1953, for instance, only a few weeks before the popular uprising of June 17, the paper reports on a verdict of "eight years hard labor for a Wall Street agent"—a deacon of the Protestant Church's Youth Ministry in Lüritz—for "war-mongering and sabotaging state activities." But even without access to the court records of these years, I have no difficulty imagining how the First Senate of the Regional Court in Neuburg would deal with this and other cases that were deemed "political." East German criminal case law of the 1950s, especially case law of the regional courts and the Supreme Court, has become a well-plowed field of historical research. This was the decade that in 1950 began with the infamous "Waldheim trials," which in secret hearings pronounced draconian penalties for more than 3000 real and alleged Nazi war criminals, among them 32 death sentences.[22] In October 1950, the Supreme Court initiated its notorious case law on Article 6 of the GDR Constitution of 1949, using a seemingly innocuous constitutional provision to fabricate a new crime against the state that could not be found in any criminal legislation: the "incitement to boycott." Article 6 (which in its first paragraph establishes equal protection) in its second paragraph indeed calls "the incitement to warfare and boycott" a "felony."[23] The Constitution neither defines the behavior that would constitute "incitement" nor—as indeed would not behoove a constitution—does it suggest a penalty for this behavior. But the Supreme Court, undeterred by doctrinal scruples, latched onto the word "felony" used in the Constitution, applied whatever penalties the German Criminal Code of 1871 (then still in force in the GDR) provided for "felonies," and sanctioned what it called "incitement to boycott" with punishments ranging from hard labor to the death penalty.

The Supreme Court used Article 6 primarily for the repression of real (or imagined) attacks on the republic, inspired, as the Court claimed, by real (or imagined) NATO machinations. Its penalties for "incitement to boycott" were very harsh, and the recipient of these penalties, in the Court's description, looked like exhibits from a wax cabinet of the Cold War: Jehovah's Witnesses, solicited and controlled by their "headquarters in Brooklyn" (1950)[24]; imperialist spies from the West German "Investigation Committee of Free Lawyers" (1952)[25]; CIA-trained agents from the RIAS radio station in West Berlin (1955).[26] In Lüritz, "incitement to boycott" does not look quite so scary. Since the offense itself always was adjudicated by the Regional Court in Neuburg, I know the Lüritz boycott-mongerers only from the arrest warrants issued by my district court. The warrants suggest that the local representatives of law and order used the "incitement to boycott" as a welcome catchall term for people causing political trouble. Someone might be arrested for "incitement" because he rants against the Russians, Walter Ulbricht, or the Land Reform, because he calls the People's Police "a pack of crooks," or because he "lures" colleagues away from their jobs "by telling them things about West Germany that are not true" (all quotes from 1956). Neither the police nor the courts are very finicky about their legal definition of the crime. Occasionally, I come across a case in which someone is arrested for "incitement" but later sentenced for a more conventional offense.

These days, the Lüritz law enforcement agencies fear many other attacks on the new state. In 1952, for instance, a slew of arson cases keep them busy. In 1954, "illegal possession of weapons" incidents fill the crime reports, almost all cases involving half-rusted handguns left over from the war. Each season's "crimes against the state" mirror the current paranoia and suspicion of the Party. In 1957, the "Law Amending the Criminal Code" replaces "incitement to boycott" with a list of slightly more specific political offenses, of which "propaganda and provocation endangering the state" (§19) and "defamation of the state" (§20) are the ones most frequently applied in practice. But even under the new rules, crimes and perpetrators look pretty much the same as before. A state that classifies its lawbreakers as either "friend" or "foe" cannot be expected to pay much attention to the legal specifics of the act it is about to punish. What counts is the defendant's opposition to the system, even if it is not acted out but only expressed in angry words. In 1957, 88.5% of all East German crimes against the state are "defamations" under §20.[27]

"Crimes against the economy" (the other category of offenses most worrisome to the authorities), just like political crimes, in serious cases are tried before the Regional Court in Neuburg. Initially, those economic crimes that remain in Lüritz deal with offenses that seem fueled not so much by wanton criminal energies but by the actor's desperate attempt to keep afloat in an economy in which the rules have suddenly and fundamentally been altered. "Keeping secret the ownership of land," for instance, is now punishable (because it affects delivery quotas for agricultural products owed the state); "hoarding" (such as the attempts of farmers to hide extra amounts of grain for the sowing season) is illegal; and, of course, all black-market deals (which might be needed to keep private enterprises—as long as they still exist—in business) are forbidden. As the planned economy spreads and solidifies, I find more and more criminal prosecutions in the files by which the state places the blame for the malfunctionings of the command economy on the unfortunate recipients of its orders: on store managers or cashiers who without proper cash registers cannot keep track of payments and end up with deficits; on farmers who without sufficient manpower and machinery cannot bring in their harvest or milk their cows. "I don't feel guilty," a long-time farmer says in the winter of 1954 who is arrested for allowing 900 hundredweights of potatoes to freeze on the ground that he could not lay in for want of staff. "I don't see why I should be the only one responsible for the mismanagement of our cattle stable," complains a foreman who, left without help, repeatedly had failed to feed the animals on time. Toward the end of the decade, Lüritz defendants prosecuted for committing economic crimes look more like people who actually deserve the disapproval of the law. By now, tricksters have learned to manipulate the many rules and regulations of an unwieldy planned economy for their own private gain: with false reports, dubious accounting practices, bribes, and the like. In 1959, a Lüritz long-haul driver is arrested who with the help of several economic functionaries in town had run a booming business selling faked receipts for the delivery of requisitioned farm products. A Byzantine bureaucracy can easily be cheated.

"Where is the supervision and control?" the *Sentinel* had asked in an article on corruption and black-market deals in 1953. Two years later, the Neuburg Appellate Court advises its trial courts in the region to use the criminal law as an instrument of "enlightenment and coercion" to keep straight those who waver in their commitment to the law and to put a stop to the machinations of the opponents of the system. Arrest warrants are part of the law's strategy to further the goals of Socialism. Among the 1953 stack I find a number of warrants apparently issued for the sole purpose of intimidating opponents of the collectivization of East German agriculture. They all approve of the arrest of farmers accused of having failed to fulfill their delivery quota for the state. The culprits are duly taken into custody; a few days later are informed that the prosecutor has ordered the sequestration of their farms; and are released after a week or two because the reasons for the arrest "have ceased to exist." Have they managed to rustle up the hundredweights of grain or beetroots needed to top up their quota? Or—much more likely—have they agreed to join one of the new collective farms?

East German criminal law of the 1950s is meant to demonstrate that there is no alternative to Socialism in the GDR. The *Lüritz Sentinel* preaches the same lesson. Its regular column "From the Courtroom" reports only on criminal trials. Sometimes, the paper publishes just the bare text of a provision of the Criminal Code, in bold print and surrounded by a wide black frame, accompanied by the warning: "Do not forget!" Lüritzers know that the criminal law keeps a close eye on them. "I've known for a long time that they would either confiscate my farm or put me behind bars," a *Grossbauer* says in 1953 when he is arrested for the nonfulfillment of his delivery quota. He had let ten acres of his land lie fallow. "Because two years ago my father was convicted of an economic crime, I should have known better than to break the law myself," a twenty-year-old salesgirl says when she is arrested in 1955. She had helped herself to cloth and stockings. "Since the defendant knew that previously, two members of his agricultural cooperative had stolen collective property, it was his special obligation

CHAPTER 7

not to break the law himself," a Lüritz judge pronounces in a 1958 trial for embezzlement.

But as the quotes suggest, knowing is not the same as acting on that knowledge. Fear of the criminal law is not the kind of teacher that encourages Socialist citizens to trust and respect their state. On the contrary: many of the crimes committed in the years before the Wall seem fueled by irritation, discontent, and the hostility that Lüritz citizens bear for their government. A surprising number of assaults are aimed at policemen or other guardians of law and order and are triggered by the mere fact that someone wears a uniform. Young men get drunk and rail against the government or the Party. "If he had been sober, fear of punishment would have persuaded the defendant to hold his tongue," the judge surmises in a trial for defamation of the state. Many of the perpetrators in my 1950s criminal files seem convinced that the GDR state will not last much longer. In 1953, a butcher threatens a policeman: "One day, we will wear the uniforms and will be the big-shots in the village." "The hour will come when we'll get even," says a *Mittelbauer* in 1958. He, too, is no longer sober. "When times will change...," someone else shouts the same year, and ends his furious rantings with *"Heil Hitler!"* I discover that in many of the state-defamation cases, the defendants' minds seem to be muddled by an ugly confluence of Fascist and anti-Communist convictions. But when would the Lüritzers have had the time and the occasion to acquire sound democratic instincts? Their hatred of politics and politicians finds nourishment in many sources.

In such a heated mental climate, the line that East German criminal law wants to draw between "friend" and "foe" is difficult to locate. Initially, the law considered everyone an enemy of the GDR who even in a minor way had trespassed on the territory of the state. But this approach left Socialism with few friends. Then, in August 1954, the Minister of Justice, Hilde Benjamin, published an article in the GDR's major law review ("On Criminal Policy")[28] that was meant to clarify the friend/foe distinction and was distributed to every district court in the country. But my Lüritz judges still have problems with the correct classification of their perpetrators. In the winter of 1954, a report by the Justice Administration in Neuburg to the Ministry of Justice in Berlin surveys the criminal verdicts in the region that "do not conform to the article of Dr. Benjamin." The judgments of my Lüritz court are mostly faulted for being too lenient. In 1955, the Lüritz/District panel of the court is reprimanded because seven of sixty-eight criminal trials ended with acquittals. "That's 10%!" an irate supervisor has written in the margins of the page. When, in December 1957, the "Law Amending the Criminal Code" introduced two new and milder penalties—"conditional sentences" and "public censure"—for crimes posing only minor dangers for society, Lüritz judges are chided for applying both forms of punishment too often. An inspector's report complains that Lüritz sentences do not contain ideological justifications for the penalties applied. Instead, they are based on "random explanations, mostly of a nonspecific, humane variety."

Nevertheless, I have the impression that even in Berlin, authorities are searching for a more humane approach to criminal adjudication. The case law of the early 1950s in the GDR was so oppressive that it seemed to give the lie to promises of a Socialist utopia. Now East German criminal policy wants to rekindle the hopes of its own better self. On March 5, 1953, Stalin dies. On June 9, 1953, the Politbureau of the SED announces a "New Course." Three days later, the *Sentinel* reports on political reforms that include important changes in criminal policy. All coercive tax collection is suspended; all prison inmates convicted under the "Law on the Protection of People's Property" whose sentences are shorter than three years are immediately released; all suspects in preliminary custody whose likely sentence will not exceed three years also are set free.

We know how the history of the "New Course" continued: with the popular uprising of June 17, 1953. But despite draconian penalties meted out in the immediate aftermath of the rebellion (mostly not in Lüritz, but in Neuburg), the liberalization of East German criminal policy continues after June 17. "Partial liberalization," I should say, because improvements for the "friends" of Socialism (now defined more generously than before) are offset by despotic penalties for its "enemies." The Manichaean world view of these years that still included hope for a "new man" justifies both lenience for those law-breakers capable of reeducation and harshness for the irredeemable opponents of the system. Hence the almost schizophrenic bifurcation of East German criminal policy in the 1950s. Between 1953 and 1955, sentences of hard labor for nonpolitical crimes decline from 28% to 10.6% of all cases, while short-term sentences for less than a year in custody rise from 13% to 43.8%. At the same time, the Regional Court in Neuburg reports to the Ministry of Justice that espionage cases adjudicated by the Ia panel of the court have risen from 15% to 40% of its caseload. The change seems so unsettling to the court that even in its confidential message to the Ministry it lists no absolute figures but only percentages of the increase.

But for run-of-the-mill criminals in Lüritz, the relaxation of the criminal law continues after June 17, 1953. I mentioned already that in 1957, the "Law Amending the Criminal Code" introduced "conditional sentences" and "public censures" as punishments that at least partially replaced the "lock-'em-up" mentality of earlier years. At the Vth Party Congress of the SED in July 1958, the innovations are proudly hailed as evidence of the humane character of Socialism. Two years later, on October 4, 1960, First Secretary Walter Ulbricht presents a "Programmatic Declaration" to the East German Parliament that in broad and optimistic brush strokes paints a picture of the future Socialist community of men and, in the process, articulates the dual purposes of East German criminal law: "When we speak of justice, we mean the patient attempt to persuade and

CHAPTER 7

educate those citizens who have not yet fully understood their responsibilities toward society. We also mean that those who threaten the life of our people and the continued existence of our nation deserve harsh punishment."

Together with the "Programmatic Declaration," Ulbricht announces an amnesty for 12,000 prison inmates in the GDR. In later years, the word "amnesty" would make frequent appearances in East German criminal legislation because the country's prisons usually were overcrowded and needed periodic emptying to make space for newcomers. But in his euphoric talk in October 1960, the First Secretary does not yet use the term. Instead, all generous and warm-hearted Father of the Nation, Ulbricht announces a large-scale demonstration of "mercy" for his subjects. Three months later (as yet, the Wall has not been built!), the "Resolution of the Council of State on the Further Development of the Administration of Justice" of January 30, 1961, describes *how* the re-socialization of delinquent citizens is to be achieved: through socially useful work and the educational strength of the collective. "In Socialist society, nobody needs to turn to crime," says the Resolution. GDR legal politics undertakes a renewed attempt to reach utopia.

For my Lüritz judges, the attempt leads to a flurry of additional activities. In April 1961, the Justice Administration in Neuburg demands to see every criminal judgment that the Lüritz court rendered since February 1 to "check whether the Council-of-State Resolution is carried out in practice." Judges are told to initiate "personal conversations" with ex-prisoners who benefited from the amnesty: did they "experience joy" when learning of the Resolution? Did lay assessors and Party functionaries working with them encounter moving "moments" in which some of those recently released expressed their happiness at the new policy? Or even better: could one or the other judge attach to his report on the local impact of the Resolution a "thank-you note that he or she might have received from someone pardoned?" If so, he should send not a copy but "the original of the letter."

The Socialism of these years wants so intensely, so desperately, to be loved and trusted by the people. But few citizens share the Party's hope for a brave new world. Despite the new "Passport Law," the border with West Germany is still not sealed shut, and it is easy for those who do not want a part in the GDR's glowing future to run away from it. In 1960, the number of East German refugees has reached more than three quarters of the number of fugitives before the passage of the "Passport Law."[29] In the Neuburg region, many of them are farmers wanting to escape the agricultural collectives that they were forced to join. Even those malcontents deciding to stay home find ways of venting their anger at the new life that they did not ask for. In the days between March 1 and July 26, 1960, 2654 collective farmers in East Germany renounce their memberships in the new cooperatives. "Top priority" messages from the police to the Ministry of Justice report on wild rumors circulating in the land: that all farming cooperatives would be dissolved this very year; that the Americans would come and take over all economic enterprises in the GDR. In the first half of 1961, 407 Lüritzers flee to the Federal Republic; among them, thirteen teachers. "Things can't go on this way," I think as I pore over my files.

On August 13, 1961, the GDR begins with the construction of the Wall. The day before, the Party and government notables of Lüritz had been called together at the Party Secretariat to be prepared for the events to come. One of those present at the gathering was the director of the District Court. The purpose of the meeting, I assume, was to assure the Party of the unconditional loyalty of its servants in the face of a decision that for all of them must have been alarming and despicable. And indeed, a few weeks later my Lüritz court is praised by inspectors from Berlin for the "noticeable reaction of justice and security agencies" when dealing with "the provocations by critics of the Government's decisions." In Lüritz, protesters are processed in "accelerated trials" and usually punished with prison sentences of between six and twelve months. Theirs must have been fairly harmless offenses such as "defamation of the state" or hasty attempts to flee the country while it was still possible. I do not know how the more serious protesters against the Wall fared before the Ia panel of the Regional Court in Neuburg.

But I can measure from the Lüritz criminal case files the impact of the Wall's construction. It took a while before the country was entirely shut off from the surrounding world. Judging by the arrest warrants (which reveal whether a suspect was actually caught by the police or not), as late as 1963 almost half of all Lüritz fugitives managed to safely reach the West. But *who* it was who tried to flee changed after August 13, 1961. Before the Wall, many deserters came from the middle classes: teachers, engineers, skilled craftsmen, and, occasionally, chairmen of the new agricultural cooperatives who in the early years of collectivization often were recruited from the wealthiest farmers in the villages. Many fugitives left with their families, and if the arrest warrants also mention violations of customs or currency regulations, I know that they also succeeded in taking valuables along. In 1958, the protagonists in the Lüritz criminal case files indicted for "fleeing the Republic" were usually older than 25, a third of them were women, and almost all successfully escaped. These were the solid and hard-working heads of families whose loss the GDR could no longer tolerate.

Once the Wall was built, "flight from the Republic" became so dangerous that only the young and daring who could not believe in their own mortality would risk it. In 1962, the average age of Lüritz fugitives wanted for arrest is 21.6 years. Now, the deserters are no longer the ambitious and industrious, but rather the foolhardy and those without social and personal ties to hold them back. Almost all *Sperrbrecher* ("wall-breakers" or, more literally, "obstruction-breakers")

CHAPTER 7

are men. Many of the attempts to flee are not premeditated or, if at all, are badly planned. When runaways are caught and asked by the police how, precisely, they had meant to cross the border, the answer often is a hazy "somehow." A seventeen-year-old boy who plans to flee across the Baltic Sea optimistically assumes that the distance between the East German and the West German shore will be about three to four kilometers. A twenty-year-old, reckoning with twenty-five kilometers, is closer to the truth: he intends to swim that stretch at a water temperature of 60.8 degrees, with no other equipment than swimming goggles and a diver's knife. One is relieved to read that an East German border patrol boat has pulled him from the water. "Why would I want to be shot dead?" a woman once responds in an interrogation when the police accuse her of planning her escape. Prudent East German citizens now stay put. The Wall has taught them, in one fashion or another, to make their grumbling peace with Socialism.

Even the crimes against the state look less explosive now that the border to the Federal Republic is no longer open. In May 1962, a meeting of the directors of all district courts within the Neuburg region discusses the question of whether previous judicial harshness toward all enemies of the state should now, perhaps, be softened. A ministerial dignitary from Berlin (who, as is usual, attends the meeting) explains that GDR criminal policy on anti-Socialist propaganda and defamation has indeed "fundamentally changed" but warns not to apply these changes "in formalistic fashion." It is one of those safe "yes, but ..." advisories. Still, even delinquents with a previous record of "defamation of the state" may now receive conditional sentences for a new offense if they "have learned" from their previous convictions. Trial judges are told to be more reticent in handing out post-release restrictions such as the prohibition not to change one's residence without permission. Between 1966 and 1969, convictions for what count as "crimes against the state" (above all "defamations," "resistance against state authority," and border-crimes) fall from 22% of the annual criminal caseload of the Lüritz/City court to a mere 12%.

When I look at the perpetrators of these case files—mostly maladjusted and rebellious young men in whose lives a lot of things went wrong and who have turned to alcohol to drown their anger against not just the Party but the world—it seems to me that, in these years, most Lüritz "crimes against the state" no longer can count as political offenses. True, many of these acts are colored by neo-Fascism. In the spring of 1962, the weekly reports of the Neuburg Appellate Court to the Ministry of Justice mention "almost daily" police investigations "of swastikas smeared on walls." But usually, the draftsmen of these Nazi symbols have not been motivated by political convictions. Their wild, beer-fueled rantings are an embarrassment for the GDR, but do not threaten the state's safety. Even the defendants themselves do not seem to perceive their acts as dangerous challenges to Socialism. In 1969, 30% of all Lüritz defendants charged with the violation of state property are represented by a lawyer, compared to only 6.4% of those defendants charged with a crime against the state. That difference could also be explained by the class differences between the two groups of offenders.

Does my impression that the Wall produced a sullen but widespread adaptation to the political restrictions under Socialism hold up when I move from my Lüritz files to those of the Regional Court in Neuburg (which, after all, dealt with the more serious offenses against the state)? The earliest criminal case files held in Neuburg date from 1968. Because I do not know what happened in the years before, I have to be careful with my claims. But at least as far as the post-1968 years are concerned, there were not many Lüritz citizens deemed dangerous enough to warrant their being brought before the Regional Court: not more than one or two "political" offenders per year, to which an equal number of "non-political" delinquents must be added whose crimes were serious enough to be adjudicated in first instance by the Appellate Court. Those were cases of murder or manslaughter and large-scale embezzlements or frauds affecting "people's property." But the word "murder" overstates the kind of violence that happened in my town. Almost all of the eleven defendants from Lüritz who between 1968 and 1989 were tried for killing or trying to kill another human being were drunk at the time of the offense, and many of the victims survived the attack. I find no death penalty for a Lüritz murderer in my files (in 1987, the GDR abolished capital punishment) and only one life prison sentence (in 1982). In non-political capital cases, the judgments of the Neuburg Regional Court were, by West German standards, severe, but they were carefully drafted and often showed real efforts to do justice to the human complications of a tragedy.

In political cases, however, the court barely seemed to care about the rights of the defendant and instead spent most of its energy on calming the paranoia of the state. Its judgments in these cases were harsh and uncompromising and became even more so as the years wore on (although East Germany's many amnesties meant also that most prisoners did not serve their full term). About two years in prison for "agitation against the state" in the 1960s, three to six years for an offense called "terror" in the 1970s, and once, in 1980, fifteen years in prison for someone convicted of "resistance to state authority"—these were the rates that Lüritz political dissenters had to reckon with if they should find themselves before the Ia panel of the Neuburg Regional Court. If the Secret Police and the prosecutor had hit it right with the selection of their political defendants, they were men and women of persuasion: solid and thoughtful people, respected in their communities, whose willingness to give expression to their political objections might have persuaded others to follow in their steps—in other words, truly dangerous opponents of the system. But since the representatives of law and order preferred to err on the side of safety rather than be sorry, and since their political angst led them to suspect subversion even in cases in which a malefactor had been motivated by boredom or a longing for adventure rather than by principled objections to the system, the number of authentic Lüritz dissidents who were convicted by the Ia panel of the Regional Court was probably smaller than the number of "politicals" in the court's index of defendants. At least in the Lüritz of my criminal case files, there was little open, articulate, and articulated criticism of Socialism. As a result, the state's fear of its own citizens visibly diminished after the construction of the Wall. Criminal law no longer had the primary task of defending an ideological system under siege. Those in control again seemed to remember their plans for educating a "new man" that prior to the Wall had been undermined by the ease with their pupils could escape the lessons.

On August 4, 1963, the Council of State issues the "Decree on the Principles and Methods of the GDR Agencies of Justice." The decree is a direct descendant of First Secretary Ulbricht's "Programmatic Declaration" of October 1960 and of the Council of State's own "Resolution on the Further Development of the Administration of Justice" of January 1961. Like its predecessors, it is an optimistic piece of legislation, claiming "education and persuasion" to be the "primary activity" of the Socialist state. But if previous East German pedagogic efforts were fueled by vague hopes for the malleability of human nature, these hopes can now, post-Wall, be given definite institutional shape. East German criminal law, in particular, is assigned specific educational tasks. All "suitable" criminal proceedings are to be staged not in a courtroom but at the defendant's place of work and are to involve members of his work collective. At the investigatory stage, neighbors and colleagues of a culprit should provide information about the conflict and its setting; at the trial, they should—as people themselves affected by a social trespass—be given the occasion to comment on it and to suggest responses. Collectives are encouraged to appoint "social accusers" or "defenders" to represent their views on act and actor at the trial and to mobilize the whole workforce to prevent similar offenses in the future. The decree also introduces "sureties of the collective": collective promises, issued at the trial, to help a wayward colleague with his re-socialization that would allow the judge to replace an otherwise expected prison sentence with probation. To further stabilize weak and unreliable defendants, the judge may order them, for a set time, not to leave their current place of work.

These are impressive and, for all concerned, labor-intensive innovations. The Lüritz judges must have greeted them with weary sighs. They know that their compliance with the new criminal policies would be spurred on and monitored by the Neuburg Appellate Court. The District Court, accordingly, is ordered to list all educational measures that it undertook in every individual decisions in order to enable the Appellate Court to check whether the State Council's "principles and methods" of criminal adjudication had been properly observed. The

1965 files of the District Court contain a set of work sheets headed "Procedural Objectives": handwritten notes on meetings prior to a trial, in which the judge and the lay assessors assigned to a particular case outline the pedagogic strategy for its upcoming hearing. And I find bundles of duplicates of *other* district courts' decisions in the wood cellar, sent by the Regional Court as examples of how to carry out the new procedural policies: mountains of pages, covered in pale, barely decipherable lilac-colored copy-print, that my Lüritz judges, too, apparently could not bring themselves to read because the sheets are smooth and immaculate and only very, very rarely marred by someone's underlinings.

Part of the reason why it was so difficult to carry out the 1963 "Decree on the Agencies of Justice" and to supervise its execution from above was the technical imprecision of the decree, which had the outward shape of a piece of legislation but whose goals were listed in inspirational, decidedly un-legal, language. The decree wanted to exploit the pedagogic strength of the collective, but never defines "collective." It contains no rules on how to select a representative of the collective for participation in a trial nor on the choice between "social accusers" or "defenders." The decree leaves open who among a defendant's colleagues may vote on these decisions and whether there has to be a vote at all. It does not state the factors that make a criminal trial "suitable" for being staged at the defendant's place of work rather than in the courtroom.

I assume that the imprecision was intentional. The "Decree on the Agencies of Justice" wanted to loosen up and humanize legal routines by infusing them with the experiences and insights of work collectives. In 1964, a letter from the Regional Court in Neuburg thus admonishes my Lüritz judges to stay true to the decree's intentions by avoiding "all cookie-cutter formulas, routines, and preconceptions" in the handling of their cases. "Attention: all judges," the letter states in its opening paragraph. But while I find, indeed, every Lüritz judge's initials on the sheet, I cannot see how the Appellate Court's instructions can have helped my protagonists to carry out their daily work. "Routine" is not only a professional vice of judges but also a professional virtue. It insures the automatic observation of formal rules and thus speeds up and equalizes their application. Now, under the decree, every judge, in every trial, is supposed to reinvent the wheel and focus on every offender's highly personal potential for social reintegration. Involving a defendant's collective in this task means a lot of extra work. An enterprise's management must be informed; social accusers or defenders must be found. Social representatives must be instructed and prepared to exercise their roles in the proceedings. In 1964, the Regional Court finds fault with a Lüritz judge who had invited an offender's *current* colleagues to his trial but no representative from his *previous* place of work. As a result, the Regional Court complains, the causes of the defendant's deviance had not been fully investigated. It appears that the Justice Decree not only increased

CHAPTER 7

my judges' workload but also placed additional burdens on a law-breaker's employer.

Still, everybody tries to do his best. Admittedly, only a small percentage of Lüritz criminal trials are adjudicated at the defendant's place of work: hearings in situ simply are too time consuming and expensive. But Lüritz judges, instead, bring the work collectives into the courtroom. They invite whoever is linked to the defendant by collective ties to his upcoming trial: the drinking buddies of a rowdy prosecuted for assault; the members of an alleged fraudster's judo club; the classmates of a high-school student accused of trying to flee the country. "Honoring the demands of the 'Decree on the Agencies of Justice,'" the invitation states on those occasions. Judges instruct and question social representatives of a defendant's work brigade, housing block, or garden commune; occasionally, they return an indictment to the prosecutor's office because no social representative showed up in court or refuse to admit a representative whose comments on the case appear too skimpy. After the verdict has been passed, judges "evaluate" offense and punishment at the perpetrator's workplace in order to educate his colleagues and to enlist them in plans for his re-socialization. I find some moving pleadings of collective representatives among the verdicts (mostly handwritten texts that someone unaccustomed to public speaking would simply read in court) in which a defendant's fellow workers ask the court for lenience and promise to help their mate avoid transgressions in the future. These years, the *Lüritz Sentinel*, too, likes to publish uplifting stories about criminals whom the collective led back onto the straight and narrow path of Socialist legality. This is how an optimistic review of East German criminal adjudication under the Justice Decree would read.

But there is another way in which the Justice Decree's story can be told: as the account of a reform that carried within itself the seeds of its own failure. In order to live up to the decree's demands, my judges had to make so many phone calls, organize so many meetings, write so many letters, and produce so many reports on their activities to enable the Regional Court in Neuburg, for its part, to convince the Ministry of Justice in Berlin that every judge under its authority contributed to the decree's success, that all this extra work could only be accomplished by resorting to superficiality and routine. Not surprisingly, the GDR Supreme Court in April 1965 issued a "Resolution on Citizens' Participation in Criminal Procedure" that criticized the often "only formal inclusion of social representatives" in trials. "True participation," the resolution states, does not consist of the filling in of forms, but must be "differentiated and fact-driven." The "Decree on the Agencies of Justice" does not aim for "busy work" but for "changing an offender's character," explains the court.[30] Easier said than done.

There were more problems yet with the decree. Did the collective representatives truly represent the collectives? Even the Supreme Court had occasional doubts. It ordered its district courts not to admit social participants in criminal trials without examining whether "the collective had given them a mandate" for their role. But how could one tell? The Justice Decree provided no procedure for the selection of social representatives. The regulatory vacuum was filled by the discretion of police and prosecutors, who during their investigations of a crime also chose and prepared the suspect's colleagues for participation in the trial. As a result, first instance criminal proceedings in the GDR involved three times as many "social accusers" as "defenders."[31] Why would the law enforcers who selected the participants look for people offering *excuses* for a perpetrator's deeds? Official pressure on collectives to send delegates to a comrade's trial as "accusers" rather than "defenders" may also explain why many of the "social accusers" I encounter in my records often made light of a defendant's guilt: the prosecutor must have told them to *condemn* an act that solidarity with a fellow worker led them to *condone*.

And these are only the positive failures, so to speak, of the decree: the cases in which collective representatives, while maybe more lenient than law enforcement officers might wish, nevertheless engaged with zeal and compassion in their tasks. In most cases, though, the briefs of social representatives in criminal trials sound as if their authors, tired at the end of a long work day, produced the texts that, they assumed, the guardians of law and order would want to see. Most statements—usually just one handwritten page—are vague and formulaic, and virtually never contain those human details that only a defendant's fellow workers would know and that could help a judge to write a sentence that took its subject's personal strengths and weaknesses into account. On the other hand: I do sometimes discover signs of long-standing animosity between a criminal defendant and his work collective, which now makes use of the occasion to try to get rid of a disliked colleague or at least to vent its anger over his not fitting in. The GDR Supreme Court, too, is aware of the possibility of personal vendettas, and in its "Decree of 1965" orders its trial courts to disallow the testimony of a collective representative against whom the defendant raises reasonable objections. I have found no case among my criminal law files in which this happened.

Again, this is not surprising. The Justice Decree's faith in collective warmth was paid for with its disbelief in the significance of legal form. The "instructions" to collective representatives by prosecutors and judges, the "procedural objectives" designed by the judge and the lay assessors to strengthen the pedagogic impact of a trial, even some of the "evaluations" of a case at a defendant's work site were arranged *before* the oral arguments had even taken place. The social representatives were thus invited to morally condemn an act whose legal blameworthiness had not yet been established. This type of preemptive populist involvement had to undermine the presumption of innocence proclaimed by

CHAPTER 7

East German criminal procedure. By the mid-1960s, GDR judges were (more or less) university-trained professionals. All "people's judges" wanting to maintain their jobs had to have passed correspondence courses at the "Academy of State and Law" in Potsdam to bring their legal knowledge up to speed. Even so, my judges' formal instincts, their taste for conceptual precision, and their understanding of the legitimating function of procedure were undeveloped and, if anything, were further muddled by the Justice Decree's intentional insistence on some undefined collective warmth.

The judges' disrespect for formal legal process has left many traces in the Lüritz files. A 1964 conviction of an exhibitionist, for instance, contains explicit praise for "several citizens" who upon spotting the offender "took him to task by dealing him several blows." The judge could find no fault with the virtuous vigilantes: "Our working people rightly were enraged by the defendant's immoral acts." Lüritz judges as a rule are careful and, at times, downright pedantic. But to them, legal form is a matter of order rather than of justice. When in 1965, the marriage of a prosecutor and a judge at the Lüritz court (Herr and Frau Bereck, both with university diplomas) repeatedly leads to situations in which Prosecutor Bereck has to prepare a case that Judge Bereck will eventually adjudicate, the Neuburg Appellate Court is worried that this marital collaboration "might cause some citizens to suspect a lack of impartiality" in the resulting judgment. The problem is taken care of by an arrangement between court and prosecution under which Prosecutor Bereck no longer *signs* indictments over which his wife might sit in judgment. Behind the scenes, the spouses' cooperation could continue. As far as I can tell, the Neuburg Appellate Court voiced no objection to this Solomonic strategy.

How can I fuse my contradictory descriptions of the judicial *policy* and *practice* under the Justice Decree of 1963—my jarring accounts of the decree's success (on the one hand) and of its failure (on the other)—into a single, convincing picture? Perhaps by adding some history to it: both versions of my story find their explanation in the construction of the Berlin Wall. The Wall assured East German Socialism of the external safety that the system needed to seriously attempt the reeducation of its citizenry. But the Wall also closed off the national classroom, kept out fresh air, prevented all external inspiration, and so produced the closeness and confinement that turned an optimistic educational experiment into self-righteous, petty tutelage. The law was supposed to prune and weed out whatever might impede the individual's integration in the collective. Time and again I discover accusations in the files reproaching a defendant for refusing to adapt, for not engaging in "regular work," for not leading "an ordered life," for standing aside, wanting to be someone special, pursuing only one's personal interests, not taking advice. Socialism could not accept an individual's detachment from the fold. In 1964, Judge Bereck adds an extra four months to the three-and-a-half years of hard labor suggested by the prosecutor as penalty for a swindler's defrauding private creditors to the tune of 20,000 Marks. The defendant "has illusions of grandeur," she writes in her sentence. "Instead of saving money, like everybody else, in order to honestly equip his home, he boastfully promised his wife new furniture." In the same year, Judge Gemmen (borrowed by the Lüritz Court from a neighboring district because Judge Christiansen is ill with tuberculosis) sentences a young man to ten months in prison (rather than five months, as demanded by the prosecutor) for repeated joy rides, undertaken on other people's motorcycles and without a license. The judge is particularly incensed by the culprit's brazen self-assertion. "Apparently he believes that every citizen is the judge of his own abilities to steer a motor through public traffic," she writes. "It did not occur to him to apply for membership in a motorcycle club."

The law wants people to become "a member" in these years: of a club, a collective, a housing organization; of society. It punishes those who keep themselves apart. Since it is no longer possible to physically escape the GDR, it is the mental and emotional dissociations from collective solidarity that the court must fight: self-aggrandizement, self-centeredness, going it alone. The pressures to conform are brought to bear not only on political dissenters or on un-integrated loners at the workplace. All "deviant" behavior, all attempts to march to a different drummer, are suspect—homosexuals, for instance, are treated harshly by the law and by the courts. Only in 1987 did a judgment of East Germany's Supreme Court call gays and lesbians equal citizens in a Socialist society.[32] But that was close to D-Day. In 1963, still unshaken in their belief in Socialism's superiority, the Lüritz police counts it as a success when in a sting to stamp out bourgeois moral filth and trash it confiscates, in six apartments on Karl Marx Avenue, a total of 174 dime novels: 151 romances, eleven historic potboilers, and twelve Wild West adventures. The booklets, with titles such as "Princess Firehead" and "You Must Not Weep," all came from West Germany. Most of them were found in bedrooms. Even the escape into a Capitalist dream world was barred to Lüritz citizens.

The Wall had redirected the interests of Socialist crime enforcement from the external enemies of the GDR to those who threatened the country's internal solidarity and order; from the outward acts of suspects to their inner life. Not that the old division of the world into friend and foe had been abandoned. But the "foes" were now pursued at home: among those who "saw no need to accept the norms of our Socialist community," or—worse, since harder to uncover—within the treacherous mind of a defendant. The notion of what constituted a "crime" became increasingly internalized until the boundaries between acts, intentions, speculations, and mere flights of fancy were blurred and, at times, all but erased. Loyalty alone, or its suspected absence, was what counted.

CHAPTER 7

Here is an example from 1971; incidentally, a case not adjudicated by the Lüritz court but in a neighboring town that the librarian of the *Stasi* Archive in Neuburg mistakenly placed upon my desk. I will use it because it demonstrates the self-referential paranoia of East Germany's criminal law enforcement of these years at its most extreme. Three young men, friends and all three good-for-nothings, complain about the boredom in their little town, chat now and then about their plans to flee the country, and for some time now have been under *Stasi* observation. One of them, who knows why, sets fire to a local barn that he himself reports to the fire station and then proceeds to help extinguish. The event leads to his questioning—first by the regular police, then by the *Stasi*—and soon to the arrest of all three friends.

And then the interrogations by the *Stasi* (which in the GDR, in line with the rules of criminal procedure, investigated all political offenses) begin in earnest. The transcripts fill seven voluminous folders. For three long months the suspects are questioned, again and again: first individually, then in confrontation with their buddies; sometimes just once a week, sometimes more often; from 9 o'clock to noon, from 1 PM to 5; always with a lunch break that the interrogator notes, precisely to the minute, for the record. It looks like a regular workday for both suspects and investigators. The questions always are the same. But the answers change over time and with every week become more dramatic and outrageous.

Soon, one of the friends is said to have had a pistol that he buried in the cemetery. His mate, who was (dishonorably) discharged after military service, allegedly pilfered thirty hand grenades from the People's Army. The third man of the trio is reported to have mixed weed killer and sugar to concoct explosives intended to blow up the local District Party Bureau. The story goes from bad to worse. The language used by the three suspects to describe their plans sounds increasingly subversive. Their choice of words gradually resembles that of their interrogators. Initially, the young man who had set the fire tried to explain his act by claiming that he wanted to "take revenge" for insufficient state support after his release from a previous prison sentence. By the end of the questioning, he claims that he intended to blow up not only the Party headquarters but also the building housing the local Secret Police Agency. Why? "Because the SED District Bureau represents the power of the Party and the District Office of State Security insures the safety of the working class." The words cannot have sprung from the culprit's own vocabulary. I find a photograph of the SED District Bureau among the pages that shows "the power of the Party" in less than brilliant light: it is a gray and modest row house in a street with other gray and modest row houses. By June 1971, the interrogations have sufficiently progressed to allow the Regional Court in Neuburg to open criminal proceedings against the three. The charge alleges what the GDR Criminal Code calls "terror": the young men are accused of arson and a planned attack on the SED Party Bureau with the intent of carrying out an armed escape across the border and, once in West Germany, of being able to claim the status of political refugees.

During the hearings at the Regional Court it soon becomes quite clear that, besides the initial arson (which the arsonist, himself a member of the town's voluntary fire brigade, did his best to help contain), none of the evil plans of the defendants ever moved beyond the stage of fantasy. There were no weapons buried in the cemetery. Nor did the hand grenades exist: the self-proclaimed owners of the weapons had only wanted to impress their friends. Whether the homemade dynamite could ever have exploded seems doubtful, too: the file contains a photograph of a bottle with watery-looking liquid, but no chemical analysis of its content. The friends' intention to flee the country (according to the prosecutor's charge "around New Year") had never led to any serious action. An early motorcycle tour to reconnoiter the border had never gotten on the road because the motorcycle had broken down. After that, the flight plan was no longer mentioned. The three malcontents had only talked and daydreamed about rebellion and escape—nothing more.

But the most amazing aspect of the story is the fact that court and prosecutor do not see the threadbare character of the defendants' enterprise as evidence of its not posing any serious danger to the state. On the contrary: to the representatives of state authority, the fact that the defendants' fantasies were unconstrained by any practical considerations of feasibility appears, if anything, to heighten their alarm. The GDR Criminal Code of 1968 in its §101 defines "terror" not as a specific act but as an "undertaking" and so, admittedly, encourages the blurring of the beginning and the end of whatever "undertaking" the judges must evaluate. But the main reason for their absurdly harsh sentences for the defendants (six years in prison each for the two older ones, three years for the youngest of the three) is the judges' outrage at the discontent and anger at state and Party that the culprits' fantasies reflect. The court reacts to their games of make-believe the way a mother would whose child pretends to fire at her with a toy gun. Of course, the mother knows that the "Bang! Bang!" won't threaten her physical safety. But she is shocked by the antagonism and aggressiveness that the game reflects. How can one even play with the idea of shooting someone whom you are supposed to love?

The judges are not alone in their surreal assessment of the case. All in the courtroom seem to understand that this is a trial not of facts but of loyalty. Even only imagined faithlessness is real betrayal. Nobody seems to notice anymore that none of the young men ever posed a realistic threat to either state or Party. "It is not thanks to them that the defendants' goals remained unrealized," says the prosecutor. "No one who favors terroristic acts like these can expect mercy," says the "social accuser" representing the culprits' work collective. And even

CHAPTER 7

the defendants speak of their castles in the air as of unquestionable certainties. "We knew that there might be casualties or bodies," says one of them. Caused by whom, for heaven's sake?

I find a number of other criminal case files in the Neuburg *Stasi* Archive in which the border between daydreams and reality, between fantasies, intentions, and the acts needed to carry out imagined plans, are so blurred that in the end, even rebellious mind games are enough to land someone in prison as a dangerous enemy of the state. A political system that insists on being loved is more deeply disappointed by the refusal of this love than by the actual aggressiveness of many ordinary criminals. In 1970, the Neuburg Regional Court thus sentences four Lüritz teenagers to prison terms of between two and ten years because they had formed a club with the unlikely name of "Clan of Rusty Clabs," in which they blew off steam by bragging about political rebellion, beat-music, and their future collaboration with the CIA. The only thing the boys had actually *done* was draft a political flyer (which they immediately tore up) and produce a membership ID card with a fake official seal. "The defendants had no scruples about committing crimes," said the prosecutor at their trial. In 1978, a twenty-year-old man is sentenced to five-and-a-half years in prison for committing "terror": he had planned to drive a car (which still needed to be stolen) to the border, overpower a border guard with a flare gun (which he had not yet obtained), and flee. The culprit had devised this scheme after watching "a utopian movie on West German television" in which the victim, hit by a flare, had "internally combusted." The prosecutor, describing the gory details of the show, deplored the "high criminal intensity" of the defendant's plan. And even as late as the summer of 1988, the Lüritz District Court hands out a penalty of fourteen months in prison for "obstructing state activity" to a crane operator who had announced that he would hang himself on the tree standing right in front of the city's Interior Department if the department would continue to reject his applications for an exit visa. The defendant had brought a rope along to give some added weight to his announcement. Never mind that the suicide threat had little chance of succeeding: the Interior Department is situated close to the Lüritz market square; the tree in front of it is high and difficult to climb; and, since "the place usually swarms with agents from 'Security,'" the alleged suicide candidate had counted on being noticed right away and—thus the plan—on finally being listened to. I assume that it was the very threat of undermining the state's solicitude by self-destruction that led the court to chose so harsh a sentence. A child who loves his parents should threaten suicide not even as a joke. The Lüritz court is so outraged by the defendant's heartless scheme that it reports the matter to the Neuburg Appellate Court, which in turn passes on the story to the Ministry of Justice. A straightforward brawl or an embezzlement would never have garnered similar attention.

PUNISHMENTS

Although the Socialist state up to the very last year of the GDR's existence continued to be easily hurt or insulted by its citizens' shenanigans, East German criminal law calmed down sufficiently after the paranoia of the 1950s and the slow consolidation that followed the construction of the Wall to turn its attention to more realistic threats against Socialist society. In the 1970s, "asocial behavior" is the crime on which the Lüritz court spends most of its attention. *Asoziale* (or *Assis* in GDR vernacular) were persons who did not earn their keep: slackers and shirkers who came late (or not at all) to work; hobos and vagrants who kept afloat with begging or the occasional odd job; young people avoiding proper jobs and instead freeloading on their parents; mothers or fathers failing to pay child support. Most *Assis* were people with no self-discipline and little staying power, many lacked a personal network of people whom they could rely on, and the majority were alcoholics. In 1973, of 297 defendants sentenced by my Lüritz court, 124 were *Asoziale*—by far the largest group of lawbreakers in the dock. In the same year, Lüritz judges adjudicated seventeen cases of "flight from the Republic" and fifteen various crimes against the state.

Most legal systems disapprove of citizens with irregular and aimless lifestyles, and the law's reaction to their being unable or unwilling to fit in can serve as a gauge of a state's intolerance and authoritarian harshness. The Nazis in the early years of the Third Reich locked up "asocial" citizens in prisons and later murdered them in concentration camps.[33] In the Federal Republic, until 1959 someone "refusing to take up work" could be remanded for up to four years to a "workhouse." Under East German Socialism, "work evasion" always was illegal: at first, as in West Germany, under the rules of the old German Criminal Code of 1871; then, under a 1961 Decree that shortly after the construction of the Wall introduced "labor education" in the GDR; and finally, since 1968, under §249 of the new East German Criminal Code, which penalized "asocial behavior." The sanctions for work evasion changed over the decades: jail or "workhouse" in the early years; since 1961, indefinite assignments to "educational work commandos"; and, after the abolition of the "work commandos" in 1977, criminal sentences of up to two (and for recidivists, up to five) years in prison.

The definitions of what constituted "work-shy behavior" changed as well. When, in August 1961, GDR trial courts were authorized, upon the application of local authorities, to sentence "truants" to "labor education," the law contained no definition of "truancy" and thus enabled every local mayor to get rid of undesirables in his town or village by denouncing them as parasites. I assume that the legal imprecision of the 1961 decree, coming right on the heels of the construction of the Berlin Wall, had been intended to allow, if necessary, the swift apprehension of people making trouble. As far as I can tell, though, the decree was not applied in Lüritz. The criminal case files of the early 1960s contain only very occasional prosecutions for vagrancy or prostitution.

CHAPTER 7

The new East German Criminal Code of 1968, in its §249, defined "asocial behavior" more extensively (though not much more precisely) as "the endangerment of social cohesion or the public order" caused by an able-bodied citizen's obstinate refusal to engage in useful work. "Endangerment" can cover many things. Most importantly: a "danger" can exist even if it is quite uncertain whether that "danger" will, in the end, result in actual harm. Section 249 of the Criminal Code allowed the system to defend itself against future hazards imagined only by the paranoia of an authoritarian state afraid of the uncontrolled behavior of its citizens. In 1974, the East German legislature extended its reach into a future fraught with peril even further by passing the so-called *Gefährdeten Verordnung* (Ordinance on Citizens in Danger of Becoming Criminals), which provided for the registration and state supervision of people whose disorderly lifestyle suggested that at some *future* point in time they might conceivably be tempted to break the law.

This was preventive penal medicine. As soon as someone strayed from the straight and narrow path of Socialist behavior, the law was to get hold of him and turn him into a well-adapted citizen. The new policy fit in well with the political atmosphere of the 1970s in the GDR, when the utopian hopes for a "new man" that had originally fueled the Justice Decree of 1961 were carried out in a more bureaucratic and—at least as far as *Asoziale* were concerned—more ruthless fashion than had been intended in the previous decade. In Lüritz, the share of convictions for work-evasion rises from 0.7% of all criminal sentences in 1964 to almost 42% in 1973, and as late as 1979 still amounts to 34.5%. Virtually all defendants prosecuted for "asocial behavior" are placed under detention pending trial. They never are represented by counsel. Often, "asocials" are tried collectively in groups of three or four, allowing for judicial economy of scale: all bums and good-for-nothings who were arrested on the same day and now have to face the court together (though usually separated by gender). Until April 1977 (when "labor education" was abolished), almost everyone prosecuted for "asocial behavior" was placed in a "work commando" (often attached to an ordinary penitentiary); in theory, until "the purpose of the educational measure has been reached"; in practice (at least in Lüritz), for an average of nineteen-and-one-third months. To compare: in 1973, the average Lüritz penalty for attempted "flight from the Republic" was seventeen months in prison; for various crimes against the state and the public order (which in only half the cases led to custodial sentences) the average penalty was 10.6 months. By 1979, Lüritz *Asoziale*, upon conviction, still had to reckon with average prison sentences of between eighteen and twenty-four months. Recidivists—and many *Assis* were recidivists because they were punished for a way of living rather than for individual acts—often spend many life-years behind bars. Of all the defendants whom I encounter in the Lüritz criminal case files, only sex offenders and occasional big-time thieves and embezzlers received harsher penalties than drunkards, bums, and loafers.

It cannot have been very easy in the GDR to successfully avoid all useful work. Socialist society did not stand idly by to watch a member sink into alcoholism and idleness. At the first sign of tardiness or absenteeism, an employee might be called in by his boss or foreman and be given a talking to and, if admonitions did not help, might be summoned by the enterprise's conflict commission, where his workmates would tell him to shape up. Sometimes members of a slacker's work brigade would appear on his doorstep early in the morning to get him out of bed. If his work habits did not improve, an enterprise could contact the city's "Interior Department" to have a lazy worker registered as someone "in danger of becoming a criminal," with the result that he would be subjected to various official impositions and restrictions: reporting regularly to the police, not changing jobs without permission, avoiding certain restaurants or bars, and cutting contacts with one's favorite drinking buddies. And even if an inveterate shirker would be fired (which under the rules of East German labor law was difficult to do), he always would be offered another job. Only if nothing else availed would the prosecutor bring a case for "asocial behavior" under §249 of the Criminal Code. The indictment almost always was preceded by the culprit's arrest. "Suspect cannot be disciplined w/o detention," the judge inevitably wrote to justify the warrant. The unstable and drifting lifestyle of an *Assi* could be corrected only by imprisonment. Maybe not even that: once safely behind bars, an *Assi* no longer had to make his own decisions.

Reading through all these case files, I cannot help feeling something akin to admiration for the obstinacy with which *Asoziale* resisted the educational efforts of the state. The records are peppered with complaints about their unwillingness to better themselves. "She absolutely refuses to accept advice and does exactly as she pleases," the boss of a defendant complains at her trial in 1976. I have no difficulty finding many similar quotes. "He ignored the many educational efforts and suggestions of his collective, the enterprise management, and the Department of Interior Affairs." "He is unwilling to admit mistakes." "The collective believes that on his own, the defendant is not prepared to fundamentally change his ways."

The complaints go to the heart of what Socialism saw as the obligation—and the chance—of every citizen: to fundamentally change. *Assis* neither could nor wanted to alter their way of life. This is the reason, I believe, why they appeared so threatening to Socialism: because every day, by their mere existence, *Asoziale* gave the lie to the pedagogic pretensions of the system. Despite its considerable efforts, the East German state did not succeed in transforming *Assis* into industrious new men and women. It cannot come as a surprise that the GDR Supreme Court called "asocial behavior" "destructive" and "demoralizing" and as late as 1979 called *Asoziale* "members of the enemy's reserve force."[34]

The latter accusation was unfounded. Capitalism, too, disapproves of loiterers and shirkers and, after Reunification, a new statute of 1992 that was intended to undo the injustices committed under Socialism, excluded convictions under §249 of the GDR Criminal Code from the list of those criminal sentences whose imposition automatically entitled East German defendants to rehabilitation. Nevertheless, I would call "asocial behavior" a "political" crime: not because the defendants thought of themselves as dissidents, but because the state so dramatized the blameworthiness of a shiftless life that it could be punished with a severity usually reserved for dangerous political offenders. Sometimes I wonder, though, whether the amazing tenacity with which "asocial" citizens refused to cooperate in their own reeducation did not contain an undercurrent of political resistance. In their personal comments on their crime (typed on the back of their arrest warrants), many *Asoziale* speak in the sassy voice of rebels. "I didn't feel like it," they often say when asked by the judge why, for such a lengthy period, they had not worked. "I have no taste for work," someone explains. "The weather was much too nice," claims one young woman. "The pay wasn't worth it," many say and well they might, because the work they were assigned usually was boring and monotonous, and, since most *Asoziale* were in debt, the court deducted regular installment payments from their slender wages. "I have to say that for 350 Marks a month I am not willing every day to go to work," one *Assi* testifies. Many seasonal slackers keep themselves above water with odd jobs here or there. "I don't think much of collective work and prefer to be paid for my actual performance," says a thirty-four-year-old carpenter, coming dangerously close to a political statement. Another sign of *Assi* obstinacy: although defendants under §249 of the Criminal Code virtually never had a lawyer, they were the group most likely to appeal their sentence. Not that it did much good: *Asoziale* almost always lost their appeals. But they seem to have found it easier than other Socialist citizens to pick a fight with the authorities. "Only the *Assis* had more freedom," I was once told by a successful Lüritz plumber who wanted to illustrate for me the ease of his professional lifestyle under Socialism.

But at least in part, the *Assis*' freedom was also founded on their hopelessness. They had nothing more to lose. "I can't tell what should happen with me," one defendant says when questioned by the court. "Now it's too late," declares another. And a third: "I'll never amount to anything." Most *Asoziale* in Lüritz have long been written off by their families. They rarely have marriage partners who might offer some support: in 1973, 63% of Lüritz defendants sentenced under §249 of the Criminal Code have never been married, and 26% are divorced. When asked by the arraigning judge who should be informed of their arrest, most of the freshly apprehended *Assis* answer: "no one." In Lüritz work collectives, where industrious members have to make good the hours lost by slackers, the general disdain and even scorn for *Asoziale* is on the rise. In 1984, to placate the hard-working majority among its staff, the Lüritz shipyard issues new rules under which workers registered as "in danger of becoming criminals" are no longer to be included in the enterprise's plan for overtime performance. In addition, collectives are to be reimbursed for the financial losses caused by the non-performance of their *Assi* members. Even outside of working hours, collectives have little patience with the good-for-nothings in their midst. "The collective gave me a hard time," a young woman explains at her trial in 1985. "When I got out of prison it was like I was marked. I never was invited to anything." "The collectives could be very mean to *Assis*," a Lüritz judge confirmed.

As a result, many of them sought the company and the support of those who also were excluded from orderly society. "I liked this kind of life better than the graveyard shift," says someone at his interrogation by the judge. But, often, hanging out with drinking comrades at a bar would violate the restrictions imposed by the Interior Department, which had registered a suspect as "in danger of becoming a criminal," or would violate court orders issued in connection with a previous conviction under §249. New violations of the law, new prosecutions. Once in prison, most *Asoziale* do reasonably well and even, willy-nilly, pay their debts in slow installments from their meager prison pay. But after their release, the hated work needs to be done again; often the kind of work that is so dirty and so badly paid that reputable people will not do it (such as garbage collection or rust removal at the shipyard) and often it does not take long before someone only recently released will, again, seek his consolation in alcohol. In 1982, between 63% and 65% of all people sentenced for "asocial" behavior in the GDR are recidivists.

Socialism could tolerate neither the freedom of its "asocial" citizens nor the human and financial costs their way of life entailed. This was a political system that would not let its children step out of line nor permit them to drop by the wayside. But criminal law and labor law both seemed incapable of resolving or even of just mitigating the *Asozialen* problem. In Lüritz the number of work hours lost through absenteeism and tardiness is rising rather than declining: in 1979, the Phoenix shipyard registers 4.43 labor hours lost per employee; in 1986, the VEB Port Authority's loss amounts to 8.4 hours per employee. Lüritz employers are no longer willing to spend much energy on their *Asozialen* rehabilitation. "We will not undertake the collective debates that you required," the VEB Wholesale Trade in 1984 informs the police, who had assigned a jobless *Assi* to their enterprise (where he had never once appeared for work and after six weeks had been fired). Many state-owned firms, saddled with loafers whom the labor authorities forced upon them, try to contain the damage by offering them (illegal) temporary work or (equally illegal) contracts on probation, or at the slightest provocation apply to the prosecutor's office for a criminal investigation for work evasion. Some *Asozialen* trials at the District Court now take place without the usual participation of collective representatives because the defendant's work brigade no longer can be bothered to send a member. Even the Lüritz Interior Department, whose job it is to monitor all "citizens in danger of becoming criminals," only halfheartedly supervises its charges. In 1981, sixty-four Lüritz citizens are on the "endangered" list, most of them alcoholics, but the enterprises don't help enough with their rehabilitation, the department's own care is superficial and entangled in red tape, and *Asoziale* ordered to appear for admonitions, work assignments, and the like increasingly ignore the summons without visible consequences.

The city of Lüritz is not alone in its battle against work evasion. In the entire GDR, prisons are overcrowded with *Assi* inmates. As late as 1988, they make up almost a quarter of the East German prison population, four times as much as those offenders punished for "crimes against the state and the public order."[35] Regular amnesties temporarily make room for newcomers. But the early release of shirkers angers the working people. "General discontent is on the rise," Frau Walter (now director of the District Court) in 1981 reports at a meeting of justice functionaries in Berlin. And what about the future of those most immediately concerned? In 1973, in Lüritz the average age of suspects arrested for "asocial behavior" is 27.3 years; in 1980 (probably because of the many recidivists) it has risen to a—still youthful—average of 29.1 years. These are not weary old people facing their retirement who can no longer be expected to contribute to society. These are men and women in what should be their prime of life. In the criminal trial records of the 1980s I find a number of *Asozialen* hearings to which the prosecutor has invited school groups in order to discuss with them, after the sentencing, the dangers of alcoholism and truancy. Is the state afraid that this illness might be catching? And if it is an illness: are criminal penalties the medicine to cure it?

In the GDR, the first doubts about the country's criminal policy on work evasion arose in the late 1970s. In June 1979, the "Third Law Amending the Criminal Code" changes the wording of §249: instead of penalizing work evasion that "endangered" public order and security, the new version required public order to be "affected" by the truant's laziness, thus implying some real (rather than just potential) damage to society. One week later, the "Decree on Citizens in Danger of Becoming Criminals" is *expanded* to allow for the supervision and control of citizens who show no inclination of adopting an asocial lifestyle but who nevertheless would benefit from "social measures of education and support" (including the order to take up a job assignment). It looks as if East German legal policy attempts to shift the war against idleness and sloth from the field of criminal law onto administrative law and welfare law. Prodded by the Supreme Court, the Regional Court in Neuburg orders its district courts to investigate more carefully whether a defendant's absenteeism had indeed some public impact and to balance days missed at work against days spent by a defendant on seasonal or temporary jobs that might reduce the social damage caused by his lack of labor discipline. In 1980, a circular from the Neuburg court addressed to all its district courts lists the many ways in which the trial judges in the region (including those in Lüritz) have mis-applied §249 of the Criminal Code: by "exaggerating the significance of a defendant's previous record," by "paying not enough attention to the wording of the statute," and by sometimes "blatant failures of investigation." In March 1983, a letter from the Supreme Court criticizes "instances of formalism" among district courts whose case law on asocial behavior reflects "the faulty tendency to expand the application of §249 of the Criminal Code." This letter, too, finds its way into the in-boxes of my Lüritz judges.

By and by, the many admonitions from above appear to bear results. During the 1980s, the *Assis'* share among all criminal convictions in Lüritz visibly decreases: from 41.8% in 1973 to 19.2% in 1980 and 7.6% in 1984. Still, I am not sure how much the legal treatment of work evasion has really changed. If I compare the criminal law statistics for 1980, 1984, and 1988 (counting separately the convictions for various crimes), it turns out that sentences for "asocial behavior" have indeed declined, but property infractions have increased, and both types of offenses put together in each of the three years consistently make up 57% to 58% of the court's criminal caseload. Most truants in the Lüritz dock had not just avoided regular work but also, if their resources ran out, occasionally had forged a check or broken into a weekend cottage to spend the night or steal a bit of food. In the 1970s, such offenses were put down to the demoralizing influence of work evasion and punished as "asocial behavior." In the 1980s, the court was more likely to overlook a defendant's lack of work and focused instead on the violation of other people's property. But it seems likely that during both decades the underlying problem remained unchanged: the social isolation and exclusion, with the help of the criminal law, of a large number of weak and unproductive men and women; unable to cope with life; unsupported by family or friends; in many cases alcohol dependent; despised by those around them; in their own eyes worthless; equally pampered and disappointed by Socialism; upon release from prison driven back into illegality by rules and regulations that they lacked the self-discipline to follow—equally the bogeymen and products of a didactic and labor-obsessed dictatorship.

In Berlin, too, government and Party authorities realize that change is needed and look for ways to reintegrate *Asoziale* into Socialist society. New questions are raised about the causes of asocial behavior. In July 1983, a letter from the

CHAPTER 7

Neuburg Regional Court orders my judges to compile—within two weeks!—a list of all criminal defendants in Lüritz whose offenses reflect "a lack of social self-management and autonomy." The order came from the GDR Supreme Court and is "based on an assignment of the Party," which, it appears, intends to ground its new *Asozialen* policy on empirical data. "Deadline must be observed!" the Neuburg letter warns: the matter is urgent. It contains a list of symptoms that the Supreme Court is looking for: diminished intelligence, disturbing behavior, difficulties in adapting, lack of social contacts, alcoholism. The objects of the search are "offenders who despite their own intentions are incapable of change," the letter states.

It is the first time that I catch the Socialist judicial system admitting doubts about its own ability to educate its people. The admission reflects the growing sobriety and rationality of East German law in its last decade. With some of its ideological baggage pushed aside, GDR jurists find it easier to look at criminal policy from the viewpoint of its addressees. Already in the spring of 1983, the Supreme Court had warned its lower courts against attaching too many "measures of control" to *Asozialen* verdicts, such as prohibiting a defendant from changing his job or residence without permission after his release from prison or forbidding contacts with his former buddies. Surprisingly, the court had justified its warning not by pointing to the fact that the restrictions increased the likelihood that the defendant, by breaking them, soon again would land in jail. Instead, it had explained its misgivings about excessive "measures of control" with reference to the defendant's individual rights: such "far-reaching and invasive interference with someone's personal life" could only be legitimate if it was truly "indispensable" for his rehabilitation. A stamp near the court's letterhead—"for internal use only"—warned the recipients of its letter not to publicize the Supreme Court's new and more liberal views on *Asozialen* rights. It almost looked as if the system was ashamed of its own attempts at reform.

When on January 9, 1985, the GDR Council of Ministers passes a "Resolution on the Measures to Influence and Control Citizens Evincing Psychologically Conspicuous and Socially Deviant Behavior"—note: the court has replaced legal with medical terminology—the "Resolution" not only is *not* published but (as I know from a letter that Frau Walter sends to the Neuburg Regional Court) is *not even made available* to my Lüritz judges. I must piece together from secondary bits of information what I know about the new East German *Asozialen* policy. At the center of the reform are so-called special brigades: "sheltered collectives," as it were, who under the leadership of a particularly able and experienced foreman are assigned the type of jobs that they are actually capable of carrying out. The special brigades are designed to display remarkable flexibility and solicitude when faced with the inevitable relapses and missteps of the workers in their care. Even seemingly incorrigible loafers are not to be dismissed.

Instead, the brigadier shall find more capable and steady colleagues to support them; shall take care of the medical problems of his charges; organize, if necessary, their admission to alcohol rehabilitation programs; and locate volunteers who can look out for a lonely misfit in the hours after work and on weekends. It is a good, an admirable plan. The fact that East German justice authorities are trying to keep it secret can only be explained by worries that so rigorous a medicine might reveal the gravity of the illness it is meant to cure.

Whether the reforms succeeded is another question. The bits of information about special brigades that I discover in the Lüritz archive are disappointing. In October 1985, Frau Walter—in response to a question from the Neuburg Regional Court—reports that the Lüritz City Council has ordered the formation of five special brigades; all of them, as to be expected, in those unloved enterprises to which "asocial" citizens had been previously assigned, such as the garbage services or VEB Road Construction. I cannot tell how many special brigades actually were created, how many Lüritz *Asoziale* were included, and whether any of them ever showed up for work. When the Regional Court, in January 1988, asks Frau Walter to provide exact data on these questions, she cannot oblige: the city government, she writes, does not involve the court in the formation and management of its special brigades and does not respond when judges offer advice or information about the kind of people now called "problem citizens" whom they have encountered in their case law. Frau Walter's letter to the Regional Court sounds a little offended. But the courts, too, do not find it easy to treat asocial behavior as an illness. When a twenty-five-year-old alcoholic, freshly sentenced to twenty-two months in prison for petty theft and work evasion, appeals the verdict by explaining that "an organically caused seriously flawed personal development" renders him incapable of feeling guilt (*Assis*, too, have taken note of the new therapeutic approach to their affliction), the Neuburg Regional Court refuses to play along: "On principle, adult offenders are expected to fully adjust their behavior to existing social norms." When, in a Lüritz case, an *Assi*'s lawyer asks for a psychological evaluation of his client ("this is a sick man"), my judges, too, deny the motion and on appeal are backed up by the Regional Court. Nevertheless, the very fact that now, in 1988, an "asocial" defendant actually is represented by counsel suggests that change lies in the air. I discover the first acquittal of an *Assi* (who had been prosecuted for "violating measures of control") in a judgment from 1984 holding that the defendant "could not be blamed" for not working since he had not been offered acceptable employment after his release. True, only five months after his acquittal I find the man again in prison. But the court's ruling—placing the blame for the unsuccessful reintegration of released *Assi* convicts not only on their own iniquities but also on omissions of the state—is followed in later cases, too. *The times, they are a-changing.*

CHAPTER 7

Not just for the *Asoziale*. To judge by my statistics, the 1980s see a relaxation and normalization of criminal law in the GDR that only in the fear and panic of its final years is partially undone. Compared to civil law, criminal law loses in significance: between 1980 and 1985, incoming criminal cases drop from 37.6% to 27.5% of first-instance caseloads in the Neuburg region. Criminal defendants are beginning to assert their rights. While in 1979, only 5.6% of all criminal defendants in Lüritz were represented by a lawyer, that figure rises to 11.8% by 1985 and to 16% by 1988. The share of custodial sentences imposed by my Lüritz court drops from 65.1% of all criminal decisions in 1979 to 53.3% in 1988.

Political criminal case law changes, too. But because politics is at the center of the rising storm and because my judges are torn between their new pragmatism and their old obedience to the Party, the development of the political criminal law in the last decade of the GDR is more tortured and more contradictory than developments in other areas of the law. If I check the criminal statistics of the Regional Court (which I can reconstruct from a collection of index cards at the Neuburg prosecutor's office), it looks indeed as if the daily workload of the Court becomes less political, less dramatic, more matter-of-fact or—seen with Western eyes—more "normal" in the 1980s than in previous years. Trials of class-enemies, counter-revolutionaries, and saboteurs, which kept the court busy in the 1960s and 1970s, in the 1980s first diminish and then, eventually, disappear. In 1968 the Regional Court adjudicated forty-four cases of "sedition"; in 1985 (the last year in which I discover "sedition" in my index cards) just one. The records of 1970 contain ten prosecutions for "formation of groups hostile to the state"—most, like the "Clan of Rusty Clabs," founded by youngsters eager to escape the boredom of an overregulated life—and after 1970 not a single one. Beginning with the year 1979, I also no longer find any "terror" cases in the criminal records that were threatening enough to be adjudicated by the Appellate Court. At least in the Neuburg region, East German criminal law seems to lose its most dramatic fears as Socialism itself is drifting towards its downfall.

A second, somewhat lesser group of political offenses by and by is also vanishing from the Regional Court's docket: the "crimes against the state and the public order," such as "resistance against state measures" (§212 of the Criminal Code); "interference with state authority" (§214); "disrespect for state symbols" (§222) and the like. This does not mean that the citizens of the Neuburg region no longer swear at their government or get into a fight with the police. On the contrary: in the 1980s, the number of clashes between citizen and state that are triggered by civic anger and disaffection, is, if anything, on the rise. Because of their political implications, these offenses increasingly are brought before the Regional Court in Neuburg and have risen from less than a handful of incidents per year in the 1970s to twenty to thirty cases in the early 1980s and to a full forty "resistance" or "interference" cases in the final year, 1989. But while these offenses still are *prosecuted* in the Regional Court, the court no longer deals with them itself but either remands them to the district court in the locality where the offense occurred or, in politically touchy cases, passes them on to the Neuburg/City District Court, which can adjudicate the matter at a discreet distance from the rabble-rouser's home town and at the same time can relieve the Regional Court from further dirtying its hands with petty political offenses. From 1975 on, the Neuburg/City *Kreisgericht* operates in fact like a branch office of the Regional Court in charge of second-degree "resistance" crimes. One can easily see why the Appellate Court judges don't like to deal with these offenders. Most of them are thirty- to forty-year-old drunkards acting out their aggression against the Party, the state, and their own unsatisfying lives with angry speeches, brawls, and the smashing of everything in reach. Once sobered up, they usually do not remember what they did. "I may have had one too many," says a defendant in 1988 who had drunk forty double brandies before kicking in the door of the Lüritz police station. One cannot call it a very honest kind of liberalization if the Regional Court, by passing on such cases to the Neuburg/City court, still sees to it that local populations remain unaware of civic unrest of this sort. But the court's remanding practice does reveal that the appellate judges would like to see themselves as normal judges, reviewing normal sentences that could be passed in any country respectful of the law, rather than as assistants of the *Stasi*.

It should be said that (upon orders from above) penalties for "offenses against the state and the public order" in Lüritz, too, are softening. Already in 1980, the Regional Court had criticized the undifferentiated harshness of its district courts' sentences for "resistance" crimes: "The authority of the state is best protected not by extreme but by adequate responses to its violation." In 1986, the Regional Court reduced from prison to probation the sentence of a Lüritz woman who had called the police "dirty scum" (and worse): even crimes against the state are to be punished "according to their actual gravity." As far as I can tell, political jokes, in the 1980s, no longer land their narrator in prison. "We weren't so uptight about these matters anymore," a former Lüritz prosecutor tells me. These days, most Lüritz political criminals are punished with fines of between 300 and 1000 Marks or with probation, including a number of (mostly juvenile) offenders who tore down the national flag (and on occasion even burned it).

My Lüritz judges' growing lenience (or maybe I should say: their relative lenience since it is easy to be overly impressed when an authoritarian system relaxes its harsh standards)—their relative lenience, then—when dealing with political insubordination is all the more surprising considering the deep disaffection and sometimes even hatred for Socialism that many of these incidents reveal. The "resisters" use language that is foul-mouthed and explicit: '"shit-

CHAPTER 7

heads," "pigs," "imbeciles, jerks, and criminals!" Often, the anti-Communism of the drunken rebels is punctuated with neo-Nazi slogans: *"Sieg Heil!"*; *"Heil Hitler!"*, "Down with Jews!" I discover a number of very worried weekly reports from the Neuburg court to the Ministry of Justice in the files in which the Appellate Court's director, Frau Nissen, tells of swastikas smeared on walls, defaced and toppled gravestones, and the abuse of foreigners in the region. One such particularly disquieting message Minister of Justice Heusinger has read himself (as I can tell from the green ministerial ink of his underlinings).

The GDR Justice Administration no longer refuses to acknowledge that many of its citizens are discontented, are uncooperative, and (if at all) are difficult to change and that the criminal law does not appear to be an effective pedagocic tool. Maybe the reformers take comfort from the thought that many political offenders (like the *Asozialen*) are not principled and articulate opponents of the system but undisciplined, helpless, and socially isolated drifters. That also may explain why a third group of political offenders—the "fugitives from the Republic"—at least in Lüritz now can count on milder sanctions than before. Whereas in 1973 the average penalty for would-be fugitives was a one-and-one-half-year prison sentence, in the 1980s roughly half of the "flight" cases end with probation or a stay of prosecution. In Lüritz, the number of these cases remains relatively constant over time: between fifteen and twenty-five offenses a year. But the number of border-crimes prosecuted before the Appellate Court in Neuburg is on the rise: from twenty-four cases in 1978 to sixty-eight cases in 1988 and 111 cases in the very last year of the Wall's existence. By the late 1970s, the Regional Court remands almost all prosecutions under §213 of the Criminal Code to the Neuburg/City District Court. Virtually all defendants in these cases are (or hoped to be) what GDR law enforcement plainly described as *Sperrbrecher* (literally: "barrier crashers"). There were many different ways in which defendants planned to crash that "barrier": by sneaking, running, climbing, and cutting through barbed-wire fences; by hiding in train compartments or in the trunks of cars; and—most frequently—by swimming, rowing, or paddling across the Baltic to the West German shore. Such ventures are more likely to be undertaken by daring young men than by solid heads of families. Almost all the defendants prosecuted in Lüritz or in Neuburg for attempted "flight of the Republic" were young, impatient, reckless, and unwilling to adapt to the many rules that more than elsewhere governed ordinary civic life in the GDR. Quite a few of them had previous convictions for asocial behavior. The attempts of these young men to run away from Socialism had to be disappointing to the Party. But their potential loss posed no threat to the state. Hence, I assume, the increasing willingness of the East German legal system to deal with these offenders somewhat more leniently (if you can call it lenient) than in previous years.

PUNISHMENTS

In the history (and the myth) of the German-German border, the *Sperrbrecher* were important victims of what after the collapse of Socialism were prosecuted as "government crimes": the placing of land mines along the boundary between East and West Germany; the order to shoot at people trying to escape; the actual shootings by border guards following that order. Statistically, the barrier crashers' prominence is misleading. Except for the first and the very last year of the Wall's existence, far more East German citizens made their way into the Federal Republic by legal than by illegal means. Even among those illegally departing, the *Sperrbrecher*, with a share of about 6.5% of all migrants, represented a small minority.[36] Most other "illegals" managed their escape by way of officially permitted travels to the FRG from which they did not return, or by tourist visits to other countries in the Eastern bloc from where it was easier to reach a Western country. Flights of this kind were called "illegal non-return" and, like the more dramatic physical escapes, were punishable under §213 of the GDR Criminal Code. But since these felons, as a rule, were already safely in the West when the police learned of their disappearance, they do not show up in my Lüritz criminal case files.

In the early 1980s, though, the criminal profile of the runaways from Socialism begins to change. In part, this is the consequence of a liberalization, initiated by the East German government itself, that (as we have seen) also spilled over into matters of the law. Two of its products were the 1982 "Decree on Facilitating Travels in Urgent Family Affairs" and, two years later, an unannounced and unexpected generosity of GDR travel authorities in permitting moves from East Germany to the Federal Republic. The number of legal emigrations to the West shot up from roughly 7700 moves in 1983 to almost 35,000 moves in 1984.[37] Already in the next year, the concessions were reduced by half.[38] But the wave of legal emigrations in the spring of 1984 made the Wall look more porous than before and gave new hope to those prospective *Ansreiser* who were unwilling to follow the breakneck example of the barrier crashers. In Lüritz, the number of applications for an exit visa to the Federal Republic rose, as did the doggedness and cheek by which the applicants were trying to pester the authorities into releasing them from Socialism.

East German citizens hoping to leave the country had always tried to break the state's resistance by the steady repetition of their demands. But now, the intervals between a visa application's denial and its re-submission were shortening, and the applicants' language changed from humble to assertive and demanding. In January 1987, someone in Neuburg refuses to leave the office of the city's Interior Department until his exit visa is approved: "I just won't leave without it." In 1988, a Lüritz man who in the last two years has submitted thirteen requests to leave the country—all were denied—tells the now only too

CHAPTER 7

familiar functionaries at "Interior": "You can turn me into a wreck but you will not be able to kill my hope to one day leave this country." The crane operator whom we have met before comes with his rope to the Lüritz market square and threatens to hang himself.

Usually, in cases such as these, the state would try to coax and, if that did not help, would try to browbeat an exit candidate into abandoning his plans. Prospective deserters are ordered to appear for repeated "discussions" at their enterprise or the Interior Department. Sometimes, an applicant's close relatives are summoned by "Interior" and told to talk some sense into their son or brother. Applicants themselves are put under increasing pressure: by some chicanery at work; by transfers or dismissals from their enterprise; by open threats of criminal sanctions. Sometimes, the state tries to entice a valued citizen to stay at home by offering him a better job or a more desirable apartment. None of these efforts seem to work. In 1985, an applicant decides to quit her job because she feels "too bothered" by the never-ending discussions at her enterprise that are supposed to win her back to Socialism. Prospective Lüritz emigrants discover ever more ingenious ways of embarrassing their state into loosening its hold: by sending copies of their applications "for further action" to West German relatives or, better yet, to icons of Capitalism such as the arch-anti-Communist Bavarian Prime Minister Franz Joseph Strauss, West German state television channels, or journals like *Calls for Help from Across the Border* that specialize in dramatizing the iniquities of Socialism. Some applicants in Lüritz try to catch the world's attention by publishing descriptions of their quest for exit visas on handbills or once, on a big banner that several young men, if only for a few minutes, manage to unfold in public view. In the spring of 1988, there are weekly "protest promenades" on the Lüritz market square in which a number of applicants, most of them dressed in black, meet in little groups, immediately disperse, meet and disperse again, and finally go home. A photographer is caught trying to film the event from a top window in one of the patrician houses that surround the square.

It very much looks as if prospective emigrants in Lüritz no longer are afraid of the *Stasi*, state, or Party. At least they are not afraid enough to avoid a confrontation with any of the three. Rather the opposite: most applicants' attempts to enforce their freedom are meant to work by way of provocation. Sometimes that provocation is in-your-face explicit: as in the case of a Lüritz ambulance driver who in 1988 denounces himself for planning to escape in order to be sent to prison and then, hopefully, be ransomed by the Federal Republic. Sometimes, the provocation is cleverly disguised, as in the Lüritz market promenades during which the protesters met only for a minute here or there and could not seriously be accused of staging a coherent demonstration. When in 1986 an applicant's sister mounts a media demonstration in West Berlin by blasting loudspeaker demands for his release across the Wall, and *Stasi* agents first arrest and then accuse the brother of having helped to plan the spectacle, he does not even bother to deny the allegation. "I fully trust my sister to adequately deal with the affair," he coolly says. When, two years later, *Stasi*-officers come to arrest another visa applicant who had tried to advance his cause by placing an emphatic poster in his window, the culprit asks to see their warrant and—since the agents came without—has them shamefacedly withdraw until they can return (now with a warrant) a couple of hours later. Already in September 1985, at a so-called "Leaders' Conference" in Lüritz (a monthly meeting of all law-and-order representatives in the district, including the director of my District Court), the *Stasi* member of the group had complained of the "growing aggressiveness" of applicants for exit visas and asked for more energetic responses by the state to their demands: "We should not have to tolerate such insolence from people like that."

But the "people like that" were different from those who previously had to face the court for violations of public order and security. "Fugitives from the Republic" used to be reckless youngsters; *Asoziale*, un-adapted loners; those who "resisted state authority," macho young men with rolled-up sleeves, mostly blue-collar, who had drunk too much. By comparison, applicants for exit visas tended to have had solid educations and, often, held down solid jobs. Many of them were brain rather than brawn: teachers, technicians, foremen, doctors, and sometimes even leading cadres of state enterprises—the kind of men and women who were confident to find a good job in the Federal Republic and whom the GDR desperately needed to stay home. Among the migrants in that unexpected and short-lived legal exodus from the GDR in 1984, the heads of families aged between twenty-five and forty had made up a larger share (compared to the general East German population) than was statistically warranted.[39] As Frau Walter told me, the Lüritz market-strollers promenading for their exit visas were mostly doctors and psychiatrists—again, a group of professionals in short supply. As they were thumbing their noses at the policemen and *Stasi* agents surrounding the market square, the Lüritz city fathers were worrying about losing too many medical professionals. In the fall of 1989, nineteen positions for doctors at the district hospital were vacant. How could the city cope?

So it can come as no surprise that panic seemed to reign behind the scenes of East Germany's Administration of Justice. Everyone stares, obsessed, at the German-German border. The weekly reports sent by the Regional Court to the Ministry of Justice in Berlin are filled with political rumors and with stories of escapes. In the fall of 1983, Frau Nissen lists a number of cases in which West German motorists, apparently on purpose, lost their way and prematurely exited the transit *Autobahn* reserved for Westerners driving to Berlin: "Considering the recently increasing pressures on our border, the incidents suggest that drivers were testing the ease of violating GDR transit regulations." A year later, another worried report alerts the Ministry to a number of phone calls by which West German lawyers directly contacted some district courts in the Neuburg region to ask for information. "I relate these incidents because the callers were obviously searching for possible 'weak spots,'" Frau Nissen writes. Her choice of words—"weak spots," with the "weakness" defensively put into question by quotation marks—reflects the system's fear for its own vulnerability. By 1985, the Regional Court's accounts of border violations are no longer contained in its weekly report, transmitted every Friday to the central Justice authorities in Berlin, but are sent by more urgent "immediate reports" (*Sofortmeldungen*). In the system's final year, three-quarters of all "immediate reports" from Neuburg deal with flight cases or with the protests of visa applicants. Whether or not someone applied to leave the country has become the litmus test for his trustworthiness. Work evaluations mention the fact that an employee has "submitted an illegal request to move to the Federal Republic." "The detainee has not asked for resettlement," the final prison reports for inmates scheduled for early release will often say (no need to spell out *where* the probationer would wish to be resettled). "Has *not yet* applied," I read in one such case file; "not yet"—who knows for how much longer the state can rely on its citizens. When on one occasion a lay assessor from my Lüritz District Court applies for an exit visa, the report on her disloyalty goes all the way up to the Ministry of Justice and, as I can tell from the green signature at the bottom of the page, is read by the Minister himself.

Since GDR authorities don't know how to stem the tide, they reach, again, for criminal law; the very law that only recently had begun to treat at least some rebellions against the state's authority in more relaxed and liberal fashion than before. The GDR Criminal Code contained a number of (partially overlapping) prohibitions meant to protect a nervous state against unwanted contact with the Capitalist world that looked tailor-made, and sometimes were, to fit the activities of visa applicants: such as "establishing unlawful contacts" (say, by writing letters to politicians or newspapers on the other side in order to mobilize West German support for one's attempt to leave the GDR); "seditious transfer of information" (*landesverräterische Nachrichtenübermittlung*: for instance, passing copies of an application to West German recipients, again to enlist their help); or "seditious agency" (*landesverräterische Agententätigkeit*: a very similar offence that penalized "cooperation" with West German authorities or individuals to advance one's cause). Despite their dramatic language, none of these provisions presupposed the transfer of information that was actually *secret*. The rules were triggered by the mere establishment of contacts that possibly might damage interests of the GDR. When, in the final years, disappointed visa applicants were turning to ever more emphatic means to advertise their plight, a fourth "applicant offense" made its appearance in the Lüritz criminal case files: "interference with state or societal activities." The young man who refused to leave the office of the Neuburg Interior Department without a valid exit visa, for example, "interfered" with the department's daily work. Our suicidal friend who chose the Lüritz market square to demonstrate his desperation over the denial of his visa "interfered" with the activities of the police. Some applicants were prosecuted for something called "interference by the establishment of contacts": a seemingly condensed and therefore doubly dangerous offense committed by insisting on one's claim to leave an unloved state.

Tracing the distribution of these cases between the Regional Court in Neuburg and the Neuburg/City District Court allows me not just to measure the emigration problem's political significance but also to show how quickly the East German judicial system lost its hope of stopping the hemorrhage with the help of criminal law. In the late 1970s and early 1980s, the Regional Court still took it upon itself to adjudicate most "contact" crimes. In the criminal case files of those years, "establishing unlawful contacts" appears to be primarily a middle-class offense: maybe because the kind of people whose daily tools are telephones, typewriters, and paper are most likely to appeal for help to equally educated people on the other side. In 1980, nine of the eleven defendants prosecuted in the region for "unlawful contacts" are university-educated; four of the nine are doctors. Their social status warrants the Appellate Court's own time and effort to be spent on their conviction. But when news spread of the impact and effectiveness of the "unlawful contacts" and when, in 1984, thirty-eight "contact" cases are brought before the Regional Court (many of them involving working-class defendants), the High Court judges helplessly raise their hands and begin to remand the "contact" crimes to be adjudicated by the Neuburg/City District Court. In 1985, the regional judges themselves decide only "seditious transfer of information" and "agency" cases: the crimes of the most tenacious and daring emigration candidates. They hand down harsh punishments for these defendants: on average, almost four years in prison. To compare: the average penalty for the "establishment of contacts" drops from thirty-two months in 1981 to nineteen months (now meted out by the Neuburg/City District Court) in 1988. For 1989, I can no longer find any "contact" cases at either the Regional or the Neuburg/City District Court. The criminal law no longer is capable of stopping the flow of information and the back-and-forth of human contacts between both Germanies. The same is true for the dramatically rising number of border crimes (1985: twenty-nine cases; 1988: sixty-eight cases; 1989: 106 cases); all now adjudicated in Neuburg/City. In August 1989, attempted flights are no longer prosecuted. Lord knows why the Regional Court in the very last year of the state's and its own existence still bothered to decide five "sedition" crimes, the last one as late as September 1989. Maybe the judges wanted to save face in the political maelstrom sweeping them and their state away. By then, Frau Nissen and her staff must have known that for the GDR, the battle of "political criminal law" vs. "emigrants" was lost.

It was lost, I believe, because by the 1980s the East German state and law had changed enough to no longer be able to apply without embarrassment that brute power necessary to keep its many willing escapees at home. The applicants for exit visas knew so, too. Judges and prosecutors were still willing to *frighten* particularly rambunctious candidates by issuing warrants for their arrest. In 1988, the Regional Court rejects one very pushy applicant's appeal against his pre-trial detention by claiming that the accused "could only be disciplined by his incarceration"—thus practically admitting that the arrest had not (as the law required) been necessary to prevent the suspect's escape but had been made in order to punish him for his assertiveness. But now, the system lacks the ideological conviction to stay its ruthless course. Instead, the state tries to avoid the confrontation with its children. Arrests usually are preceded by several warnings. On one occasion, a protest poster is allowed to hang in a private window for almost three months before the police officially take note of it. The participants in the Lüritz market promenade are arrested in February 1988, transferred to the *Stasi* prison in Neuburg, released after two weeks, and in the end are each fined between 2000 and 3000 Marks. The man who tried to photograph the happening loses his film to the police, but the prosecutor drops criminal charges against him. Visa applicants sentenced for "establishing contacts" and the like often are granted early releases from their prison sentences (or are ransomed by the Federal Republic) and are allowed to resettle in West Germany. "Purpose of sentence accomplished," a note in the prisoner's probation file will state in those cases. But it seems that it was the prisoner's purpose rather than the prison's that was "accomplished."

Lüritz arrest warrants, too, can demonstrate how in the last decade of its life East German political criminal law is gradually losing all its punch. They also show how the law's decay is hastened by the state's own unsteady and reluctant concessions. Again, would-be emigrants are at the center of the story, but this time not the barrier crashers (whose number, as we have seen, in the 1980s dramatically shot up in the Appellate Court's statistics), but those who left the GDR by way of "illegal non-return." The method was arduous but involved no physical risks and efforts: you obtained (by whatever personal inventiveness and pull) a temporary travel visa to the Federal Republic and, upon arrival, informed friends, relatives, or, directly, the police that you did not intend to return to the GDR. Like any other "flight from the Republic," "illegal non-return" under §213 of the Criminal Code was punishable by up to two (and in aggravated cases, up to eight) years in prison, and the police, as soon as they got wind of someone's "non-return," issued an arrest warrant for the runaway. These warrants—thick bundles of pink forms that on their back page inform me of the age, the gender, the job of the fugitive, and the date and method of his or her escape—are part of my wood-cellar treasures. All I need to do is count the number of "non-returners" in each year.

A reminder: "non-return" required, by definition, the cooperation of the Interior Department, which had to issue a much longed-for temporary travel visa that allowed the offender's departure in the first place. Prior to the 1982 "Decree on Facilitating Travels," such travel visas to the West must have been rare. The state was tight-fisted with such permits; heads of families were allowed to travel only on their own so one could be sure of their return, and police and *Stasi* were on the look-out for symptoms of illicit travel fever. As late as 1984, my Lüritz court convicts two friends of "acts preparatory to aggravated illegal non-return": they had applied for travel visas to Hungary and not kept mum about the ulterior purposes of the intended trip. "Method of committing crime: train travel" says a 1976 police report about another intended getaway. For many years, the GDR was a country in which "train travel" could get you into trouble with the law.

All that changes, quite suddenly, in the last few years. For 1987, I find among the fourteen arrest warrants issued for "flight of the Republic" five "non-returners"; 1988, of seventy-five fugitives wanted by the police, thirty-two are "non-returners"; and among the 111 warrants for escapees in 1989, eighty-one are for "non-return." All eighty-one of those one-way travelers must have been assisted by permits issued by the state. And these runaways no longer are the reckless young men whom I previously encountered as defendants in the Lüritz dock. My stack of arrest warrants shows the average age of men wanted for violations of §213 of the Criminal Code in 1973 to be twenty. By 1980, that average age had risen to 23.6 years. But in 1989, only 40% of the fugitives were younger than twenty-five; 28% were above forty years of age; and almost a third were women. In Lüritz and elsewhere, those solid and industrious citizens were turning their backs on the GDR whose grumpy loyalty, until then, had held the land together.

My impressions are confirmed by the overall migration figures for the GDR. Between 1963 and 1988, roughly a third of all relocations from East to West Germany were illegal, a percentage that only in 1984 (the year of the East German government's unusual largesse in granting exit permits) dropped to 14.6% because in that year it was no longer so necessary to leave the country on the sly. In most years, about two-thirds of all emigrants (and in 1984: 85.4%) thus transferred to the West with the permission of the Socialist state. One might say that in those years, both East German *right* and *might* did their intended jobs: the law allowed a small number of malcontents to leave the country in supervised and regulated fashion (with that miraculous year of 1984 being the exception to prove the rule), while the sheer power of the state kept the silent (and increasingly, the grumbling) majority securely at home. In 1989, both law and power come adrift. The number of emigrants shoots up to almost ninefold that of the preceding year. But most of these migrants—70.4%—now *illegally* move West,[40] tolerated (and even assisted through the issuance of travel visas) by a state that no longer finds the totalitarian gumption to defend itself with ruthlessness and violence. Nobody cares anymore that "non-return" is called "illegal." The law has lost its power to scare a citizenry whose loyalty has crumbled into supporting a distasteful state. How is the SED to keep the country in its grip?

CHAPTER 8

THE PARTY

I wonder whether I should have introduced the Party in an earlier chapter of this book. Did anything ever happen without its blessings? West Germans never doubted that in the GDR all matters of any importance were decided by the Party. My East German conversation partners shared this view. They, too, believed that in their country in the end all depended on the Party. Does that mean that I ought to describe the East German judicial system and the Party in one breath, as it were, to achieve an accurate portrayal of both?

Whatever its role in the adjudicatory process, the Party left surprisingly few traces in the Lüritz archive. Until now, we only rarely met it in the flesh: as for instance in 1959, when Judge Steinmetz let Frau Hille's lawsuit flounder in the face of opposition by the "SED District Bureau/Department Fishing Industry"; in 1983, when the Supreme Court—"honoring a specific task set by the Party"— tried to impress upon the Lüritz court the need for a less punitive approach to "asocial' behavior; or in 1984, when in "Orff vs. VEB Phoenix Shipyard" the Lüritz District Party leaned on Herr Orff's union representative to make him testify *against* his client's interest at the trial. Such chance encounters produce a very conflicting portrait. The Party contemptuous of the law in matters "Fishing Industry"? A force of law reform as far as "asocial" defendants are concerned? A puppeteer pulling his strings in "Orff vs. Phoenix"? Up to this point, the Party rather looks like a Cheshire cat whose disembodied smile (or frown) turns up out of the blue and vanishes again before a reader of the files can get hold of the apparition and question it about how to anticipate its future moves. To really understand the Party's role in everyday legal life, I have to start a systematic search for it.

In the Lüritz case files, that is: as a visible and openly acknowledged participant in the resolution of legal disputes, the Party shows up only in the very early years, when a motley crew of people's judges and old bourgeois lawyers like Herr Curtius tried as best they could to process the law suits flooding the Lüritz court and when the new political authorities in town did not yet know how to handle their suddenly acquired powers. In 1948, for instance, in a fight between a widow and her brother-in-law over a bicycle left by the plaintiff's husband, the defendant, obviously a Party member, informs the court that the SED District Bureau "had taken an interest" in the matter. The hint has the desired impact.

CHAPTER 8

Herr Curtius no longer looks for legal grounds to decide the dispute but simply awards the bicycle to the comrade defendant. But I find not only compliance but also open criticism of the Party in the early records. In a 1952 criminal case involving unexplained losses in the cash registry for Party literature and pamphlets at the SED's Lüritz headquarters, for example, the court sentences the unfortunate cashier to no more than "probation at the workplace": "The court took note of the fact that at the time the takings in the registry no longer matched the sales, confusion and disarray existed in the District Party office." In the same year, District Judge Schlumm tells the parties in a civil dispute that "they would have done better composing more convincing legal briefs than running to the SED for help." Admittedly, Herr Schlumm, one of the old "bourgeois" judges, in 1953 disappears from the files; his colleague, Herr Curtius, had already been removed from office the year before. But in the very first years of the GDR there clearly existed variations in my judges' responses to the demands of power. And it was not only the SED that tried to meddle in affairs *sub judice*. The State Control informed the court how it should decide; housing authorities put in their two bits' worth; the Farmers' Party came to the defense of a Party member being sued and asked the court "to please take the necessary steps for his vindication." One gets the impression of a legal landscape in which individual plots have not yet been measured and assigned, where no fences delineate the boundaries between the various inhabitants, and where the general lack of orientation encourages the more energetic and ruthless players to invade other people's territory.

With the consolidation of political conditions in the GDR, the Party begins to disappear from the Lüritz case files. Of course that does not mean that it is no longer interested in what happens at the court. But the nature of its interest changes. As I can tell from reading the minutes of the Lüritz SED District Bureau's meetings (now a short train trip away at the state archive in Gronau), the District Secretariat in the 1950s was still quite willing to meddle with the daily work of the Lüritz court. In April 1953, for example (just a few weeks after Stalin's death and before the New Course that would soon be followed by the June rebellion), the District Party bosses criticize a number of criminal sentences for "new farmers" accused of violations of state property as too harsh and order the prosecutor to "take immediate measures" to overturn a particularly heavy-handed judgment against one of the defendants. It seems that the offending judges even were invited to the meeting. Item 10 on the day's agenda: "The Secretariat explains to the Comrade Prosecutor and Comrade Döring from the District Court the Party's concrete approach to this problem." The key word in this sentence is "concrete." The ideological climate at the District Court will occupy the Party leadership also in later years (more on this in a moment). But that the District Bureau reprimands the court for faulty decisions in specific cases seems to happen only in the 1950s. That judges are even present at the Secretariat's meetings becomes rare as well. If I encounter them in the later minutes, it will be either just for the discussion of a specific part of the agenda (for example, an upcoming election of judges in the district) or for the annual report of the court director to the district leadership that was one of his ritual duties in the GDR. Since the early 1960s, specific cases on the Lüritz docket are at least not officially enough debated by the Lüritz District Party Leadership to leave a trace of the discussion in the Bureau minutes. Incidentally, a similar development took place at the Party center in Berlin, where the Politbureau in the 1950s discussed an average of about ten specific criminal trials per year; a number that dropped to two by 1963 and by 1964 (with the exception of a single case in 1971) had shrunk to zero.[41]

The political style begins to change. Already in 1959, when the "SED/ Department Fishing Industry" intervenes in Frau Hille's suit to protect her warehouse against the leaking salt-fish barrels of her tenant, the comrades may have been a little embarrassed by their brazen interference. At least they do not directly tell the judges what to do but only allow the defendant to boast of their protection in his brief. When, a year earlier, in a labor law dispute, the Party organization of the plaintiff had written to criticize the court's investigation of the issues ("If testimonial evidence does not succeed in clearing up the matter, our Party organization will take the case in hand and set the record straight"), someone at the court had underlined the sentence in red and the comrade whom the offensive letter was intended to support ended up by losing his case. By 1958, his protectors already realized that their immediate intercession was against the rules. "Although you seem to object to our involvement..." the Party Secretary writes in the opening sentence of his letter and ends his request by asking "to keep this correspondence strictly confidential." By now, the role assignments among the various players in government and Party apparatus are more settled than in the early years of the Republic; the judges are better educated and more confident about their place within the system; the Party is better able to control its members. Both constitutions of the GDR (the first from 1949, the second from 1968) described East German judges as "independent" and "subject only to the law."

Seeing is believing. But in any case, that is what their demeanor in the courtroom is supposed to look like. When, for instance, in 1961 a house owner suing to evict one of his tenants calls her "an old witch" and tries to improve his own case by accusing the defendant of celebrating national holidays by hanging not the GDR flag "but her knickers in the window," the court pays no attention to the political implications of the case. The plaintiff's local Party organization had eagerly repeated the accusation and in a letter to the court had spoken of "an act of sabotage and an attempt to ridicule our social order." But Judge Steinmetz (a people's judge) deals with the case as he would with any other serious collision between hostile tenants: he terminates the landlord-tenant relationship between the parties, asks the city's Housing Office to find a new apartment for the defendant, and orders the costs of the trial to be paid by the plaintiff/landlord. Because —as all participants are well aware—new housing will be unavailable, the decision means, in fact, that the "old witch" will stay right where she is.

At least as far as appearances are concerned, the boundaries between the judiciary and the administration have become more clearly marked than in earlier years. When, for instance, in 1966 a Lüritz plaintiff writes to the city's Housing Administration to enlist its support in a landlord/tenant dispute currently before the District Court, the office replies with a polite refusal: regretfully, a branch of the city's administration was "not authorized to intervene in a judicial matter." Until the last days of the GDR, reference to the "independence of the courts" served as a convenient formula for state and Party authorities to rid themselves of citizens' requests for help in a specific lawsuit. Adjudication is a business for the courts, and in judicial matters both judges and state functionaries seem to find it increasingly embarrassing to be encountered in too close cooperation with each other. In 1988, six employees of the Lüritz port complain in a 32,000-Mark lawsuit over innovation bonuses that "their suit had received no support whatsoever from the Party" and that a petition to the First District Secretary in the matter "to this date had received no reply." In the same year, the Ministry of Justice informs a petitioner complaining about the outcome of his divorce case: "The Ministry cannot comply with your requests to exert some influence upon the court. Courts are independent in their jurisdiction."

So far the official story. I do not have the impression that East German citizens believe it. While the Party increasingly takes care to keep its name out of judicial records, the citizens, from the first to the last day of the GDR, call for its help if their litigation seems to flounder. True, in the early days their political incantations sound a bit more brazen than in later years. "Speaking as a comrade ..." is a phrase I am more likely to encounter in case files from the 1960s than the 1980s. There is more political swagger to the arguments advanced to demonstrate a writer's political loyalty in the years before the Wall than after. "As far as we are able, we, too, are helping to preserve international peace," a plaintiff writes in 1951 in a landlord/tenant dispute, and a defendant, also in a housing case, claims in the same year: "Regarding the issue from a Socialist viewpoint, I am of the opinion that this lease no longer fits into our anti-Fascist–democratic social order." But necessity at all times spurs the imagination. "I regret my behavior and think that I have made a good start improving myself by studying [while in preliminary detention] the documents of the IXth Party Congress," says a defendant in 1976, hoping for a suspended sentence. In the 1980s, political arguments often have economic undertones: such as "to do socially useful work one also needs a good apartment."

But the references to the Party and its clout are still amazingly outspoken. As late as 1985 the loser in a lawsuit between neighbors over the height of a hedge between their gardens tries to achieve the reopening of his appeal by threatening the Regional Court with a petition to the Party's Central Committee: "Since the plaintiff cannot obtain support for his case at the regional level, he will have to place his trust in the central authorities." The Regional Court in Neuburg is unimpressed by the suggestion, and the Central Committee, when the petition does indeed arrive, returns it to the Regional Court "for further action." But the plaintiff fires off a second petition to the Central Committee, this time in order to prevent the execution of the judgment, because he simply refuses to believe that in judicial matters the Party should not have the final word. "We did not dare to press our case by turning to the Party," the six innovators write in 1988 when they appeal their lost case over bonuses to the Regional Court. But it is not true: they "dared" indeed to ask for the Party's help; petitioned the First Secretary while their case was still pending before the District Court; and saw no reason not to mention their unsuccessful application to the Party in their brief to the Regional Court. The judges were not surprised by such political advances, either. "We had to laugh about them," said Frau Nissen, the director of the Regional Court, about the countless attempts of both parties in the hedge dispute to advance their case by entreaties to the Party, the Secret Police, the National Front, or whatever other Socialist authority to one or the other supplicant seemed to be worth a letter. Frau Nissen was amused by the campaigns to influence the court, but not outraged. None of the various functionaries who in the hedge case were approached by either party took the petitioners to task for the illegitimacy of their pleas.

"Under Socialism, there were five times as many strings that you could pull [as] there are today," one of the three pre-*Wende* Lüritz lawyers once explained to me. On the other hand, those strings, in the eyes of many, *needed* to be pulled to get things moving. As one of the antagonists in the hedge fight put it: "You needed connections for everything." Occasionally, I even find a lawsuit in the files in which the court itself acknowledges the legal significance of "connections." In 1966, for instance, a veterinarian sues a Lüritz city employee who had promised to obtain a local license for the plaintiff's practice. The defendant had advertised his help by claiming that "he was a member of the District Council and personally knew all the gentlemen who had a say in these matters." When the license does not materialize, the plaintiff goes to court and successfully retrieves the 200 Marks disguised as a "loan" that he paid for his intervener's promise. And in 1979, in a reverse case, Herr Taddäus holds an evidentiary hearing to

CHAPTER 8

establish "whether the plaintiff's intercession" with the Housing Authority (this time at the expense of 700 Marks) was indeed the cause of the defendant's successful exchange of flats and whether the defendant therefore owed the plaintiff the promised sum. A representative of the city's Housing Office testifies that, yes, the plaintiff's advocacy in the matter had indeed persuaded the office to approve the change. Both plaintiffs, by the way, win their cases not through judgments (for which the judge would have to write a reasoned legal argument) but by simply settling for the full amount of the payoff sum (requiring just the formal approval by the court). Moreover, in both cases, the "connections" honored by the court were meant to sway administrators but not judges, and, as far as I can tell, the Party (beyond the likely Party membership of the bureaucrats involved) had no hand in the decisions. But one could understand if in a legal system that itself proclaimed the "unity of powers," citizens, too, did not attribute much significance to the subtle distinctions between buying favors from the second or the third branch of government or from that power overshadowing all three: the Party.

Were Lüritz citizens right when they believed that the Party, if it only chose to, could steer the outcome of their litigation any way it wanted? It is too soon for me to tell. The Party was such a slippery and multi-headed Hydra, the judges were so adept at reacting to its changing moods with changing strategies, that any unambiguous evaluation of the relationship between the Party and the courts is likely to be false. Here is a lawsuit from 1971 that can show how in confrontations between political power and the law both sides—the judges and the Party functionaries—felt themselves on uncertain territory and therefore chose their steps with care. The case—"Reimann vs. Roadworks Cooperative"—features the most insolent attempt by a Party member to sway the outcome of a case that I encountered in my files. It is also the last case of this sort, since later political interferences with judicial decision-making tended to take place outside the courtroom.

Here are the facts. Herr Reimann, Captain with the Secret Police in Neuburg, sues the Roadworks Cooperative for damage to his motorcycle that he incurred when he collided, late at night, with an unexpected street barrier that the Cooperative had neglected to mark with lanterns. Herr Reimann's legal case is sound. But nevertheless, his father, Reimann senior, worries about the outcome of the suit and sends two letters to the District Court that leave no doubt about the writer's intentions. The first, addressed to the secretary of the court, begins: "Although, considering my post as member of the Party District Secretariat, my time is precious, I will be happy to inform you of the details of the accident." The condescending introduction is followed by references to "Comrade Petzold" (the judge who at the court's weekly "Legal Advice Session" allegedly already had confirmed the damage claim); to "Comrade Kaufmann" (the district prosecutor, said to be of the same opinion), and "Comrade Kosewitz" (the First Party Secretary of the District, who "always has an open ear for the concerns of his colleagues"). The final sentence of the three-page letter: "We shall see how quickly Comrade Kosewitz will cut through the red tape and together with Comrades Petzold and Kaufmann will resolve the issue."

The court's initial reaction to the assault is cool and collected. A note of two short lines, signed by the court's secretary, informs Herr Reimann senior that he lacks legal authority to represent his son and that the court therefore "considers this matter closed." But Herr Reimann does not give in. He sends a second letter, this time addressed to the court's director, Herr Taddäus; reminds Herr Taddäus that another member of the District Secreatriat had already spoken to him about the case; mentions that the *Stasi*, too, supports the lawsuit of his son; asks "for understandable reasons please not to mention the State Security in this connection"; and closes with a confidential nudge among colleagues: "Isn't it sad, dear Comrade Thaddäus, with what unnecessary problems we have to struggle everyday? As if we comrades wouldn't need our time to deal with more important issues." Then, at the end, just one more sentence doing duty as an alibi: "Of course I respect the authority of the court." All this in the informal and familial *Du*, the second person singular, that Germans use among relatives and friends and that was customary among Party members.

Herr Taddäus does what every judge might do to avoid unwelcome complications in a lawsuit: he resolves the case informally by persuading the Cooperative to acknowledge the claim against it and the plaintiff to withdraw his suit. Whether it was his father's gall that ensured Herr Reimann's victory is hard to tell, because he should have succeeded with his claim in any case. But the story shows the difficulties of maintaining judicial independence in a political system in which all actors from the word go are intertwined in an inescapable and sticky network of political connections. All of them—the judge, the prosecutor, and the Party functionary—are comrades; all know each other well from many previous encounters; almost all of them address each other with the trusting *Du*, which personalizes the rejection of a favor and lets it appear more hostile than the refusal of cooperation among strangers; and all are dependent on the same superior Party authorities. Herr Taddäus clearly was annoyed by the brazen intervention of the father: the curt response to Herr Reimann senior's first letter to the court could not have been written without the court director's approval. But neither he nor the district attorney whom Herr Reimann senior also tried to lean upon had refused to discuss the son's case with the father. The Party is everywhere; its many incarnations cannot be shaken off. It does not need to be present in the courtroom to make its influence on what happens there be felt.

If in the second half of my Lüritz legal history, I virtually never encounter the Party *in persona* in the files, the reason for its absence may have nothing to do with a new-found reticence to interfere in judicial matters but may simply be due to the fact that it by now has learned to use its influence more discreetly and effectively outside the courtroom. "It"? I always talk about the Party as if it had a clearly defined identity and solid outlines. But "the Party" stands for the Politbureau in Berlin, Herr Kosewitz in Lüritz, as well as all the other comrades who play a role in "Reimann v. Roadworks Cooperative," including Herr Reimann *père* from the Lüritz District Party Office no less than Herr Kositzki from the District Court. The fact that it is not always obvious at what level in the Party hierarchy someone has taken an interest in a particular issue further complicates the interactions between the immediate participants.

There were many occasions at which representatives of both the Party and the court in Lüritz could meet and talk about matters involving law. In a judge's ordinary work day, the Party unit at the court itself represented the most intimate conflation of law and politics. It included the judges, prosecutors, and notaries connected with the court and usually was led by the District Attorney as the unit's secretary. That meant that Herr Kosewitz as the court's director as a rule would *not* be present at the weekly "Secretaries' Meetings" in the office of the Lüritz District Party Leadership. However, he would—together with other Lüritz "security forces"—attend the monthly "Security Conferences," in which a number of city authorities met to discuss public safety issues: the prosecutor; one representative each of the regular and the criminal police; the head of the "Interior Department," Herr Rost (an important figure because his department was responsible for asocial citizens and for people applying for exit visas, both groups of interest to East German criminal law); the SED "District Security Officer"; and, last but not least, a *Stasi* representative. I know about the "Security Conferences" from Herr Fechner, the Party's last "Security Officer" in Lüritz: a slight, gray man with his hair slicked back who first worked for the police, then the military, and finally, since 1976, as the Party's liaison to Lüritz "security forces" who were responsible for law and order in the city. The fact that the Lüritz court director was included in the "security" group suggests what kind of help the Party expected from the judiciary.

Herr Fechner also tells me about the topics discussed at the group's meetings: above all, matters involving "flights from the Republic" and applications for exit visas; all fires in the district; juvenile delinquency; "asocial" behavior ("we had great cooperation on asocials," Herr Rost told me on a different occasion); and everything else that might cause unrest and confusion in the population. Here was an occasion for Herr Thaddäus to mention what was going on in court, and for Herr Fechner to let the court director know about the Party's viewpoint on the issues raised by those proceedings. Only as late as May 1989 did the director of the Regional Court in Neuburg, Frau Nissen, advise her judges that "faulty decisions by a district court may not be [the] subject of 'security conferences.'"

Until that date, we can assume that specific court decisions *were* debated at the meetings or at least were thought to be suitable objects of "security" concerns. Moreover, all "security conferences" took place in the office of the District Party Leadership, that is, on Party turf and under Party control. Only in 1989 were the monthly meetings moved to the office of the District Prosecutor—a late and largely symbolic change of venue meant to create, I guess, a little physical distance between law and political power. But since in Lüritz the District Party Leadership and the Prosecutor's Office shared the same address (they occupied the big white building on the market square that today houses a "Savings and Loans"; the SED the first, the prosecutor the second floor), it is unlikely that the move did much to level the authority relationship between the participants. In both places—thus Herr Fechner—the *Stasi* took part in the discussions but did not sign the resolutions of the group.

If Herr Reimann wanted to talk with influential comrades about the legal problems of his son, he thus had multiple occasions to do so. As a member of the District Party Leadership, the *Kreisleitung* (usually abbreviated as KL), he had a short-cut to First Party Secretary Kosewitz, with whom he shared office space at the Party's District Bureau; a place where he also, at one of the weekly "Secretaries' Meetings," might buttonhole Herr Kaufmann, the District Prosecutor, and enlist his help. Herr Reimann could ask the predecessor of Herr Fechner, another KL member, to raise his son's case at one of the monthly "security conferences" and bring it to the attention of the court director, who would be present at the meeting. Herr Reimann could use one of the many informal contacts between Party functionaries to further his son's cause. Since the SED District Leadership and the District Prosecutor were housemates, a chance encounter on the staircase might provide a good occasion for a personal chat. Important comrades would meet each other at the town's political and cultural occasions that required the presence of dignitaries. They socialized together: Herr Rost of the Interior Department, for instance, regularly played cards with Herr Thaddäus from the District Court. As Herr Rost told me, he learned about the story of the suicidal visa applicant and his rope at someone's birthday party. Who else was there?

And finally, there was the telephone. Officially, "telephone law" was frowned upon: as a rule, a call suggesting that the court do this or that would leave no traces; such calls, therefore, escaped Party control; they allowed local bosses to undercut central decision-making; and they undermined the respect for the law. Nevertheless, is seems likely that my judges at least occasionally discussed critical cases with Party authorities. "Because of the significance of this litigation [a group complaint involving wage issues], the SED District Bureau has been informed orally and in writing," I read in a 1986 account by Frau Walter (now the new director of the District Court) addressed to the Presidium of the Regional

CHAPTER 8

Court in Neuburg. By the mid-1980s, such—as Frau Walter calls them—"focused informations" for the Party are quite infrequent; in the field of labor law (the only area where I have data) I find no more than one or two reports a year, which, to do the court justice, seem to have been submitted to the KL Bureau not prior to but *after* the court's decision in a case. Quite possibly the "oral information" (why does Frau Walter even mention it?) was supplied at an earlier stage. In any event, the Party had enough eyes to be well informed about whatever shirty issues were before the court.

But did some bigwig *tell* the court how to decide a specific case? A 1977 letter by Herr Taddäus suggests that, as a rule, the Party's influence on individual decisions was exercised more discreetly. The letter deals with a landlord's eviction suit against one of his renters: ordinarily a fairly hopeless case because East German law ranked housing needs over property rights and therefore tended to favor tenants over landlords. In our case, the plaintiff hoped to move into one of the flats of an apartment house that he recently had bought. It seems that the local Party authorities were on his side: perhaps because of his connections; perhaps for the more innocent reason that the plaintiff was a carpenter and that a run-down apartment house (a safe bet since most apartment houses in the GDR *were* run down) would be better maintained if an owner capable of fixing things would also live in it. I find a memorandum in the case file recording a conversation between the current tenant and the housing authorities trying to talk her into leaving the apartment voluntarily (a suggestion that is emphatically rejected) which, at the bottom of the page, lists the names of people scheduled to receive a copy of the memo: "1 x Comrade Taddäus, District Court; 1 x Comrade Liebermann, District Party Bureau." That means that the Party is informed of the dispute.

But it seems that the District Bureau does not do enough to find alternative housing for the tenant that she might be willing to accept. Hence the letter from Herr Taddäus to the local Housing Authority asking when the defendant will be assigned another suitable apartment. If acceptable new housing will not become available to her in the near future, "I shall be forced to continue the proceedings currently before the court which I suspended after our conversation with Comrade Liebermann." That means that the Party (in the person of Comrade Liebermann from the District Party Leadership) had asked Herr Taddäus to adjourn the eviction suit in order to gain time to arrange a peaceful resolution of the conflict. Comrade Liebermann had not ordered Herr Taddäus to forget about the interests of the tenant and decide in favor of the plaintiff: that would have been against the law. Nor was Herr Taddäus willing to shelve the case beyond what seemed to him a reasonable time for the Party to get its act together. Even Comrade Liebermann seemed to assume that if the court reopened the proceedings and arrived at a decision, it probably would not conform to Party wishes. But Herr Taddäus had been willing to suspend the case in order to give Comrade Liebermann a chance to fashion a resolution more to the Party's liking than the otherwise predictable rejection of the plaintiff's eviction suit. Instead of a straightforward legal resolution, the court had helped to achieve what was called "a political resolution" of the conflict.

I find a lot of cases in my files that, I suspect, have been resolved "politically." They are marked by the unexplained suspension of a hearing that never is resumed because, after a few weeks or months, the complaint is withdrawn and the proceedings are closed. Sometimes, an innocent extrajudicial settlement between the parties may have caused the delay and the eventual termination of the suit. But in many instances the administration or the Party (and often both) must have had a hand in the affair. Especially lawsuits that could reveal political tensions or embarrassments often were terminated by "political" solutions. Here is an example: a 1978 suit by the Lüritz Youth Authority against a young single mother who had left her four-year-old son in her mother's care and fled by way of Hungary to the Federal Republic. "That was bad of her," the grandmother admitted to me when we spoke about the case. She loved the boy and had helped to raise him, but she, too, disapproved of her daughter's in-the-dead-of-night defection. As in other cases of this kind, the Youth Authority sought to terminate the mother's parental rights to free the child for adoption: in part, because the Agency believed in placing small children with young parents but also, I suspect, in part as retaliation for the mother's unpatriotic (and, under GDR law, criminal) "flight from the Republic." But the Agency had not reckoned with the resistance of the grandmother, who wanted to raise the child herself and passionately opposed the Youth Authority's termination plans. *Stasi* attempts to paint her as an accomplice in her daughter's flight were unsuccessful: the grandmother had known nothing of her daughter's planned escape. Repeated interrogations by the police and house visits by the Agency's social workers failed to discourage her. "What do you want: it is not even your child," the Youth Authority's director had complained one day, exhausted by the grandmother's tenacity. "Yours neither," she had replied. While the fight went on, the Youth Authority's termination suit lingered, suspended, at the District Court. After eight months, the Agency threw in the towel and withdrew the suit—not, I am sure, without first having cleared its capitulation with the Party District Bureau.

And another example. In the 1980s, the number of "group litigation" cases increased in Lüritz: collective suits by groups of employees from the same enterprise who got together to challenge the validity of management decisions that had curtailed the wages or bonuses to which the plaintiffs felt entitled. Socialism disliked "group litigation," especially if the suits were brought by employees against their enterprise: such cases smelled of class war and rebellion, and the rejection of such suits, even if justified by law, would leave the plaintiffs even more dissatisfied and hostile than they had been at the outset of their litigation. Hence a number of communications I discover in the files by which my District Court informs the Regional Court in Neuburg that it would suspend the litigation in order to attempt a "political resolution" of the dispute. This meant in practice that the plaintiffs, the enterprise, the union, and a Party representative would sit down together with the judge to negotiate the terms of a solution that could both appease the usually angry plaintiffs and be politically acceptable to the Party.

In some respects, these compromises resemble settlements in Capitalist courts. But unlike a settlement, the "political" resolution of a conflict was initiated neither by the parties' lawyers (because they wanted to reduce the costs of litigation or the risk of an unfavorable outcome) nor by the judge herself (because judges on both sides of the Wall liked to save time and labor). Instead, these compromises were fueled by the interests of functionaries who were less concerned about the welfare of the parties than about the state's authority and reputation. Sometimes, the court adjourned a touchy lawsuit at its own initiative to seek advice from higher-ups about how to handle the delicate political issues that it might involve. "I have not yet set a date for trial," the court director in these cases would inform the Regional Court in Neuburg.

Often, the citizen who brought the suit must have been unaware of the fact that his case had been taken into hand by higher powers. In 1987, for instance, in a suit claiming unfair dismissal, the plaintiff, a musician and "applicant" (meaning someone who had applied for an exit visa to West Germany) complained to the Regional Court in Neuburg that the District Court had intentionally "delayed" his case, that it sat on its hands, and that for months now it had been inactive in the matter. He did not know that the Regional Court, legally speaking, agreed with the plaintiff's claim that the firing was in violation of his contract. Nevertheless, the judges did their best to keep the dispute out of court. In November 1987, the Regional Court writes to the Ministry of Justice: "We have approached both the administration of the Neuburg Region and the Regional SED Secretariat in our effort to promote a resolution of this conflict that would avoid a trial and a judgment. A judicial decision in this case can only result in the continued employment of the plaintiff since his employment relationship has not been legally dissolved." "Political" resolutions of disputes served the dual purpose of keeping courts out of embarrassing political affairs and of protecting judges from actually having to break the law to satisfy the Party.

Even if the "political" resolution of a conflict satisfied a particular complainant, he nevertheless had been manipulated in the Party's name. The tenant whose eviction from her old apartment Comrades Taddäus and Liebermann discussed in the summer of 1977, for example, found in the end (as she herself admitted) a place "that suited her interests." In many other instances (lawsuits by "applicants" against their landlords or employers, for example), the "political solution" of a case may have consisted mainly of the court's attempts to talk the plaintiffs out of their intended litigation. The unexplained withdrawal of a suit that in my files may often follow many months of equally unexplained delays thus will hide both successes and defeats. In any case, they signal the transfer of a problem from the realm of law to the realm of politics. The law's authority as arbiter of individual conflicts, and the experience of individual self-assertion which successful litigation may entail, were limited to non-political disputes.

To restate what the preceding sections tried to show: if the Party was interested in the outcome of a legal dispute, it exercised its influence behind the stage, with both the Party and the judge intent on keeping Party influence out of the courthouse. If a legal dispute remained on judicial territory, judges would do their best to keep their judgments within the letter of the law. Within the four walls of their own courtroom, East German judges were positivists. After all, the statutory texts had come into being with the blessings of the Party and offered the greatest assurance that the judge who stuck to them would make the "right" decision. Outside of the courtroom, other rules applied. Away from the bench, a judge was also a comrade among others and had to do his share to realize whatever goals the Party was pursuing at the moment. One might call this arrangement a division of labor between judges and politicians; between a small enclave under law's control and an extended hinterland of Party politics in which the law had no authority. The judges, as both jurists and as comrades, had a foot in each of the two camps.

Is that how the Party saw its role as well? I decide to go for an expert opinion on the matter and to ask Herr Kosewitz himself about the relationship between the Party and the court. Klaus Kosewitz served from 1960 to 1988 as First District Secretary of the SED in Lüritz or, as he says himself, "I governed this town for almost thirty years"—a potentate in charge of the 80,000 souls who lived within the city and the district. Even after the *Wende*, the people of Lüritz talk about him as one would of the sovereign of a small, early nineteenth-century principality. Adherents praise his affability: how approachable he had been; how tenderly he had taken care of his sick wife in her wheelchair; how, unembarrassed, he had walked through town with a shopping-net in his hand. Opponents criticize his imperial leanings and his vanity: his endless speeches; his insistence on deciding everything himself; his greed to see his picture in the paper. Even Herr Kosewitz's detractors, by the way, admit that he did not meddle with judicial business. But with the schools!

Herr Kosewitz is a slight, energetic, and combative man with whom I quickly get into a lively conversation. Had he intervened in the work of the District Court? No, not of the court. He had cared more about the schools. But "links" between the District Bureau and the court happened only if one or the other side

CHAPTER 8

initiated the connection. Can he give me an example? Yes, an "intricate and tangled scandal" involving the fraudulent accounting of *Feierabend* (after-hours) work (which given the perennial shortage of labor under Socialism was an important source of manpower in the GDR). Several members of the District Council had enriched themselves, a number of SED comrades among them. A judge had been sent by the Regional Court in Neuburg to investigate the mess. But Herr Kosewitz instead had used Party methods to clean the Augean stables. A number of people had to face disciplinary proceedings; a couple of "severe reprimands" were issued; one of the culprits lost his office. Only one CDU member of the District Council had been interrogated by the court. But, in the end, the CDU man, too, had been dismissed, and with no more work to do the judge from the Regional Court had returned to Neuburg. It seems that he had no complaints about Herr Kosewitz's drawing the line between the Party and the law; between the jurisdiction of the court and that of the Lüritz District Party Leadership. I assume that even the offender from the CDU was not displeased with Herr Kosewitz's "political" approach to the affair: it saved him from having to endure a criminal trial. It also saved the court a lot of time and work, saved the CDU and the SED the embarrassment of seeing their functionaries publicly exposed, and saved the Party worried speculations about what, had there really been a trial, the court might have unearthed and, who knows, even might have punished in the end. Herr Kosewitz's solution left the court out of the loop and thus unsullied by political advances from the Party. The occasional "links" that the Party Secretary mentioned seem to have dealt with jurisdictional issues: will you take care of this particular issue or shall we?

That means that by the time a conflict was decided by the court, whatever political aspects it might once have contained had been already filtered out. As a Lüritz union functionary once told me: "Judges were not supposed to deal with politics." This division of labor between law and power did not apply to prosecutors; especially not to the prosecutors attached to the Ia Panels at the Regional Court in Neuburg, who used the criminal law to suppress criticism and political deviance in the GDR and in so doing worked closely together with the Party and the Secret Police. In 1968, for instance, the Party's First Secretary's office, the prosecutor, and the *Stasi* organized a military-style campaign against a group of workers from the Lüritz shipyard who were accused of sympathizing with recent political developments in Czechoslovakia. To judge by the many references to the suspects' subversive utterances that are listed in the file, political conversations at the shipyard must have been surprisingly unguarded. The men had criticized the dishonesty of East German television reports about events in Prague; had railed against "the shitty behavior of the Russians"; had speculated full of hope about a possible intervention by the Americans; and had watched full of pity as the Soviet occupation had put an end to the Prague dream:

"Poor people. They were on such a roll." It seems likely that the fourteen dissidents listed in the file were not the only ones to think so at the shipyard. Probably the actions directed against them were meant to prevent the spread of dangerous opinions among the 6500 other employees.

In any event, the operation to subdue the rebels was arranged with and coordinated by the Party. Even before the culprits were arrested, Herr Kosewitz (now District First Secretary for the last eight years and in this office more protective of the state's authority than he had been in his previous incarnation as a union man) suggested that "the results of the criminal investigation should be propagated by all primary Party groups both in the district and the shipyard." That way, everybody would be warned. A similar case occurred in 1978 when a particularly obstreperous bricklayer (again, a shipyard employee) was arrested for "defamation of the state." The arrest had been carefully coordinated between the Party, the prosecutor, the Secret Police, and the offender's own enterprise. In 1978, however, the powers-that-be felt safe enough to limit to mere threats their efforts to make a rebel toe the line. "After consultation between the prosecutor, the SED District Bureau, and the District Office of the Ministry for State Security," the arrest warrant was lifted two days after the man's imprisonment; he was warned and released; and an "educational meeting" at the culprit's work place hammered the need for "aggressive indoctrination and improvement of political-ideological opinions" into his and his colleagues' minds.

The courts participated in such operations, if at all, only at the final stage. In our 1968 case, for example, the Lüritz District Court sentenced the "ringleader" of the Prague supporters—following the suggestion of the prosecution—to three years in prison for "agitation against the state." In 1978, the rebellious bricklayer —following the suggestions of the prosecution—received no more than a suspended sentence for "public denigration." In these and other cases of this sort the court thus, in a way, legitimated the preceding operations by putting the judicial seal of approval on an outcome that, already at the outset of the story, had been determined by the Party. The necessary legal rules for the court's decisions could easily be found in the Criminal Code's vague and elastic sections on crimes against the state. Since the judges had not been present at the preparatory stages of the enterprise and may have been ignorant of its most objectionable details, they could define their own role in the story as nothing more than applying legal rules to factual circumstances. They may not have liked those rules, and sometimes they may even have sympathized with the defendants. But I do not have the impression that they were bothered by their conscience. In any event, most political cases of this sort that arose in Lüritz were adjudicated by the Regional Court in Neuburg.

In the final years of the GDR, there were few contacts left between the District Court and the Party leadership in Lüritz. In January 1987, a letter from the

CHAPTER 8

Neuburg Regional Court addressed to all district courts in the region summarized the rules for their cooperation with the SED (in itself, a surprising move, since in the past, leaving the rules *unarticulated* had been an important feature of the cooperation between the Party and the court). The letter listed no more than four occasions officially requiring contacts between both: the monthly "security conferences" (at which the court director would meet with a Party functionary and law enforcement delegates to discuss law and order issues in town); the court director's annual report to the SED District Bureau (which sometimes was delivered on request but which in most years amounted to no more than one of those annual rituals in the life of a presiding judge); the obligation to provide the First Secretary with copies of all "court censures" issued in connection with a judgment (which were sent *post festum* and therefore at a time when the Party could no longer try to influence the court's decision); and the cooperation between court and Party in something called the "Committee on Legal Propaganda and Education" (which was run by the Party but which I never found mentioned elsewhere in the Lüritz files and which may not have existed in my town at all). But that was in the declining years of Socialism in the GDR. In earlier years, the demarcation between law and power must have been fuzzier.

At all times, the system could work without friction only if the judges felt comfortable in their dual roles of jurists and comrades; if the right hand knew and approved of what the left was doing. Hence the enormous significance of cadre policy in the GDR, for the judiciary no less than for other branches of government. Of course, district judges and prosecutors could not be appointed without the approval of the SED First Secretary. One needed people to whom, if necessary, the Party could establish "links" and who, in the relative seclusion of the courtroom, did not have to be kept on a tight leash. One needed true believers. If West Germans imagine the Party, they like to think of it as a spider in its net: a poisonous creature that controls all around it, pulls all strings, entices its victims into its domain, entangles them within its sticky filaments, and then proceeds to swallow them. But the Party did not want to be a spider. If there were such a thing as a self-portrait of the Party, it would have rather resembled the image of a Pope: that of a priest and administrator of a secular religion. As disciples bowing toward Rome or Mecca, comrades were meant to turn toward Berlin to find the answers to important questions. "Pope" and "spider" resemble one another insofar as both inhabit the center of their respective universes: all roads, all threads lead up to them. But like the decisions of the Pope, those of the Party were supported by moral claims.

Beyond the teaching of professional skills, the education of East German judges, from the very beginning, thus focused on the inculcation of true beliefs. In the early years, when students with often no more than a grade-school education were trained to serve as "people's judges," those beliefs were simpler, more colorful, and intertwined with more political legends than in later decades, when all law students needed the *Abitur* (the highest level of high-school graduation) to be admitted to university. Up to the very end, East German legal education included a heavy dose of ideology. But the relative weight of political and legal subject matters shifted over time. In Frau Rüstig's days (judging by the number of pages covered), about half of her tests dealt with topics like "The Collapse of Imperialist Colonialism and its Impact on Imperialist Contradictions"—themes too exotic to be even recognizable as law school tests to Western readers. The other half—questions about the differences between murder and manslaughter, contractual error, the liability for traffic accidents—would have been equally at home in Western classrooms. By the 1980s, the ideological portion of law school examinations had sobered and shrunk down to about a third. The schizophrenia of the split between the ideological and legal curriculum remained until the end, but students spent more time on law—about the same number of hours as law students in the United States. The ideology came extra.[42]

Once in office, East German judges had to keep up with their political training. The Ministry of Justice, which was responsible for the continued ideological education of its judiciary, seems to have found it difficult to hit the right pedagogical note. Too rigid indoctrination might undermine judicial self-respect and creativity; too little indoctrination might endanger loyalty. The files suggest some back-and-forth between the two. I find a decree from 1956 in the Lüritz archive that orders the "reorganization" of the training program; another one from 1958 announces its immediate "resumption." Initially, the basic topics for study were provided by the Ministry: in May 1957 the topic was "The Law of Proof in Criminal Proceedings"; in June 1957 "The Violations of Legality in the Bonn Republic and the Arbitrariness of West German Courts." A memorandum from 1958 suggests that the list of subjects provided by the Ministry "obviously is intended to be no more than a recommendation for the Party organizations in the district." Back in Berlin, the Party would rather be "Pope" than "spider" and hopes for self-propelled political enthusiasm and curiosity even at the grass-root level. In 1981, the Presidium of the GDR Council of Ministers discusses the "state-political training program" for its public servants and issues a "Resolution on the Implementation on the Continuous Marxist-Leninist Education of State Cadres," which affirms, once again, that the topics for study should be selected "under the own responsibility of the district courts." But my Lüritz judges prefer to stick to the list of themes sent every month by the Regional Court in Neuburg. Now, in the 1980s, most training sessions are likely to focus not on ideology but on the economy: "The Economic Plan as a Decisive Governmental Steering Mechanism" (thus the suggested discussion topic for December 1983); "The Schwerdt Initiative to Increase the Productivity of Labor" (January 1984); "The Consistent Strengthening of the GDR's Export Performance" (February 1984).

CHAPTER 8

The judges must take turns reporting on the topic of the month—and not just they: the court secretaries, too, have to contribute to the sessions. They take place on the first Monday of each month; according to some judges' desk calendars that I discover in the wood cellar, discussions begin at seven o'clock in the morning: an early Socialist morning chapel with, I assume, a sleepy congregation. The monthly "Party seminar" (an ideological study meeting just for Party members which, at the Lüritz court, included every judge) took place in the evening after work (another drowsy period of the day) and lasted two to three hours.

The Party also took care of its judges' morals. In their personal life, judges were expected to be models for ordinary citizens. In the 1950s, two people's judges living together without the benefit of clergy are told that they must marry if they want to keep their jobs—the Party objects, if not to "sin," at least to unconventional lifestyles. Impending divorces within the judiciary are reported all the way up to the Ministry of Justice in Berlin. In the early years, a Lüritz people's judge and a prosecutor are fired because they falsely had denied their previous membership in Hitler's NSDAP (and it appears that lying to the Party had condemned them more than being fellow travelers under the Nazis). Even in the summer of 1989, only a few months before the system's final breaths, Judge Rodewaldt is ordered to withdraw his civil suit against a neighbor because a judge is not supposed to publicly engage in quarrels over personal advantages.

But the Party also could be counted on when judges needed help. In 1963, First Secretary Kosewitz personally comes to Frau Rüstig's aid when she gets into trouble with the law-and-order forces in the city because she cannot persuade her bourgeois landlady to turn the TV-antenna on the roof of her apartment house toward the East and thus away from Western television channels. The owner is an old lady close to ninety and in Frau Rüstig's eyes too old to be reeducated. And so Herr Kosewitz assuages Frau Rüstig's critics; praises her steadfast labor for the Party; and arranges a three-week rest cure for the judge during which the uproar in Lüritz over Frau Rüstig's indulgence of class-enemies can quiet down. The antenna is never turned around. When, in 1982, Herr Taddäus cannot get an official permit to run a 1000-watt electric heater in the ice-cold porter's lodge of the Lüritz courthouse (energy conservation!), he approaches the District Bureau of the SED, which sees to it that the heater is installed. When, two years later, Herr Taddäus wants to quit his post because he is tired of the constrictions of his work and of the enmity between himself and the director of the Regional Court, Frau Nissen, he turns to the First Secretary personally who achieves the impossible and obtains Herr Taddäus' honorable discharge from the judiciary. Without the Party's help, one could not escape it. As late as the fall of 1988, the Regional SED Bureau in Neuburg and the District Party Leadership in Lüritz are enlisted to resolve an eruption of personal hostilities within the Lüritz prosecutor's office that led one woman prosecutor to contemplate her resignation. The warfare, which was fueled by rumors and malicious gossip, had absolutely nothing to do with politics: just a love affair, some defamations, a macho head of office, and the like. But the Party—all Pope—insisted not only on the right beliefs among the faithful but also on their brotherly relations with each other.

The division of labor between law and politics required the judges to effectively internalize the messages of Socialism. The Party needed to be certain that its judges (like missionaries in the field) could do without immediate supervision in the courtroom because their ideological conscience alone (now called "Party spirit") would lead them to the right decisions. That meant that the Party had to be concerned about its judges' inner lives. The training of consciousness was an important part of politics. When in the late 1950s and early 1960s, it becomes increasingly improper for local Party bosses to meddle with specific court decisions, the Lüritz Party Leadership spends all the more energy on training its judges' consciousness. The court's own party organization (called GO, for *Grundorganization* or basic party unit) and, in particular, that group's First Secretary (almost always a prosecutor) provided the link between town and judicial gown. It was the GO Secretary who participated in the weekly "Secretaries' Meetings" in Herr Kosewitz's office; it was he who reported to the District Leadership on the political atmosphere at court; and it was he whose task it was to boost his colleagues' ideological morale.

Thus the official *agitprop* ambitions of the Party. The minutes of the SED Secretariat meetings that dealt with the ideological conditions at the District Court tell a different story. They read like a litany of failures. As far as I can tell, the Lüritz Party raises its first alarm in the fall of 1958. A Party "brigade," assigned to investigate the situation at the court, uncovers a "weakly developed commitment to Party work," "too little political consciousness," and too much "coziness" among the judges. According to the report, the court's case law (specific decisions are no longer mentioned) hovers between "excessive severity" and "indulgence." The examiners complain that the court's work lacks a political compass: instead, "it seems to vacillate between extremes." The report does not give one the impression that the judges have internalized the teachings of the Party.

In 1965—now on the coattails of the "Decree on the Administration of the Courts"—the SED District Bureau arranges for two new investigations of the District Court. The results of both are discussed at a Secretariat meeting in June 1965 and are included in the file: a report on "the realization of Party resolutions" that is signed by both the chief of police and the district prosecutor, and a summary of the Party Control Committee "on the moral-political condition of the GO District Court, Prosecutor's office, and State Notariat." Both reports

CHAPTER 8

criticize "bourgeois objectivity," "remnants of old habits of thought," and the "ideological calm" within the judiciary. Until the end of 1964, the Party meetings at the court "had discussed nothing but professional issues." When confronted with their lack of political engagement, judges had claimed "to serve the Party every day through their professional work." That was not how the Party understood the division between law and politics. Where was the faith that helped a judge to focus on the teachings of the Party? Herr Bald, then the director of the District Court, receives a "severe reprimand" and is relieved, not of his judgeship, but of his position as director of the court; allegedly, because of personal shortcomings, but very likely because of his lack of ideological fervor. In September 1965, there is another meeting with the Party secretaries of the court, the prosecutor's office, and the state notary's office in the First District Secretary's headquarters near the Lüritz market square. I find a handwritten note among the pages of the file that one of the Party big-shots at the meeting must have used as a crib sheet for his sermon to the errant comrades at the court: "Why aren't you capable of taking critical positions yourself? ... The state must engage in a critical relationship with its judiciary."

That looks as if an intensification of the missionary pressure on the courts is in the offing. But to judge by the minutes of the Secretariat meetings of the following years, the ideological renaissance at the courts does not take place. Instead, I discover something that one might call "relaxation through routine." In June 1965, the Party group in the Lüritz court had been criticized for its failure to inform the District Leadership of the political discussions and the mood among the staff. Occasional reports had come haphazardly and only by word of mouth. After the shake-up, the information pattern changes. Now there are written reports on the state of the ideological consciousness of the judiciary. Their author is the prosecutor (in his role of Party Secretary of the group), who, in the peace of his own study and with the authority that is inherent in the written word, composes beautiful accounts of exemplary political morale among the judges. He describes, in eager and submissive words, his colleagues' enthusiasm for the most recent Party policies; outlines their efforts to translate those policies into judicial practice; occasionally admits a few mistakes; and usually ends with the assurance that in the future everyone will try even harder to live up to the expectations of the Party. From the prosecutor's report of May 1969: "We have increasingly made it a practice to center our party work not on professional questions, but on serious ideological concerns." From another report of November 1977: "Our fundamental task: to strengthen the combativeness of our Party group and to intensify its political-ideological work." Lord knows how much of the protestation is actually true. The minutes of a Secretariat meeting of September 1968, for instance, reveal that lively discussions at the courthouse had expressed sympathy for the Prague Spring. The faux pas is corrected by a GO meeting focusing explicitly on events in the CSSR at which "all comrades welcome the invasion by the five Socialist countries" and that ends with the promise that "political conversations at the court will be intensified." Now the Party has it in writing. Such declarations "are accepted by the District Leadership" which adds them to their files, where I will find them more than thirty-five years later. For the 1970s and 1980s, I can find no other traces of interactions between the Party and the District Court. Occasionally, the Secretariat plans "legal conferences" in the district, but they do not involve the court but are arranged under the stewardship of the District Party's "Security Delegate."

As the District Party Bureau is moving out of the business of safeguarding ideological correctness at the court, the task increasingly is handled by the judicial bureaucracy alone. From Berlin, the Ministry of Justice sends lengthy "directive documents" that outline the ideologically accurate approach to legal issues. Additional instructions come from the Neuburg Regional Court, which often attaches to its lessons the copies of particularly praiseworthy decisions by other courts in the region that can serve as examples to their sister courts. I find thick bundles of these model cases in my files. Their pages, like old carpets, are shot through with bare spots in places where the copy machine's ink ran low, and their immaculate smoothness after forty years tells me that they cannot have been handled by many readers. Apparently, authorities in Neuburg and Berlin feared the same and repeatedly admonished the recipients to carefully study every document. In 1965, when the East German judiciary, on orders from Berlin, engaged in a statewide discussion of the draft of a new Family Code, the Regional Court found it necessary to send a critical circular to all its district courts: "It has been shown that a true debate can only be achieved if the participants are actually familiar with the text under discussion." "To the attention of all judges," I read on the copy of a court censure that the regional court in 1964 distributes among all its district courts. "Perusal has to be documented by judge's initials." And on another text from 1976: "To be studied and discussed in depth."

Easier said than done. The "Guidelines for the Realization of the Resolutions of the IXth Party Congress of the SED," which the Lüritz judges are supposed to "discuss in depth," are thirty-seven pages long; printed on silky, milk-coffee–colored GDR copy paper that keeps rolling up as you try to turn the page; and strewn with liturgical incantations that, like incense, cloud whatever topic might be buried in the text. "The comprehensive strengthening of our Socialist state of workers and of farmers as a form of the dictatorship of the proletariat." "The leading role of the working class and its Marxist-Leninist Party." The monstrous definitions go on and on. By the time you have finished the page, you have trouble remembering what it just said. One of the recipients of the tract did take the trouble to underline with a red pencil everything of note. But on page twenty,

CHAPTER 8

his good intentions fizzled out, and in the remaining seventeen pages I find only two more red marks. "Start reading from the back," Herr Kosewitz had advised me when I complained to him about the impenetrability of Socialist party documents. Sometimes, the method helps, because many of the papers are following the same rhetoric pattern: some general remarks on the Party's historic role; a sketch of global political conditions; something on the position of the GDR; and only then, almost as an afterthought, a reference to the specific issue that provided the occasion for the message in the first place. But "starting at the back" is different from "discussing a text in depth." The wordy jumble of the Party documents crowded out whatever tiny seed of ideological conviction they might have contained and, instead of convincing their exhausted readers, taught them to spend as little time on Party literature as possible. Suspecting that many of its admonitions fell on deaf ears, the Party asked for evidence of its students' attentiveness, demanding that all judges sign a document or that the court send a report on its debate to the Regional Court and to the Supreme Court in Berlin.

But even in the fairly faithful 1950s and 1960s, justice officials in Berlin complained that it required "endless telephone calls" to get the district courts to regularly report on ideological schooling sessions at the courthouse. I find many reminders in the files for information that has not yet been received. To bring some shape and order into the reporting system, the Ministry of Justice, in the 1970s, introduced questionnaires on the continuing political education program, with empty spaces for the various aspects of a training session that a session's chair only needed to fill in: "main issues discussed"; "problems encountered"; "preparations"; "conclusions." "It was concluded that the training session was of interest to all participants," I read in a questionnaire from November 1976. And on a meeting six months later: "Conclusions: more intensive preparation through self-study." But soon the entries are becoming more laconic. The "conclusions" drawn from a Marxist-Leninist study session of March 26, 1979: "The current training system can be continued." Of January 21, 1980: "None." Of November 30, 1981: "None." Of November 25, 1982: "As before." At a Marxism-Leninism schooling session in December 1988, a third of all court members obligated to participate do not show up, two of them "repeatedly without excuses for their absence."

But even those who properly attend the meetings do not appear to spend much time on the discussion of Marxism-Leninism. In a judge's desk diary from 1986 (a wood-cellar find) I discover that many monthly meetings on the teachings of the classics are noted with a slash: "ML/lay assessor training"; "ML/ communal issues." Apparently, the ideological instruction hour was used to talk about more practical concerns. The entries confirm what Frau Walter had already told me: that in the final years, the ML morning hours were almost exclusively devoted to discussing the daily business of a trial court. That means that at the end, my judges had, again, arrived at the conditions that the Lüritz District Party Control Committee already had condemned in 1965: that party meetings at the court "discussed nothing but professional issues." Obviously, one cannot conclude that Lüritz judges and prosecutors were political opponents of the system. But one can infer that most of them (with the possible exception of the early people's judges) probably cared more for the law than for politics. The Party that so dearly wanted to be "Pope" could rely less and less on the faith of its disciples. It became increasingly suspicious and controlling of its judges.

Among my most revealing finds from the wood cellar are two official lists of the qualities that a GDR judge needed to possess: the first from 1969, the second from 1988. The differences between the texts reveal the ideological disenchantment that took place during the two decades that separate the documents. The first list, headed "Guidelines for the Evaluation of Candidates," was sent by the regional courts to all its district courts in preparation for the election of new judges by the legislatures. It enumerates the many criteria that Socialist judges are expected to live up to. In place No. 1 on the long catalog I find "a comrade's behavior at work": ability, commitment, self-reliance, reliability, realistic self-assessment, and the like. Then, under No. 2, come "the candidate's political behavior and world views." But as the following sub-categories suggest, the political virtues expected from a judge are not focused on ideology but quite pragmatically on his willingness to cooperate in the creation of a new society: "willingness to fulfill social obligations"; "openness for innovation"; "leadership abilities and methods." Putting the feasibility of this new society aside, I get the impression that those who composed the list were rational and practical administrators. The 1969 document does not mention West Germany.

The 1988 list, again, contains "Criteria for the Evaluation of Judicial Cadres" drawn up by the Ministry of Justice. This time, the first issues to consider when assessing a person's suitability for judicial office are his "ideological position and development"; more specifically, his "attitude toward the SED," his "willingness to put Party decisions into practice," and his endorsement "of a policy of antagonism towards the imperialist Federal Republic." The next place on the list is taken up by "issues of Socialist labor morality," seen not as a matter of commitment to one's work but, again, as a question of political loyalty, reflected in such virtues as "state discipline" and "concerns for security and vigilance." Only in place No. 4 on the long bill—and even then only at the very end of the paragraph are those qualities mentioned that a judge needs to expertly and timely do his job, such as "efficiency at work" or "knowledge and experience." By 1988, the GDR Justice Administration no longer dares to hope for judges with legal sophistication and experience. Nor is the true belief in Socialism a prerequisite for an appointment. What matters now is solely a judge's loyalty, defined not as internal obligation and attachment but—as in the case of a lover who

CHAPTER 8

knows that he has lost his lady's affections long ago—as reticence toward other suitors. A Socialist judge may not flirt with the West.

Throughout its entire life, the East German legal system was obsessed with comparisons to the Federal Republic. It stared West with the intensity of a rabbit staring at a snake. While it was almost impossible for GDR judges to be kicked out of office for incompetence, during the forty years of Socialist legal history in Lüritz, three judges had to leave the bench because of "contact problems"—not their own, by the way, but as a proxy, as it were, for relatives who had gotten entangled with the West. Frau Döring had to step down in 1953 because her daughter had escaped to West Berlin. Herr Machnow lost his office in 1982 because his stepson, through an intermediary, had received some wristwatches from an aunt in the Federal Republic and had sold them on the black market. To me, the most incomprehensible relegation is that of Frau Christiansen—yes, the capable and loyal people's judge who had always served Socialism with so much conviction—who in 1965, from one day to the next, disappears from the Lüritz files. I have to ask Frau Rüstig to discover why: because her sixteen-year-old son Lars, an apprentice with the GDR Merchant Marine and, as Frau Rüstig tells me, "always a headstrong boy," had made use of his ship's passage through the Strait of Gibraltar to jump overboard in order to reach the West by swimming, and had drowned. The story gets even worse. Of all the Lüritz judges dishonorably dismissed from their positions, only Frau Christiansen is not only punished but is also abandoned by the system. The others, like disobedient children, after their spanking are again accepted in the family fold. Frau Döring, after her dismissal, is appointed head of the Lüritz Youth Agency. Herr Machnow moves to a new position as legal counsel to the City's Housing Department. And even Herr Taddäus, who had left his office with the reluctant blessings of the Party but in clear violation of its policy opposing the self-initiated resignation of a judge, with Herr Kosewitz's help finds a new job as in-house attorney of the Lüritz district hospital. Only Frau Christiansen disappears not only from the Lüritz files but also from the city. I ask Frau Rüstig to explain to me the Party's hard-hearted reaction to her crime. "They could do this only to a single woman," says Frau Rüstig. How am I to understand that? Did Frau Christiansen's frequent run-ins with her male colleagues from the Lüritz prosecutor's office make her position at the court more vulnerable than it would otherwise have been? Or was she so cruelly cast out for the very reason that, before her fall, she had been one of the Party's favorite children?

But even if, throughout the entire history of the GDR, "contact problems" were cause enough to expel a judge from his position, there was a difference between the early and the late East German phobia of everything connected with the West. In the 1960s, the Federal Republic not only is attacked but also is taken seriously as an ideological competitor. I find frequent comparisons between the

East and West German justice systems in my files, stressing such differences as the lower crime rate in the GDR or its more energetic prosecution of Nazi criminals. Occasionally, East German texts betray the timid hope that the much maligned big brother might actually recognize some legal achievements in the GDR. After the passage of the new Criminal Code of 1968, the Ministry of Justice, in a confidential circular to all East German courts, asked for reports on "the reactions of West German, West Berlin, and foreign newspapers" to the new code. Next to angry responses to West German criticisms, I also find some proud citations of West German expressions of muted praise. When, in 1969, a West German dissertation—in an unexpectedly neutral and nonjudgmental voice—describes East German difficulties in trying to transform an inherited bourgeois legal system into its ideological opposite,[43] the Party takes the academic neophyte's report so seriously that it sets up a scholarly committee to deal with the thesis' arguments.[44]

By the late 1970s and in the 1980s, East German authorities seem to care almost exclusively about their country's unqualified and almost panicky dissociation from the West. In May 1978, the Ministry of Justice issues a *Rund-Verfügung* (internal directive) that establishes—as far as I can tell, for the first time—the obligation of all judicial functionaries to entertain no contacts with West Germany. "RV 7/78" is classified, and I find only a copy of its most significant provisions in the Lüritz archive. The directive forbids all non-professional contacts with the West and all travel to the West by Justice employees. Exceptions for contacts by mail and for personal visits with immediate relatives (in the first degree) may be approved of *orally* by the director of the regional court. The exception does not apply to the directors of district courts. They have to wait three years after they retire from their office before they can apply for permission to visit close family members in the Federal Republic. When the directive is reissued in December 1985, the Regional Court sends along a note inquiring whether its prohibitions "had been the subject of special discussions among the colleagues." That I cannot tell. But I do know that in the fall of 1986, Herr Taddäus, by now no longer director of the Lüritz court but for the last two years legal counsel at the district hospital, applies for permission to attend his brother's silver wedding anniversary in West Germany, and that his application, with reference to RV 7/78, is rejected. Even a petition addressed to the Pope personally in Berlin brings no relief. Herr Taddäus' letter to Erich Honecker, a seven-page-long emotional description of the writer's many sacrifices for the cause of Socialism, is soured with the bile of disappointment. He is ashamed, Herr Taddäus writes, that he obeyed the Party's order to cut the ties to his parents, who now are dead, and to his siblings in the Federal Republic. "Sometimes, when reflecting upon the meaning of our lives, we think that we have lost respect for ourselves."

CHAPTER 8

But the letter is to no avail: it is referred from Honecker's office to the Neuburg Regional Court, which instructs Frau Walter, now the new director of the District Court, to inform her former colleague in a "clarifying conversation" of the rejection of his plea. Frau Walter tells me that it was an embarrassing encounter. But rules are rules, for judges even more than for other people. When, in June 1986, RV 7/78 is lifted with respect to other Justice employees, the easing up does not apply to judges. For them, all contacts with the West remain forbidden fruit. "You won't believe what would have happened if I had come to work without the Party pin on my lapel," a former justice of the Supreme Court of the GDR once told me when we were talking about his last years and months in office. With judges' faith in the Party's moral authority now fading or extinct, external demonstrations of loyalty have become all the more important.

In Lüritz, ideological stagnation and routine lead to a greater appreciation for the professional aspects of a judge's work. That does not mean that judicial autonomy is on the rise. But by and by, the hierarchical structures in which judges operate are transformed. While in the early years Party control of the judiciary was local and direct, it now increasingly is mediated by professional experts from the Ministry of Justice and the Supreme Court. In the 1950s and 1960s, the SED District Leadership had occasionally engaged in its own judicial policy (first, by simply telling judges what to do; later, by trying to raise their ideological consciousness). In later decades, legal policies are centrally designed at the Ministry of Justice and the Supreme Court and passed down to the district courts by way of the regional appellate courts.

Even before the streamlining of the judicial chain of command, the Ministry of Justice had entertained an army of inspectors to keep a watchful eye on the daily work of its trial courts. Given the half-baked legal education of the people's judges and their lack of experience in administrative matters, the supervision, in the early years, may have been necessary. Frau Christiansen (who started her career as an inspector before she was promoted to the bench in 1953) used to send worried assessments to Berlin about the judges she investigated. "Barely capable of additional training," she writes in 1952 about a people's judge in Neuburg. "Passable knowledge of the law," says her 1953 report on a newly baked district court director in Neuburg. But "he has difficulties with the German language," and that the examinee occasionally helps out at the counter of his in-laws' haberdashery shop "is inappropriate."

In the 1950s, Frau Christiansen and her inspector colleagues from Berlin thus travel the Republic: visit courthouses; read decisions; talk to judges; ask about workloads, staff problems, and the reactions of citizens; check on "watchfulness and order" at court and on the judges' accounting and orthography; praise and criticize; and try to bring their charges' ideological convictions up to speed.

Lüritz family law decisions "do not correctly appreciate the essence of marriage," I read in an inspector's account of 1954. And in the evaluation of a criminal decision from the same year: "The District Court has failed to see that the defendant's act was a typical manifestation of agricultural class war." In November 1953, two inspectors and a para-legal together need seventy-two work hours to thoroughly examine the output of the District Court of Lüritz/City. In March 1955, another group spends 100 work hours on the sister court of Lüritz/District.

In the beginning, the inspectors' accounts for their superiors in Berlin are matter-of-fact and filled with useful details, contain no lengthy political introductions, and even in their ideological critiques are practice-focused. Considering the haphazard medley of barely trained judges that the justice administration has to deal with, one can understand that those up high want to know what is happening on the ground. "We thank you for your good and thorough reports," I read in a letter from the Ministry of Justice addressed to Frau Christiansen in 1952. But as the professional legal education of judges in the GDR improves, the system's political concerns move to the forefront. A round of inspections in August 1958 is centered on the reception and the lessons learned after the Vth SED Party Congress. The inspection topic for September 1961 is "Reactions by Justice and Security Organs to Provocations in Response to Steps Taken by the Government"; or, in plain English, to the building of the Berlin Wall.

But the regular appearance of nosey officials in the courthouse and the cooperation between the various inspectors from the Ministry of Justice, its regional representatives, and the Regional Court also cause problems. High Court judges and functionaries from the Ministry do not agree on whether the inspections would be better handled by administrators coming from outside or from within the judiciary itself through supervision by the higher-ranking courts. The Ministry worries about the spontaneity and informality of many of the revisions. In April 1957, Chief Inspector Weise from the Ministry of Justice complains about "a certain tendency" of the inspectors to rely too much "on chats across a desk and personal notes" instead of on the written records of an official consultation. "This method of proceeding does not only hamper control and self-control, but also leads to the somewhat haphazard character of our work." Inspection reports reveal that some judges complain of the many obligations to provide information on their work and that others occasionally try to play off one report against another. An assessment by the Ministry of Justice of February in 1972 finds fault with the "inconsistencies" of the inspection system that make it difficult to keep an eye on the inspectors themselves. "One general weakness are the attempts of some inspectors to exert immediate influence on the judicial work itself. This is due to a lack of operative activities of the regional courts and to their insufficient attendance of trials." In other words: instead of overlapping and diffuse attempts to investigate the work of courts from the outside, it might be better to leave the supervision of trial courts to the (geographically and professionally closer) regional courts.

And that is what happens. In the course of the 1970s, visits from ministerial inspectors to the Lüritz court become less and less frequent. The 1979 annual plan of the Ministry of Justice provides for the inspection of only two trial courts in the Neuburg region; my court is not among them. The only inspection reports from the late 1970s that I can find among the Lüritz files describe financial audits under the supervision of the Regional Court in Neuburg that check up on the observation of all those rules by which an overregulated and impoverished state tries to keep down the costs of justice. They do not deal with ideology.

Instead, the political education of the judiciary now takes place, more efficiently and more elegantly than before, at numerous colloquia, retreats, and conferences of all sorts at which judges of district and regional courts are kept current with the professional and political developments in the GDR. The teachers at these meetings are not inspectors, but professors, Supreme Court justices, or ministerial officials. There are "DCC conferences" for all district court directors in the region; "area specialist meetings" focusing on a specific area of the law such as criminal or labor law; and a host of "work" or "administrative" get-togethers at the Lüritz courthouse. All these gatherings were hierarchical affairs: someone from higher up told my Lürtz judges on the ground how they should think or act in a variety of circumstances. The speakers at "director meetings" usually came from the Supreme Court, a Ministry, or from a university; "area specialist meetings" could be joined by judges from the regional court; and "work" or "administrative" meetings at the courthouse were chaired by the court director and occasionally backed up by a visitor from the regional court. At least at gatherings outside of one's own courthouse (and much of the time, within) there was no opposition from below. Frau Nissen, the former director of the Neuburg Regional Court, told me that the conferences "were tightly organized." "There was no frolicking about," Frau Nissen said. A "Trainee Cadres Colloquium for Future District Court Directors" of August 1983, for instance, lasted three weeks, with lectures from 8:00 AM to noon and from 2:00 PM to 6:00 PM, a reading list of twenty-three titles, and one single "weekend leave." There was no time for the back-and-forth of objections and discussions. "Overburdening was one of the methods by which we kept our judges on a leash," said Frau Nissen. She was referring to a judge's ordinary work week, but her description also holds true for the many education meetings East German judges had to endure.

I found a bunch of notebooks from such meetings in the Lüritz wood cellar; among them, four college journals used by Frau Walter between 1981 and 1990. To keep up with legal developments, East German judges did not rely on the academic "commentaries" to a code traditionally used by German jurists (which quickly age unless the publisher keeps up with new editions and of which only a few existed in the GDR) but on handwritten notes and memos that they collected, each under his or her own cataloging system, in file folders, drawers, shoeboxes, and the like. The source of their collected wisdom was not what West German lawyers call the "H.L." (for *herrschende Lehre*, or majority doctrine, reflecting the latest viewpoints held in the academy and case law) but whatever higher-ups in the judicial hierarchy had told them at the most recent conference or workshop. As in West Germany, a judge's starting point when dealing with a case was the letter of the law. But the correct *interpretations* of the law came from Berlin. Because these interpretations, together with the Party line, were subject to change, it was important to keep current. Hence the attentiveness and care with which Frau Walter took down whatever she was taught at her many seminars and conferences.

I can tell from her notes that Frau Walter's teachers left no aspect of a judge's work unattended. Many lessons dealt with practical problems. "If larger households are evicted, the court must hire moving company and arrange for insurance," Frau Walter wrote in July 1983 in her notebook. I find guidelines on the interpretation of statutes ("illegal preparation of flight from the Republic also to be found in cases in which defendant transferred property from GDR to non-Socialist economies for later use"); on sentencing practices ("penalties for §249 of the Criminal Code [asocial behavior] often too high"); on procedural issues ("in the future, §249 defendants not to receive copies of their sentence; oral communication counts as delivery"); on the reintegration of defendants after their release from prison ("border-crime offenders to be treated the same way as other offenders"). The teachers also try to rekindle the ideological fervor of their pupils. "The primary task: preserving peace," Frau Walter notes at an "area specialist meeting" in March 1983. And a year later, at a similar occasion: "All men and women must be dedicated to our noble goals." Do I detect something like irony in her word-for-word copying of the admonition?

So much for the *prescriptive* methods of what was called the "steering" (*Anleitung*) of East German judges: instructions on how to deal with certain problems in the *future*. But "steering" also covered the judges' *past* behavior by way of evaluations of their work and criticisms of mistakes. At the meetings and colloquia for court directors and area specialists, the docent's criticism of faulty judgments was usually couched in general terms: he would not mention a specific case decided by an identifiable judge but rather chastise some generic fault of East German adjudication (such as: "must place more emphasis on preservation of state authority" in criminal law decisions). As a rule, in-house work meetings or administrative meetings might fault a specific judge not for individual judgments but for the nonjudicial aspects of her work. "Neu. for several months in arrears with statistics," I read in the minutes of one such work conference in

CHAPTER 8

March 1983 (what? the capable and resolute Frau Neumann?). Or, in March 1986: "Processing of divorce proceedings too slow." (The sluggish pace of civil law proceedings was a problem for all East German courts. The combination of overwork, red tape, and leisurely Socialist didactics led to growing judicial backlogs everywhere.) But sometimes the disapproval uttered at an in-house work meeting could be very specific. In one such meeting in March 1985, for example, a guest from the Neuburg Regional Court (who, it appears, has come down from Neuburg especially for this purpose) criticizes several Lüritz sentences for rape. There is a record of the meeting in the files. "Surprisingly, suspended sentences by Dist. Ct," I read. "Checked case files. In two instances, decisions wrong. In rape cases, suspended sentences should be the exception. To be discussed with Jdg." "Jdg."—in this case, Herr Sailer, one of the old judges, on the bench since 1963 and often absent due to illness—from now on will be careful not to give suspended sentences to rapists. Nothing wrong with that, I think. But what about Herr Sailer's "independence," guaranteed by the Constitution of the GDR? It should be noted in this context that the minutes of every work and administrative meeting at the Lüritz District Court had to be sent to the Regional Court in Neuburg so that the Neuburg supervisors could stay close on the heels of every Lüritz judge.

Even in Berlin, the East German Justice Administration seemed at times concerned about the "independence" of its judges. The "steering" of the GDR judiciary—the neverending obligations of all judges to report to their higher-ups; the countless inspections, reviews, critiques, directives, admonitions to which the judges were exposed—offered numerous occasions at which a High Court judge could simply *tell* a foot-soldier from a trial court how to decide a specific case. But that was not the way things usually happened. As a rule, judges would not be ordered to render a specific judgment, or, if they were, the order was phrased noncommittally enough to leave some room for noncompliance, and, in any event, orders of this sort usually would come only in politically touchy cases and, even then, seem to have caused discomfort to the system. The rules for prosecutors, as we saw, were different. Before the trial, each proposed penalty was discussed, and signed off on, by the prosecutor's district office, and in cases considered politically sensitive, had to be approved of, and sometimes even was suggested, by the regional prosecutor or even the Prosecutor General (who had the most immediate backing of the Party).

But the "steering" of the judiciary was more discreet, more veiled, and probably also more embarrassing to judges than to prosecutors. I know about it not from the Lüritz files but from the weekly reports in which the Neuburg court had to inform the Ministry of Justice of current happenings at the district courts within its region. The only traces of some meddling by superior authorities that I occasionally find in the local files are little slips of papers—"returned by B.G."

(for *Bezirksgericht*) with an added date—that reveal that a particular case file had attracted the attention of the Neuburg court, was sent there, and now is restored to the Lüritz archive. But even in these cases, the Regional Court may have done nothing that affected the immediate decision of my court. If a garden-variety judgment was considered "faulty" by those checking up on it, the normal way to correct it was by way of an appeal by either the parties or the prosecutor (who, as in other civil law countries, could appeal a criminal conviction). If the deadline for an appeal had passed, the criticized decision would be left as is. "Too late for cassation" (a second, state-initiated appeal available in Socialist legal systems), for instance, said the overseer's report on Herr Sailer's way-too-lenient sentences for rape. At this point, what the state would do is merely try to forestall a repetition of the error. It would have been far too costly to avoid derailments of this sort by an *ex ante* supervision of the judges. The loss of legitimacy, of judicial satisfaction, the sheer administrative expenses of a system of preventive intervention, would have been far too high.

Often, state actions to deter judicial deviations were not even necessary. In complicated cases, my Lüritz judges would on their own call up a colleague from the Regional Court to ask how to handle an intricate or touchy legal issue. The Regional Court, in turn, might pass on the inquiry to the Supreme Court or the Ministry of Justice. The tone of such exchanges was cooperative and polite. "It is our opinion...," the Regional Court might write and outline what it took to be the best solution to the problem. "We see no objections..." might be the answer from Berlin. Until that answer came, the District Court would delay setting a date for trial. By the 1980s, the procedure was so well rehearsed and tuned that I can find no resentments and no signs of tensions between those at the top and at the bottom in the files. Instead, I see a tightly led but amicable system of cooperation. All participants are workers in the vineyard of Socialist justice and each, at his or her own pace, does what is needed to produce a case law that can serve its goals. When, on one occasion, the Neuburg Regional Court favors a solution to a labor law dispute that would conflict with the advice suggested by a popular East German television show on daily legal problems, it doesn't simply tell its district court to follow its own advice but checks with the Ministry of Justice first—apparently, the television lawyers, for their part, had based their opinion on the authority of the East German Under-Secretariat for Labor and Wages, and the Regional Court does not want to break rank with other state authorities. Never mind that the judges have a mandate to resolve legal disputes and the TV-people do not. In a system obsessed with finding the one right answer, questions of jurisdiction are less important than the display of collective harmony. In such a climate, judicial independence—which is best practiced, as it were, by going it alone—must be vulnerable even if, in theory, it is approved of by the powers-that-be.

CHAPTER 8

And so it was whenever judicial independence conflicted with other social or political ambitions of the state. Here is one example. In January 1985, the Regional Court in Neuburg learns that a Neuburg hospital has sued one of its patients for the costs of her delivery, which in her case were not carried by the state health insurance system because the woman had been unemployed. Thus the hospital's claim. The Neuburg judges are not willing to accept that, under Socialism, a young mother, employed or not, should have to pay for giving birth in a state hospital. Since the district court has already set the date for trial, it is too late to suggest its postponement. Instead, the Regional Court directs the presiding judge to hear the case but not to decide it before the superior judges have had occasion to contact the Social Security Administration to clarify the legal issues.

So here we have a case of failed coordination: the Regional Court received no timely notice of a lawsuit that might give Socialist health care a bad name. Things continue to go wrong when the patient's husband declares during oral argument that he is quite prepared to pay the bill, and when the appellate judge sent by the Regional Court to "guide" the lower court through the intricacies of the case is told by the Regional Public Health Department that claims like the hospital's were not unusual and generally should be paid. So the judge decides to ignore the orders from her court's director to push for a delay and lets the District Court proceed with its judgment in favor of the plaintiff hospital. As a result, the Neuburg Regional Court finds itself in the embarrassing position of having to spell out to the Ministry of Justice why its own judge disobeyed her clear-cut orders to prevent the trial court's decision.

I know all this from Frau Nissen's weekly report to the Ministry. The court director does her best to cover up for the unauthorized decision of her colleague. Given the Public Health Department's information, she explains, "the presiding judge [from the District Court] and the member of the [Regional Court's] Civil Chamber delegated to participate in the district court hearing had felt themselves legitimated to deviate from the directive of the Regional Court." The unusually detailed excuse confirms in black and white what ordinarily I could only have guessed. Apparently, the "guidance" of the lower court's handling of the sensitive case had been officially discussed and settled at a meeting in the Regional Court. The court had sent a deputy to the trial court charged with the task of supervising its handling of the case. The watchdog even had participated in the hearing. And, most interesting to me: neither the "guiding" nor the "guided" judge had found the supervision process threatening enough to refrain from reaching a decision that, while conflicting with the Regional Court's directive, nevertheless seemed to be supported by the evidence and by the agreement of the parties.

The continuation of the story also is instructive. The Regional Court does everything in its power to prevent the trial court's objectionable decision from being carried out. It immediately requests the case file; orders the trial court to not yet provide the parties with copies of the judgment; begs the director of the district hospital to wait with the collection of the debt; advises the defendant not to pay it; and asks the Ministry of Justice to please investigate whether state health providers may indeed charge uninsured patients for the costs of services. A handwritten note in the file reveals that the inquiry is passed on to the competent official. I cannot find his answer in the file.

In this particular instance of politically motivated interference with the course of law, the Regional Court's behavior was motivated not by the fear of criticism and dissent but by a sense of social responsibility and justice for the unemployed and uninsured. Moreover: the High Court judges do their best to stay within the limits of the law and do not frontally attack the lower court decision that they disapprove of, attempting only to delay its execution. I assume that the Regional Court hopes for professional support by the Ministry of Justice and wants to gain time and arguments for a "political" resolution of the conflict. Maybe the judges plan to persuade the hospital to voluntarily withdrawal its claim. Or maybe the Regional Court hopes for the Supreme Court to overrule the trial court's decision by way of a cassation—that is, a court-initiated review that is independent of the parties.

But the case also shows that the East German judiciary's respect for law—here demonstrated by the Neuburg judges' tiptoeing around the law rather than stepping on its feet—was, at best, a respect for *substantive* law. The judges show little understanding for the autonomy-preserving function of *procedure*. They are not interested in autonomy but in the factually correct and useful resolution of social conflicts. Such as it was, the "independence" of East German judges covered only the individual decision of specific cases and even then extended only as far as a judge's "guidance" by the superior court and his or her own judicial backbone would allow. The enclave of freedom in which judges operated was not secured by indisputable legal rules. It offered no reliable shelter against the wind and rain of political weather changes. And in the 1980s, the weather was getting worse.

I find in the files a growing number of letters from the Regional Court to the Ministry of Justice in which the Neuburg court informs the Ministry that it has "taken control" of a Lüritz case, or, in translation, that the Neuburgers—by way of advice, suggestions, warnings, and dilatory maneuvers of all sort—were seeing to it that the Lüritz judge arrived at a resolution of a legal conflict that was politically acceptable. "The District Court will receive continued guidance during the litigation of this case," the Regional Court assured the Ministry when, for instance, in 1981, a citizen of Lüritz sued the state for compensation for water damages caused by faulty street repairs. Although only a civil case based on the obligations of ownership, the dispute came close enough to the state's authority to require watchful supervision. In 1987, a collective suit by seven agricultural workers for temporary wages between job assignments is similarly "taken control of" by the Regional Court: "The Labor Law Panel of the Court will continue to provide guidance to the district judge." Many of the growing number of "group complaints" by which, in the 1980s, employees tried to enforce the promised payment of premiums, wage supplements, and the like against the state, were litigated "under the control" of superior judges. But the type of litigation thought to be most urgently in need of supervision in these years were lawsuits by so-called applicants: cases brought by or against people who had applied for exit visas to the West, had consequently been dismissed or transferred to a less desirable job, and now contested their demotion in labor court. "The district court has not yet set a date for oral argument," the Neuburg court informs the Justice Administration in Berlin when a teacher dismissed for "unsuitability" (in other words: for having asked to be allowed to join her family in the FRG) sues for her reinstatement. "The trial will take place under the control and guidance of the Regional Court."

If the regional judges themselves are uncertain about how to deal with an inconvenient case, they, too, turn to their higher-ups for help. "We intend to dismiss the plaintiff's claim as 'obviously unsubstantiated' under §28 of the Civil Code," the Neuburg court, in 1983, informs the GDR Supreme Court; again, in a matter involving the dismissal of an "applicant." "Date for trial not yet set"—apparently, the Regional Court wants to wait until its handling of the matter is approved by the Supreme Court. "The District Court has followed our suggestion and adjourned further proceedings in this case," the Regional Court writes in 1987 concerning a civil suit against a black market car dealer—ostensibly, to wait for some information from the Lüritz City Price Department, but also to give authorities in Berlin a chance to provide some guidance for dealing with the growing anarchy of second-hand car markets in the GDR. When the Lüritz court in 1988 rejects a quasi-class-action by thirty-four shift-workers claiming additional vacation days—it should be said, *after* the Lüritz judges had "consulted" with their higher-ups about the legal merits of the case—and the plaintiffs are "dumbfounded" by their defeat, the Regional Court, again, brings the matter to the attention of the Justice Administration in Berlin. "We plan to affirm the District Court's decision," Frau Nissen writes. Even so, the anger of three dozen workers against the workers' and peasants' state is a disquieting political event, maybe even a warning sign, that must be reported to those in control and firmly taken in hand.

And so, as the years wore on, the "steering" of the East German judiciary increasingly served to control whatever possible political dangers might be in the offing. A supervision system that ideally was meant to guarantee the rationality, the uniformity, the *social rightness* of the law, became the watchdog of an anxious state. Keep a tight grip on everything, its motto seemed to be. Leave nothing to chance. Always stay alert. After all, the judiciary was one of the "security agencies" of the state. During the Xth Party Congress of the SED, for instance, the Regional Court reports in one of its weekly briefings for the Ministry of Justice: "On Saturday, April 14, 1981, all district courts in the region were tested for their readiness for action. Measures were taken to ensure that district courts are also operational after hours and on weekends and all times are able to issue arrest warrants and handle accelerated criminal proceedings." Not that a lot of violations of the law occurred during the days of the Party Congress: all I can find is four police notices about flags pulled down from flagpoles. But something *might* have happened. Many of the Regional Court's weekly reports to Berlin sound like sighs of relief that, once again, nothing had gone wrong. "On occasion of the Spring Meeting of the Free German Youth Movement in Neuburg, no significant events occurred," I read in the account of June 11, 1981, or, in the Court's report of June 18, 1982: "We are of the opinion that the [recent] national elections went very well and without incidents."

This constant and pervasive fear of societal disorder is also evident in a letter sent in December 1981 by Frau Nissen, the director of the Regional Court, to the Minister of Justice in which she reports on the Neuburg visit of a group of Polish High Court judges. Frau Nissen had invited the visitors (together with "some comrades from the Party leadership") for dinner and some "quiet conversation" in her apartment. The visitors—two of them members of Solidarity—"very openly" had talked about the developments in Poland: the country in turmoil; "the almost complete collapse of state power"; the "economic chaos." Frau Nissen's description of the visit to her Minister sounds sober but critical: the Poles are friends, but they are on the wrong path. "I got the impression," writes Frau Nissen, "that the Polish comrades see the creation of a smoothly running economic system as the key to solving all their problems. They do not take into account the need for firm guidance by the Party and the state." The result, she thinks, is "unrest" which "does nobody any good." Two weeks after the visit, General Jaruzelski declares the state of emergency in Poland. In the Neuburg region (a relieved Frau Nissen reports to Berlin) the uproar in the neighboring country had not triggered "any special incidents" at home. The East German legal order—all order—had held fast.

But this is only one side of the story. The files do not just tell of rising worries about how to keep East German courts on a tighter leash. In the 1980s, they also show surprising steps in the direction of a rule of law: efforts to sharpen the requirements for the admissibility of evidence in criminal proceedings; admonitions for judges to show more respect and to listen more attentively to defense attorneys; warnings against the trial courts' too eager approval of arrest warrants. Both the attempts to tighten and to liberalize the law originate not at the bottom of East Germany's pyramid of justice but at the top. In my files, the institutions that most visibly push for more formality and precision in the work of judges are the Ministry of Justice and the Supreme Court. At the seminars and training sessions that every judge in the GDR regularly had to attend, distinguished speakers from Berlin (and, in their name, appellate judges from the Neuburg Regional Court) explain to my Lüritz judges that they must show "more judicial independence" in their work. At one such lecture in October 1983, Frau Walter writes into her notebook: "Court must on its own authority examine prosecutor's indictment. Must establish substantive truth. Crucial: judges' growing accountability for their decisions." And a year later, at a "directors' meeting" with Frau Nissen: " Individual responsibility of judges must be strengthened."

In the final years of East German Socialism, the rule-of-law talk at judicial teaching conferences increasingly addresses issues not just from the state's, but from the citizen's perspective. "Citizen measures 'legal certainty' by the enforcement of his personal rights," Frau Walter writes into her notebook at a continuing legal education course in October 1986. Two years later, at a 1988 Supreme Court meeting on preliminary detention practices in the Neuburg region, Frau Nissen speaks of the social costs of restricting individual freedoms. We must learn "to better balance society's interest in protection and ... the basic rights of the accused," she says. It is the first time that I discover the term "basic rights" mentioned in the context of criminal proceedings. In the past, rights-talk had always referred to *social* rights such as the right to work or housing. If the discussion turned on a defendant's imprisonment prior to trial, "legal security" had been understood not as the defendant's right to a procedure ruled by law but as the interest of law-abiding citizens to be protected against criminals who—because of lackadaisical police work—had in fact *not* been arrested.

But how do you teach judges who for so long have been led firmly by the hand that they should be autonomous and reach decisions based only on their own assessment of a case? Obviously, through judicial guidance. Frau Walter and her judges at the Lüritz court are *told* that they should be more independent, and if they're not, it must be because they did not properly follow directions from above. In 1984, at the same meeting at which Frau Walter wrote "individual responsibility of judges must be strengthened" in her notebook, she also took down other reproaches by the speaker—such as "main criticism: central documents are not put into practice in judicial work"—and underlined the sentence with a heavy pen. Frau Walter, for her part, "urges" her judges toward greater independence and reports back on her efforts to the Supreme Court. In 1987, Frau Nissen reports from the Regional Court (which serves as liaison between the reformers in Berlin and her own trial judges) that "a tight system of controls and guidance" seems to have improved the hoped-for individual autonomy of judges. She tells her supervisors from the Supreme Court: "We have used a variety of managerial techniques to strengthen judges' professional expertise, their feelings of political responsibility, and their courage to reach decisions. In the process, we have reinforced the district court directors' own authority to control and guide the practice of detention pending trial."

Is Frau Nissen right when she claims that, in the final years of Socialism, Lüritz judges have become more confident and self-sufficient in their work? The preliminary detention practice that Frau Nissen mentions to support her claim can serve as an example of how difficult it is to achieve judicial independence by command. Already in earlier years, the GDR Justice Administration thought it necessary to monitor the detention practice of its trial courts. How closely did they pay attention to the legal rules that governed the remand of suspects pending trial? In the spring of 1981, a "Control Group of the Central Justice Organs" (Supreme Court, Prosecutor General, and Ministry of Justice) had inspected detentions in the Neuburg region and had found "no faulty practices." But the 1980s' hopes for liberalization, coupled with worries about how to deal with East Germany's rising number of unemployed (and unemployable) "asocial citizens," led to a revisiting of the detention issue. Many "asocials" were recidivists. After release from their first prison sentence—now marked as *Knastis* (jailbirds) and probably assigned the same kind of distasteful work that they had ducked before—they often would fall in with the same old friends and the same disreputable lifestyle. This time, they very likely were arrested more quickly than before. "For purposes of enforcing discipline," the arrest warrant would say. How else could the police keep *Asoziale* off the streets? In 1976, 86% of all defendants sentenced for "asocial behavior" had been imprisoned prior to their trial, compared to 29% of all other offenders. If prosecutors or police wanted an *Assi* rearrested, they could count on the cooperation of the court. It was extremely rare that judges rejected their application for a warrant. At a meeting in February 1988, a Neuburg judge revealed that, to his knowledge, there were some regions in the GDR where applications for arrest had never been denied.

The campaigns for judicial independence that were orchestrated in Berlin and that in the 1980s reached the Lüritz court were meant to put an end to the accommodating attitude of trial courts toward the representatives of law and order. "Don't let yourself be awed by prosecutors!" a lecturer says in 1988 at a three-day "directors' meeting" for the Neuburg region whose only topics are the preconditions for arrest. "If in doubt, deny a prosecutor's application for a warrant," admonishes a Regional Court judge (and qualifies his advice by adding "once in a while"). At the same meeting, Frau Walter reports that her Lüritz judges now have come to realize that some of their warrants probably "should not have been issued." In the winter of 1988, again at a "directors' meeting," a representative from the Regional Court announces that the judiciary now "had come to grips" with the vexing issue of detentions. Frau Nissen, who a few months later has to report to the Supreme Court on how her trial courts are doing, repeats the message of success: in the Neuburg region, the campaigns to strengthen "the personal responsibility of judges has led to ... greater dependability and consistency in the imposition of arrests."

In Lüritz, indeed, the share of "asocial" defendants who by the time of trial had already been in custody dropped from 85.4% in 1980 to 52.6% in 1984 and 43.8% in 1988. Overall, arrest warrants were denied a little bit more frequently than before: while in 1987 the court had rejected 4% of all prosecutorial requests for the detention of a suspect, that figure rose to 5% in 1988 and 7.6% in 1989. But the sum total of all arrest warrants issued by Lüritz judges *rose* in the final years of Socialism from 121 warrants in 1987 to 170 in 1989. If we don't focus on "asocial" perpetrators but look at everyone who got into trouble with the law, the share of those who were imprisoned prior to their trial remains pretty constant at about a quarter of all defendants. So what has actually changed since some people at the upper echelon of East Germany's justice administration began to talk about a liberalization of the law?

The contradictions and the tensions in the system have become more visible and more intractable. For every relaxation that I discover in the files, I find a clamping down; for every "giddyup!" a sharp pull on the reins. The liberalizers in Berlin who want to steer East German law in new directions are both courageous and timid: they want reform, but they do not want to offend the Party with their innovations. They talk of human rights and worry about their reputation. "We must not offer any openings for attacks," the Vice-President of the Supreme Court says at a seminar in October 1986, and a year later, at a meeting again about arrests, Frau Walter writes in her notebook: "Need to conform with rules of international law. Foreign countries pay attention." My Lüritz judges—in the same breath—are admonished to show more independence *and* to be mindful of the Party. "Always focus on realization of central resolutions. Apply own evaluations," Frau Walter notes at a "directors' meeting" in July 1984. In 1986, a Justice from the Supreme Court explains to his audience at the Judicial Academy in Wustrau: "Judicial independence is a postulate of the Constitution. Judicial decision-making, too, is governed by the primacy of politics." And in April 1986, Frau Walter writes down this Delphic sentence into her diary: "Unity of democratic centralism, self-responsibility, and independence of the judiciary." "Important" she adds in the margins of the page. What could she possibly have understood by the message that she so carefully recorded?

But what about the Party? Wasn't this chapter meant to deal with the Party? We seem to have lost sight of it by spending so much time on the "guidance" of East German judges by their superiors in Berlin. But the Party was always present during our detour. After all, the judicial steering mechanisms *served* to translate Party goals into court decisions. What changed over the years was not the

Party's influence on the judiciary but the methods by which this influence was exerted over courts and judges. When the Party was unquestioned in its role as "Pope," it could operate with open appeals to the faith and loyalty of its judiciary. The 1963 "Decree on the Basic Tasks and Methods of the Justice Organs" (*Rechtspflege-Erlass*), which tried to involve the citizenry in the administration of justice, for example, was such a rallying call that openly connected law and Party politics. But in the waning years of Socialism, faced with a judiciary whose political faith had crumbled as its legal skills improved, the Party chose to pull its strings from behind the scenes and was reduced to being a "spider": lying in wait, keeping an eye on everyone, hoping to paralyze its prey by fear, and only now and then scurrying out of its hiding place to snap up a victim or to repair its net. Here is a case that demonstrates how in its final year the relationship between the Party and its judges has gone to seed:

In November 1988, the Lüritz prosecutor brings a charge of "causing harm to the economy" against Walter Ockham, the director of a gigantic poultry farm about half an hour's drive from Lüritz. Like everywhere else in the industrialized world, in the GDR, too, chicken meat was processed more or less on the assembly line. Herr Ockham's enterprise, a state-owned cooperative, was in charge of the first phase of production of about a third of all *Broilers* (the East German term) consumed at lunch and dinner tables in the GDR: that is, the hatching of the chicks and their care in the first week of life. The birds then were passed on for fattening to enterprises that also took care of the slaughtering. The hatching, feeding, and slaughtering of the chickens and, above all, the staggered scheduling of their production throughout the planning year, were coordinated—not very efficiently—by the "GDR Poultry Combine," whose targets often were at odds with supply and demand among the participating state-owned enterprises. Very likely, the "GDR Poultry Combine" was less to blame for whatever bottlenecks occurred than the inflexibility and inertia of a planned economy. In any case, the poultry enterprises in the region often had complained about discrepancies between their various production targets.

In October 1988, Herr Ockham's enterprise found itself in a more dicey situation than usual. A *Broiler* glut in the entire GDR meant that the firms to which he ordinarily delivered the week-old chicks could no longer sell them, once fattened, and therefore cancelled orders that for months had been part of Herr Ockham's production plan. Between July and September 1988, Herr Ockham lost orders for about 500,000 birds. When, on October 10, he receives a telegram from one of his partner firms canceling reception of another 40,000 freshly hatched chicks (no state-owned grocery in the GDR is willing to buy and store any more chicken meat), he is at the end of his tether. An SOS-telephone call to the "GDR Poultry Combine" takes five hours to be finally put through. His teleprinter has been broken for days. So Herr Ockham decides to help himself: he

CHAPTER 8

orders the removal of 60,000 eggs from the incubators and the killing of 40,000 recently hatched birds. His staff buries the chickens in a nearby wood, where hikers discover the mass grave and inform the newspaper of their find. Now, a year before the Turnabout, the story is actually printed. This must be how the district prosecutor and, very soon, the Party bosses in Berlin learn of the massacre.

Nobody in Lüritz thinks that Herr Ockham's desperate decision is reason enough to drag him into court: not the prosecutor; not the judges; not the First District Secretary of the SED. All know that the intentional destruction of food-stuffs that cannot be sold is supposed to happen only under Capitalism. But people in town also know that Herr Ockham found himself between a rock and a hard place and that it was the planned economy that put him there. Nevertheless, on orders from above, the district prosecutor brings his charge of an economic crime, and the Regional Court in Neuburg "takes control of the case." Not just the Regional Court. At Herr Ockham's trial in December 1988, the audience in the courtroom included not only emissaries from the Neuburg court but also several observers from Berlin. That much I know from the director of the Regional Court, Frau Nissen (who seems to have resented the investigators from Berlin as invaders onto her own court's territory). The reason for their presence in the Lüritz courtroom: two weeks before the trial, at the 7th Session of the Central Committee, Party Chief Erich Honecker had talked about the coordination problems of East German chicken-breeding enterprises. To avoid impasses, some comrades "resorted to illegal solutions by destroying 100,000 chickens," he had said. "That's unacceptable and it was correct that the prosecutor intervened." Honecker's speech settled Herr Ockham's fate: his trial could not result in an acquittal. The "spider" had flitted out from behind his leaf.

In Lüritz, people do their best to neutralize its poison. Frau Walter, who presides at Herr Ockham's trial, sentences him under §166, para. 1 of the Criminal Code to six months in prison, grants probation, and sets a probationary period of one year—the shortest time that is permissible under the Code. I assume that the penalty had the blessings of someone higher up. Frau Walter's judgment mentions with approval the contributions of Herr Ockham's lawyer at the trial who helped "to throw light on the complex situation and on the defendant's motivation." Originally, Frau Nissen had determined that it should be *her* delegate from the Neuburg Regional Court who should draft Herr Ockham's sentence. Frau Walter angrily rejects the suggestion. In the end, she and the watchdog from the Regional Court agree on a compromise: Frau Walter would herself compose the judgment, but the Neuburg overseer would tell Frau Nissen, his director, that it was *he* who wrote it. I have the story from Frau Neumann, who was present in the Judges' Room when her colleagues—both, I assume, embarrassed about the reason for their fight—negotiated its resolution. In the last year of its existence, the East German judiciary's dependence and independence are jumbled and interwoven like a rat's nest.

More than a decade later, I talk with Herr Ockham about his trial. Did the court do you an injustice? I ask. "The court!" Herr Ockham says contemptuously. Back then, he was an important man in whose life the SED must have played a much bigger role than judges did. "Until then, I always got my rights from the Party!" It was the Party that he felt betrayed by, not the court. But it is a court, a Capitalist court, that in November 1990 rehabilitates Herr Ockham.

CHAPTER 9

HOPES AND LIES

Up to this point in my story, I have paid no attention to the sense of reality and to the truthfulness of the administration of justice in my town—not unlike a skater who knows that she is gliding on thin ice and hastens to move on before the ice should break. The strategy will not have alleviated the occasional suspicions of my readers. So now, finally, I should address the amazing dishonesty of the East German legal system: its utopian hopes; its tendency to whitewash failures and disappointments; its obsessive secrecy; its pretenses and evasions; its outright lies. In Socialist law, hopes and lies reinforced each other: the hopes gave rise to promises that were impossible to keep; the lies at first were meant to advance the promises' fulfillment and in the end could only serve to cover up the hopes' collapse.

I should state at the outset that my contemporary witnesses' reports must be taken with quite a few grains of salt. Some of their reports are patently untrue but inoffensive, such as when someone who under Socialism held an important post tells me that he never was a member of the Party. Usually, this type of lie quickly collapses on its own. In most cases, it is not mean to prevent me from uncovering the truth but to establish the trustworthiness of my conversation partner, who fears that I will not believe a former member of the SED. "I was not in the Party" means: "Don't write me off." But I don't write him off, whatever a witness's political affiliations, and I never ask whether someone willing to help me with my questions was or was not a member of the Party. The lie "I was not a Party member" always is offered without prompting from my side.

I am more likely to be led astray by another kind of lie—also well-meaning and also meant to safeguard a speaker's self-respect: the rosy recollections of a witness who needs to justify his former self both in his own and his conversation partner's eyes. In those cases, the unadorned account of my paper records may help to counterbalance personal memories that, like pebbles in a river, have been smoothed and polished over time. Frau Rüstig's recollections of her final examination at the academy for people's judges, for example—"all law; no politics"—are contradicted by documents found in the wood cellar that even list the topics of her papers on ideology. Her proud description of the bunch of roses presented to her by a grateful couple who had made peace after one of those optimistic reconciliation procedures urged upon divorcing couples in the early 1960s is put into question not only by Frau Rüstig's own admission but by an index card in the Lüritz archive recording the couple's divorce in the following year.

But the lies proper worry me; lies intentionally told to hide whatever the speaker would prefer me not to know. Sometimes I catch these lies with the help of another speaker's truthfulness. Frau Walter, for example, tells me about the "market promenades" of Lüritz applicants for exit visas in early 1988, but Herr Kosewitz, First District Party Secretary, whom I also ask about the protests, has never heard of them. Herr Kosewitz also cannot remember that Frau Christiansen, hard-working and straight-shooting Frau Christiansen (as Frau Rüstig told me), in 1965 had to leave the Lüritz bench and the city altogether because her son Lars, in an attempt to flee, jumped ship in the Mediterranean and drowned. "Was that not a promotion?" Herr Kosewitz asks, apologetically, when I remind him of Frau Christiansen's departure. No, Herr Kosewitz; it was a cold-hearted giving-the-boot to a loyal (and at the time, grieving) servant of the state. In this case, at least, I know what happened. But I will not be able to correct all misinformation with the help of other sources.

Sometimes, my own suspicions are stoked by the suspicions of the witnesses themselves. Gisela Nissen, for example, daughter of Ruth Nissen (director of the Regional Court in Neuburg) and in the final years of the GDR a young district judge on the Lüritz bench, warns me not to place too much faith in the police records of searches and seizures. The two "independent witnesses," she says, who under §113, para. 1 of the Criminal Code were supposed to observe the search, often were *Stasi* agents whom the police had brought along and who were told to wait on the sidewalk until, as "random pedestrians," they were called in to attest to the proper observance of procedures. Is the accusation true? I spend an afternoon leafing through a thick bundle of judicial confirmations of search-and-seizure protocols (one of the wood-cellar finds) and check the names and addresses of all "independent witnesses." As I can tell from street names and from the house or apartment numbers of people participating in the search, many "witnesses" were indeed bona fide neighbors or fellow tenants of the suspect. But among the roughly 150 searches undertaken by the Lüritz police in 1980, there are, admittedly, fifteen cases in which a witness was not just an accidental bystander: his name also shows up in other searches, undertaken in other parts of town. So here is someone who in one way or the other previously has cooperated with the police. But does that mean he is a *Stasi* agent? Are suspects accused of having stolen "one pair of dark blue gentlemen's trousers" or "forty-eight rolls of toilet paper" the kind of criminals "The Firm" would bother to keep track of? Could not the police have simply brought one of their own, to save the time and trouble of having to locate an "independent witness"? That would have been illegal, too, but less sinister than the involvement of the Secret Police. When, on one occasion, the police are confiscating genuinely political items on their search ("two Wolf Biermann posters; one handwritten page containing excerpts of UN articles, Helsinki Conference"), the protocol is signed by witnesses whose names and addresses I have never met before. Which does not mean that they may not be *Stasi* agents, after all.

I find a lot of other odds and ends in the Lüritz files that give me pause. Omissions, for example. In 1984, an *Asozialer* complains in his appeal to the Neuburg Regional Court that at his Lüritz trial the judge had berated him and shushed him up just because he had applied for an exit visa for the FRG. But when I check it, the record of the trial shows no exchanges of this sort at all. When, in 1986, Herr Taddäus (the former director of the District Court) is refused permission to attend a family celebration in West Germany and writes a long and angry letter to First Secretary Erich Honecker describing, in great detail, his disappointment with the Party and with Socialism, I find that letter, together with others of its kind, in a folder marked "Petitions" in the Lüritz archive. But Frau Walter's annual court statistics for 1986 lists under the heading "Petitions Dealing With Ideological Concerns": "none." Although I know from several "weekly reports" that, in the final years of Socialism, many prospective emigrants would beleaguer the court's "Information Office" to learn about the legal possibilities of leaving the country, the office's "Visitors' Book" makes no mention of their inquiries.

Yes, looking closely, I might discover similar white spots in West German court files. And even my suspicion that Party members receive better treatment from the court than average citizens might apply (with a slight change in the definition of privilege) to dignitaries in a Capitalist democracy. In 1964, for instance, a Lüritz locksmith—SED member and often-decorated "activist"—is given a one-and-a-half year prison sentence with probation for the long-time sexual abuse of his stepdaughter, while (also in 1964) an eighteen-year-old apprentice, for a very similar offense, is punished with fourteen months' worth of hard labor. The locksmith, a "model worker" and foreman of his collective, needs no deprivation of freedom to be successfully rehabilitated, my court declares. If Party members are prosecuted for substantial felonies (such as large-scale embezzlements), they usually are first expelled from the SED and then, upon conviction, are sentenced to what look like appropriate punishments for their offense. But in the case of lesser violations of the law, defendants with Party pins and offices do better in my court (or so it seems to me) than ordinary mortals. How suspicious is their treatment? In every legal system, a defendant's orderly and successful previous existence (which in the GDR included someone's Party membership) makes him appear more capable of rehabilitation than an undisciplined and shiftless life at the fringes of society. That cannot come as a surprise. I am more concerned about the legal problems of Party members that never come to my attention because they are resolved not by way of law but by politics and thus do not show up in court files.

This much is certain: the legal system of the GDR could not tolerate publicity. East German justice was more afraid of criticism and dissent; more fearful of curious glances of their neighbors or of the curiosity of citizens at home; more apprehensive about fresh breezes that might lift a curtain or flashlights that might shine into a corner than a justice system governed by the rule of law would be allowed to. Its secretiveness was easier to ensure. When, in 1982, the head of the Neuburg Housing Office is prosecuted for corruption in the Neuburg/City District Court, the Regional Court assures the Ministry of Justice in Berlin: "Measures have been taken to make certain that information about the trial will not leak out. There will be no press reports. The trial will be guided and controlled by us." "No extended public" at hearings in which defendants are likely to "make provocative statements," I read in an instruction from above. And in a Regional Court circular to its district judges of 1980: "We have repeatedly instructed trial courts" in sentences under §249 of the Criminal Code not to make mention of an asocial defendant's political motivation for his refusal to engage in useful work. When, in 1987, the nephew of a famous (or infamous) East German television personality, through large-scale bogus sales of desirable sporting goods, manages to defraud a large number of trusting Lüritz citizens and then escapes their restitution claims by going West, the Regional Court advises my judges not to inform his angry victims of his whereabouts but simply speak of an "unknown location."

The East German justice system was obsessed with secrecy. It played its cards close to the chest and passed on as little information as possible. In criminal trials that might reflect badly on political conditions in the GDR—flight attempts, cases of neo-Nazi hooliganism, sometimes even asocial behavior—the judgment was not handed out to the defendant but only given him to read and then returned to the safekeeping of the court. The reason: the Party feared that someone might send a copy of the sentence to a West German newspaper or television station. Since East German bureaucrats were Prussians and believed in order, the convicted man on those occasions would be given an official form to sign: "I herewith confirm that my sentence was announced to me today. I have received an instruction sheet informing me about the requirements for filing an appeal." "I do not care to read my sentence," an *Asozialer* in the fall of 1984 writes on the sheet—perhaps because he does not want to legitimize the procedure with his signature; perhaps because he has experienced it all too often. But even with respect to people whom Socialism ought to be able to rely on, it seems at times to find it necessary to protect itself by avoiding saying things in print. At a legal meeting in February 1988, for instance, Frau Kerstin, director of the

CHAPTER 9

Neuburg Appellate Court, only *reads* to the assembled judges in the audience "instructions made available by the Supreme Court relating to the deviant and unlawful behavior of certain persons or groups of persons in the GDR." It seems too risky to say more about the case in print. Only the mention of a judgment by Frau Kerstin ("against Müller and seven co-defendants") allows me to guess at the topic of her talk: she must have spoken of the recent violent attacks by right-wing skinheads on concert goers at the Zions-Church in East Berlin.

But relying on oral communications comes at a cost. Oral statements leave fewer traces than the written word but are more difficult to monitor by supervisory authorities. My judges must be constantly reminded to let defendants in politically touchy cases only read their sentence (instead of allowing them to take it home). A judges' conference in the spring of 1983 thus advises all attendants: "Please note: Sentence must be handed over to defendant for perusal. Defendant's acknowledgement of sentence must be recorded in file." A few weeks later, notes from an in-house meeting at my Lüritz court repeat the admonition: "Defendant *himself* must have read the sentence." Still, there seemed to be some chance involved in whether or not a defendant was allowed to take possession of the sheet of paper that spelled out how he would spend the next months or years of his life. Attention to another order of the Supreme Court (again, as far as I can tell, communicated only by word of mouth to its recipients) was also somewhat chancy: the rule that suits by applicants for exit visas contesting their dismissal should not—like other labor law disputes—be handled by the conflict commission in the plaintiff's enterprise, but should go directly to the District Court and, without oral argument, should be dismissed as "obviously unfounded." A former justice of the GDR Supreme Court once showed me the only written version of this order that I have ever seen: typed on a sheet of paper that bore no letterhead, no date, no signature, no mark that could have linked it to any GDR authority. The purpose of that order must have been the wish to guard against the criticism (by fellow workers or the world at large) that might have followed public knowledge of political dismissals. I can't believe that the court's attempt at secrecy did its intended job. But when, in 1984, a prospective emigrant's dismissal suit mistakenly is tried by the plaintiff's conflict commission and when, even worse, the plaintiff appeals his case to the Lüritz District Court whose labor judge is *not* informed of the dangerous political connotations of the case, the whole affair seems so embarrassing that the Neuburg Regional Court sends a humble and apologetic report about it to the Ministry of Justice in Berlin.

East German justice even hid its solicitude and generosity from public view if well-intentioned measures could reveal the mistakes or weaknesses that gave them cause. Some unduly harsh criminal sentences of my trial court, for instance, are not *overruled* by the Neuburg Appellate Court (which would imply an erroneous decision by the trial judge) but are corrected, *sub rosa*, as it were, by a Regional Court instruction to my district court that orders the defendant's "accelerated" consideration for probation. In such cases, the "good-conduct certificate" usually required for an early release should not hold the prisoner to "exaggerated" expectations of good behavior, writes the Appellate Court. When, in 1980, the Ministry of Justice issues an internal directive that authorizes state compensation for certain crime victims who cannot obtain redress from their attackers, one of my Lüritz judges finds herself in hot water when she encourages one such victim (half blinded by a vicious batterer) to apply for compensation under Directive RV 2/80. He follows her advice. By return post, the Ministry responds with heavy criticism for my judge: she was not authorized—so she is told—to encourage the victim's application since doing so "undermined the confidentiality of an internal ministerial directive." The victim should have been informed only once an application by the court was granted. A few months later, the Regional Court admonishes my judges, in a similar vein, to only *orally* inform those victims whose compensation claims had been denied. To pass out any written statements about the eligibility (or lack thereof) for compensation might encourage citizens to believe that they might actually be *entitled* to those benefits. The socialist state wants to look generous; wants to *be* generous, too, if it can afford to, but does not want to lose control over its own munificence. When a 1958 amendment to the Passport Law rescinds the penalties for certain border-crimes in order to encourage fugitives to return to the GDR, the Ministry of Justice tries to hide the intended leniency as well it can. "SECRET" says an instruction that is meant to explain the new policy to trial court judges. "Not to be passed on!" Thirty years later, the creation of "special brigades" for *Asoziale* (meant to at least partially replace the former punitive repression of truancy with therapeutic social care) is hidden from Western eyes as if it were a dirty secret.

In the GDR, even the humdrum instruments of any orderly administration of justice, the dates and figures marking the work day of the judges and administrators at my courthouse, were kept under lock and key. Apart from six meager pages in its Statistical Yearbook, the East German government published no judicial statistics. When Frau Walter, in October 1985, is asked by the Women's Commission of the District Party Leadership in Lüritz to provide data on the court's divorce adjudication, she must—officially—decline: she is "not authorized" to release divorce statistics. But she could provide the desired information orally, Frau Walter's letter helpfully concludes. The incident reveals that the GDR Justice Administration's insistence on avoiding paper trails not only facilitated but also undermined its own obsessive secretiveness: much information intended "for internal use only" will have been passed on not just "from hand to hand" but also "from mouth to ear" and thus spread further, and in more distorted fashion, than its originators ever had intended. With the result, I reckon, that much of the official decision-making in my town was based not on public knowledge but on rumors. Guidelines for the calculation of performance premiums and bonuses, for instance, often were only to be found in unpublished ministerial directives. Instructions by the Ministry of Justice that directed a judge's daily work were "for internal use only." In the court's ledger for "Incoming Matters," the fact than an inquiry or complaint concerned an application for an exit visa could only be deduced from a code number assigned to emigration issues. The social class of plaintiffs making use of the country's half-hearted and belated judicial review of administrative acts (introduced less than a year before the fall) was also identified in code.

Even the decisions of the GDR Supreme Court were shielded from inspection by the outside world. Beginning in 1977, the Court's case law was no longer published in book form (good paper was expensive and in short supply and the East German printing process too slow-paced to keep the volumes current) but in mimeographed booklets, usually five to six a year, that were distributed directly to the courts. Each issue of the *Informationen des Obersten Gerichts* (OGI or Supreme Court Information) was numbered (so its distribution to unauthorized recipients could easily be traced back to the original source of an indiscretion), and in the early years of the decisions' publication (if you can call it that) attorneys could consult Supreme Court case law only by studying the one and only copy of the *Informationen* that each attorneys' college in the country was assigned. In later years, the collection's distribution improved a little. But even then, a lawyer could not *cite* Supreme Court case law in his briefs since—thus the preface to the series written by the Court's President himself—"explicit references to the OGI in any publications or court decisions are not permitted."[45] Herr Mohr, one of three attorneys who in the 1970s and 1980s had offices in town, described the use of Supreme Court case law as "a permanent headache."

It was not the only headache caused by East German legal literature. Oh, the linguistic contortions of this judicial system! In the early years, when most of my Lüritz judges were unpolished and ideologically eager "people's judges," their language was professionally vague but politically unambiguous: as, for instance, in the description of defendants prosecuted for economic crimes as "parasites feasting on the people's labor" for whom "there was no use in our GDR." People's judges did not always find it easy to correctly use the new Socialist terminology. In one of my early labor law judgments that had called "human labor power the most important production power," for example, an inspector's red pencil has crossed out "production power" and replaced it with "productive power." But it seems to me that the pedantic correction missed the *Zeitgeist*. In its first decade, GDR legal language was made to mean just what the speaker chose it to mean. A report from the Neuburg Appellate Court on the social background of all 1955 offenders in the region, for instance, distinguishes between "real workers" and "workers" (with the result that the proletarian share of crime is reduced from roughly half to no more than about a third of all offenders).

In later decades, the linguistic dishonesty of East German law-speak loses its transparency. By and by, the rules for how to disguise legal realities with words become unarticulated but established custom. At a 1958 trial for "defamation of the state," Frau Christiansen still reads in court all of the defendant's objectionable political jokes to be included in the trial record. Six years later, in another criminal case involving witticisms at the expense of those in power, the Lüritz judge refers to the offensive jokes only with cautious circumscription: the defendant had "disparaged the Chairman of the GDR Council of State by using an expletive referring to the Chairman's appearance" (like most of his landsmen, he must have called Walter Ulbricht "the Goatee"). In 1980, finally, in the dismissal suit brought by Herr Orff, the cheeky booklet of jokes found in the plaintiff's desk is only mentioned discretely and fleetingly as "a collection of aphorisms."

In the Federal Republic, too, the legal language, especially of the 1950s and 1960s, was politically loaded and served not only to convey specific information but also to ideologically assert and justify the political context that gave rise to it. In a 1958 child support suit against a Lüritz father, for instance, who had left wife and child behind when he absconded to West Germany, the West German Magistrate Judge in Bad Dürckheim (who, by way of inter-court assistance, questions the father) speaks of the child's home country as "Middle Germany" and so implicitly denies not only the GDR's legitimate existence but also the postwar loss of Germany's former eastern regions to Poland. The Lüritz mother in her brief calls the GDR "the Eastern Zone," thus demonstrating her lack of faith in her own government. And the Lüritz Youth Agency, assessing the child's welfare, speaks of "our workers' and farmers' state." The three expressions stand for three different political world views. But while West German legal language, as the years wore on, gained in professional detachment, East German legal language perfected its political dissimulation. My judges become increasingly adapt at glossing over disagreeable facts and happenings. A 1964 criminal judgment, for instances, explains that the defendant "failed to appreciate the security measures of August 13, 1961"—in other words, he must have railed against the building of the Berlin Wall. In 1982, the Regional Court in one of its weekly reports to the Ministry of Justice in Berlin mentions a fugitive who was "injured in execution of his crime" and needed a leg amputation—he probably stepped on one of the land-mines that, almost until the end, secured the so-called deathstrip along the East German border. Toward the last years of Socialism, the euphemisms meant to paraphrase its undesirable realities are so banal and nondescriptive that they don't even any longer reveal the system's disapproval. If

CHAPTER 9

someone applies "for a permission for a change of residence," I know in which direction he plans to move. If in a labor law dispute the plaintiff was fired "for objective reasons," I can be sure that he had applied for an exit visa to the Federal Republic.

Sometimes, the choice of words meant to embellish or disguise a certain situation or a set of facts might almost be called brazen. A term much used in East German civil or criminal procedure, for example—"extended public" (*erweiterte Öffentlichkeit*)—referred to judicial hearings held before a specially invited audience of citizens who were thought in particular need of the lesson that the trial would convey: railroad workers, for instance, were told to attend the criminal trial of a colleague whose violation of safety regulations had caused an accident, or defaulting tenants were asked to witness the rent-collection case against an equally delinquent fellow tenant. The term "extended public" thus described an audience that was in no way widened or expanded but that on the contrary: that was intentionally *restricted* to those similarly placed as the defendant. The "public" thus created was not meant to supervise and check the proper use of state authority but rather was itself the *object* of state education and control.

Every once in a while, an unexpected ray of honesty enlightens the linguistic maze that I encounter in my records: when someone has forgotten, or simply does not want to take the trouble anymore, to embellish information that might be objectionable to official eyes. In 1974, for instance, a report from the Neuburg Appellate Court to the Ministry of Justice describes "the boilerplate protestations of their reverence for Socialism" by which some plaintiffs or defendants in divorce suits try to win the court's support. And once, in an endless position paper from the Ministry of Justice, a Freudian slip, like a flash of lightning, pierces the foggy text: instead of the established term used to describe the Berlin Wall—"anti-Fascist protection barrier"—someone has typed "anti-democratic protection barrier." Since nobody seems to have read the paper, though—its pages, as usual, are smooth and without blemish—nobody has corrected the mistake. The first time that I find "protection barrier" to be replaced by the plain "Wall" is in a Lüritz criminal judgment of 1988. Even then, the word is apologetically encased in quotation marks.

But that was in the last year of the GDR's existence, when the quotation marks no longer were meant to deceive the reader, but only to protect the writer against official disapproval. In the beginning years of Socialism in East Germany, the falsehoods uttered by my Lüritz judges were more energetic and more optimistic. It actually is a misdescription to call them "lies": for someone marching in the direction of a shiny future, even the gray present is bathed in a rosy light. In the dawn of the new state, my judges used the bench as a platform for announcing a new age and, in the process, focused on future glories more than on the problems of the present. In 1958, Frau Christiansen tells a criminal defendant that he "never had it so good in his entire life" because the East German Land Reform endowed him with his little "new farm" of twelve acres—never mind that the poor man had actually received two such allotments in succession and had been unable to make a go of either. Again Frau Christiansen, a year later, enjoining someone convicted of drunk driving to make more fruitful use of his leisure time: "There will come a day when the defendant no longer will be able to keep pace with the rapidly advancing technology of our agriculture if he neglects to acquire the necessary training."

These were the years in which the meetings of the SED District Leadership in Lüritz were concluded with the singing of the *Internationale* and when new agricultural cooperatives were given wishful dream-names such as "World-Class Standards" or "Free Life." Hope lay in the air. The Lüritz court was ruled by the conviction that men can be educated and that judges should do their part to prepare citizens by way of admonitions (and, if necessary, by way of threats and pressures) for life in a more perfect society. Socialist "new man" should be industrious, selfless, and thirsting for knowledge, should not be driven by consumerism and profit-seeking, should not be focused "on his own advantage," and should experience labor as a need rather than a burden. "The defendant misses out on life," a criminal judgment in 1959 sums up the existence of a stay-at-home housewife. In 1958, Frau Christiansen, in a sentence for multiple theft, tells the convicted man that, above all, "he must learn to work." "Then he will notice in a few months' time that work will bring him joy and will allow him to satisfy his needs."

Since my judges were no wild-eyed revolutionaries but despite their proletarian protestations were good-willed and solid citizens, their Socialist "new man," too, was supposed to be good-willed and solid: someone who led "a clean and proper life," who constantly improved himself "by reading good books and studying the current press" or by "attending cultural events such as plays" or concerts, and who, when chatting among comrades, would not tell "dirty jokes" or use "suggestive language" but whose "primary topic of conversation would be plan fulfillment." "New man" as painted in my judges' verdicts and admonitions looked pretty much like its old middle-class bourgeois cousin, cleansed of Capitalist self-interest and self-determination. The fundamental change in human nature that East German law aimed for in these years was driven not by civic hopes for a better future but by the very present political intentions of the government.

Nevertheless, even their modest educational goals caused revolutionary changes in the daily work of courts. In its first two decades—that is, in the years between the utopian optimism of the very early days and the slackening of ideological energy that had been boosted, if only temporarily, by Ulbricht's

CHAPTER 9

Programmatic Declaration of October 1960—GDR legal policy tried to instill human warmth and comradely concern into its judicial system. You might say that the Party wanted to "de-ice" the professional aloofness of the law and make the administration of justice accessible, trustworthy, and convincing to its addressees. The policy required judges who were close to the people; a simple and intelligible legal language; pedagogically sensitive procedures; the involvement of laypeople who could connect the parties and the court with the work collectives in which the legal disputes were embedded; and post-operative care by judges who even after rendering their judgment were available to help the participants to adjust to the court's decision and who spread its message.

The "people's judges," created in the first years of the new republic, fit in well with the new scheme. Unlike the middle- and upper-middle-class judges of a bourgeois state, they did not differ, in class background and education, from most of the people who sat before them on the plaintiff's or defendant's bench. Most of the privileges and insignia of judicial office were abolished by East German Socialism. During her years as Minister of Justice, Hilde Benjamin ("red Hilde") did her best to put an end to the traditional predominance of men in the German judiciary. In 1950, 15.3% of all East German judges were women; ten years later, the women's share had risen to 30.4% and, in Lüritz, to half of the six judges of the district court. By 1989, 51.3% of all trial court judges in the GDR were women. In 1954, judicial robes were done away with—much to the satisfaction of that new people's judge, Frau Rüstig, who (as she tells me half a lifetime later) wanted to win her pupil/citizen's support for Socialism not by way of "dressing up" but through education and persuasion. The new East German judicial policy also took care not to allow its functionaries' daily desk-work to blot out memories of what it meant to earn your bread by the sweat of your brow. In the late 1950s, the Party introduces campaigns of "physical labor" in the GDR that send all government officials, including judges and prosecutors, for several weeks a year to do their share in factories or on collective farms. In 1958, the Lüritz court receives official praise for having over-fulfilled its target of 200 labor hours by nearly 300% while, in addition, having taken "five acres of sugar beets under the judges' personal care." In the following fall, Herr Kellner, for three weeks, joins the crew of a trawler fishing in the Baltic Sea while Frau Christiansen spends (probably more useful) days working in an agricultural cooperative.

But even if its judges already lived the hopes of Socialism, the written law that they applied was, in most cases, still the law of the old codes inherited from the bourgeois past. Criminal law was an exception to this rule. To defend the state against potential Capitalist aggression and subversion, the criminal statutes thought to be necessary for the task had been passed early in the GDR's existence, in some cases even before the new state was founded in 1949. In October

1952—together with the Law on the Protection of People's Property (which we encountered in the chapter on criminal law)—the East German legislature passed a new law on criminal procedure that provided the rules for class war in the courtroom and gave the state great leeway in prosecuting its presumed opponents. The new Criminal Procedure Code permitted, for instance, the warrantless arrest of certain suspects; allowed the court to ward off uncomfortable motions for more evidence; authorized hearings behind closed doors if the court "considered it appropriate to exclude the public"; provided for trials *in absentia*; and legitimated the non-disclosure "of any fact and circumstance alluded to in the proceedings." The desire to educate "new man" had played no role in the drafting of these rules.

But in civil law disputes between law-abiding citizens (whom Socialism wanted to win over to its cause) my judges, until 1975, had to make do with the old German BGB (*Bürgerliches Gesetzbuch*, or Civil Code) of 1900 and the even older Civil Procedure Code of 1877 (*Zivilprozessordnung*, or ZPO)—codes that embodied Capitalist beliefs in individual autonomy and the legitimacy of self-interest and that resolved disputes between such interests in a formalistic play of legal point and counterpoint. These codes could be no help in structuring a trial that could thoroughly investigate a social conflict, identify its underlying causes, and prevent its recurrence. Socialist judges were taught not to look for "formal truth" in civil litigation—that is, for those factual bits of evidence that were needed to support or rebut the arguments of lawyers—but for the whole, the comprehensive, the "material truth," by which was meant a photo-realistic portrait of a conflict, including not only all its facts and circumstances but also its social roots and likely consequences. Only the thorough diagnosis of a conflict could lead to its effective therapy. Non-political crimes were dealt with by the same approach. If a defendant was to find his way back into the social mainstream, the judge, like a good doctor, had to probe the pathology of his former life. The very first sentence addressed to the defendant in a criminal trial was: "Describe to the court your own personal and social history." As one judge put it to me: "We started out at the primordial bog."

How do you penetrate to the primordial bog under the rules of bourgeois civil or criminal procedure? By interpreting these rules as expansively and as flexibly as possible. Already in December 1954, the Ministry of Justice had ordered GDR court libraries to be cleansed of all but the indispensable bourgeois legal literature. Apart from statutory texts and a few other basic volumes, each district court was to retain only *one* civil law textbook, *one* civil procedure commentary, and *one* BGB commentary on its shelves. It took a while before the Ministry's instruction was carried out—a 1956 inventory of the Lüritz court library lists among its holdings numerous titles from the bourgeois past but only a single year (1947) of the new East German law journal *Neue Justiz* (New Justice). One

CHAPTER 9

of the reasons for the book-laundering delay must have been lack of money. But the *interpretation* of the bourgeois rules that GDR courts, for want of new law, still needed to apply, under the guidance of East Germany's Supreme Court could be more easily adapted to the new reformatory purpose of a trial. Provisions that allowed the judge to get to the bottom of a dispute now were applied extensively. Provisions aiming for procedural economy by allowing the conclusion of a case without a thorough scrutiny of all the facts were read restrictively.

Here are some examples. The Capitalist judge's right to question parties before the court (*richterliches Fragerecht*) under §139 of the ZPO is turned into a Socialist *richterliche Fragepflicht*: the judge's *duty* to ask all questions necessary to lay bare the social structure and implications of a conflict. Bourgeois rules distributing the burden of proof between the parties (spelling procedural defeat for parties who do not meet their burden) are ignored because they allow the rendering of a decision without a total exploration of the facts. My Lüritz judges have little sympathy for testimonial privileges that obstruct the judge's efforts to get to the bottom of a case ("It is highly indicative that the defendant's wife resorted to her right to refuse to testify," I read in a 1952 criminal decision). Procedural deadlines are not taken very seriously: they speed up trials, but they bypass the thorough investigation of an issue. Until the last days of its operation, my court is generous with granting motions for deferment of a hearing: because a litigant is on vacation; because an attorney has to attend another meeting; because a summons allegedly was lost in the mail; and on one occasion—this is a legal system striving for human warmth!—because the prosecutor has a birthday party. If your goal is to untangle social conflicts, it indeed makes more sense to wait a bit than to insist on punctuality, which may only increase hostility between the parties. Sometimes, judicial even-handedness is motivated not by bourgeois principles of fairness but by Socialist concerns for the pedagogic impact of a trial. Frau Rüstig, for instance, tells me of a rape case she adjudicated in which both of her lay assessors had been women. The defendant, facing a phalanx of three women on the judges' bench, had complained about the court's likely gender bias. Frau Rüstig had gone and found two male lay judges to replace the female lay judges on the bench. What was her reason? I inquire. "Why, how could the man learn anything from his sentence if he did not trust the court?"

I wonder whether this story, too, over the years has been cast in a rosy light by Frau Rüstig's memory, because I find it doubtful that her defendants in those days could always be expected to trust their judge. Whatever the court's persuasiveness, however, the search for the "material truth" must have engendered a lot of extra work for my Lüritz judges. In the long run, the burden had to be too heavy to be carried every day. Instead of looking for the formal—the *legal*— truth, judges now had to come up with a persuasive factual scenario of a case. Their decisions, accordingly, contain few references to specific sections of a code, but lengthy and down-to-earth descriptions of the object of a legal fight: such as "a portable tile oven, new, conforming to the requirements established by the Production Association for rooms of the size and load-carrying capacity of the apartment in question." Consent decrees, judgments by defaults, and withdrawals of complaints—all types of resolutions of disputes that allow a bourgeois judge to quickly terminate a suit and move on to the next case on his crowded docket (after all, a party unwilling to fight for his or her own right deserves to be defeated)—now must include lengthy descriptions of the legal issues and the merits of a case to allow supervisory authorities to check on the social legitimacy of its outcome. In 1965, Frau Dankwarth justifies a labor law settlement (which obligates the employee-defendant to pay 150 Marks of compensation, in four installments, to his enterprise) with a *seven-page* single-spaced description of the controversy and its didactic disentanglement. Often, decisions are concluded with a moral commentary and some general advice: "The plaintiff would do well to draw a lesson from today's deliberations."

Some of my Lüritz records from the 1950s and 1960s read indeed like protocols of a successful teaching session; primarily those of labor law disputes, in which the favorite children of the system—blue-collar workers and their proletarian bosses—were amongst themselves. But civil law files, too, reflect the hope for social harmony. Procedurally, this is reflected in the fact that the court avoided contested judgments—that is, fights ending in the knock-out of one or the other party—and instead aimed for settlements. Bourgeois judges, too, prefer time-saving settlements to labor-intensive judgments. But Lüritz judges did not save time by talking the parties into compromises: they had to add extensive reasons to their settlements, and when I consider Frau Dankwarth's consensual case resolutions of these years—often hammered out in several intensely pedagogic hearings—it seems implausible that her efforts were motivated by procedural economy. No, she wanted to reestablish something like social peace between the parties. In 1975, the new East German Code of Civil Procedure replaced the term "settlement" with "mutual consent" (*Einigung*), thus stating plainly what the law was hoping for: no calculated splitting of gains and losses between the parties but the repair of human ties between them.

Judging by statistics, it looks as if the ambitious experiment succeeded. Not just in Lüritz, but in the entire GDR, a process of "legal warming" seems under way: the legal process is beginning to look less confrontational and more constructive. Civil and labor litigation is decreasing: between 1956 and 1968 (their lowest point in East German legal history), civil law caseloads of district courts fall by almost two thirds.[46] At least in court, East Germans fight less with their fellow citizens than their West German cousins do. In West German magistrate courts, over the decades, the share of settlements (that is, the bargained resolutions) among incoming cases drops while the share of contested judgments (fought to the bitter end) is on the rise. The opposite is happening in East German district courts: settlements (and, since 1975, "mutual consent" decrees) rise and contested judgments fall in number. In 1985, 43.3% of all civil law disputes in Lüritz are resolved "by mutual consent." In the same year, just 8.1% of all first instance civil cases in West German magistrate courts are settled in court.[47]

Legal disputing in the GDR seems to become not only more peaceful but also more personal in character. In the Federal Republic, civil courts function primarily as collection agencies enforcing money claims of creditors against defaulting debtors. Most plaintiffs and defendants have come into contact with each other by some impersonal transaction on the market. In Lüritz, on the other hand, many plaintiffs and defendants know each other closely, often more closely than they now would care for. Throughout the years, roughly 45% of all civil litigation takes place between ex-spouses, ex-cohabitants, other family members, neighbors, or colleagues. Since the records will not always tell me how well the parties are acquainted, the actual share of litigation between (former) friends and relations probably is even larger. Even exchange relationships have become more personalized. More than a third of all Lüritz lawsuits over money do not involve commercial debts but arise from private deals between ordinary citizens. The use of lawyers (who like a wedge might come between a citizen and his parental judge) is also on the wane. In 1979, only 15.3% of all civil parties and 5,6% of all criminal defendants in Lüritz are represented by counsel.

Are all these changes evidence of a new familiar warmth in the relations between citizens and state? Of course, one could think of other explanations for the figures I just listed. The East German drop in civil litigation rates, for instance, might just as likely (if not more so) be the result of the gradual disappearance of private property in a planned economy. The increase in personal (rather than commercial) litigation over debt collection might be due to the shortage of desirable consumer goods in a Socialist economy that forced Lüritz citizens to buy used items from each other rather than new merchandise from stores. The decrease of commercial suits against defaulting citizens might be caused by the fact that the Socialist consumer industry was not very interested in exacting payments from citizens that—for want of goods—a state-owned creditor could not profitably spend. If I want to find out whether the legal climate in my town has indeed warmed to a humanly more comfortable level (or whether the legal weather only has become more sticky and more close), I need to study my files more closely and in greater detail. Can I tell how my Lüritz litigants felt about the court's didactic efforts to better human nature, and whether those efforts affected their behavior?

My search for clues takes me, once again, into the wood cellar. Like all East German judges, my Lüritz judges, too, had to spend a considerable part of their daily efforts on the education of their clients. That education could take place in many venues: in trials staged before an "extended public" at the court or (less frequently because even more demanding of the judges' time and energy) at the enterprise or housing unit where the conflict happened: in discussions of a verdict with a defendant's work collective; in lectures about the law presented in schools, agricultural cooperatives, union meetings, garden clubs, what have you. The more undertakings of this sort, the better. The subsequent reports sent by my judges to the Regional Court in Neuburg are part of the wood-cellar treasures and give me some idea of what these meetings were about, who attended, and sometimes even of what was said in the discussions. Since in the 1980s, judges no longer had to send full-scale reports to their superiors in Neuburg but only had to fill in the blanks in a form provided by the Ministry of Justice, I know less about the judicial education sessions of the final decade of the GDR than about the sometimes enthusiastic and dramatic efforts of the early years. Often, I can only guess at what the audience thought about the meeting. What would I have thought had I been present?

Even from the far distance of another time and place, some of the lessons look reasonable and, possibly, effective. In 1961, for instance, on the occasion of a tort suit against a farm cooperative that was triggered by overloading a transformer, Frau Rüstig invites a network engineer from VEB Energy in Neuburg to present a talk on electrical circuits to the members of the cooperative. Many of the farmers "still felt uneasy about the handling of electrical equipment," Frau Rüstig writes. I am quite willing to believe that the invitation of the speaker, in Frau Rüstig's words, "also was desired by the cooperative."

Some educational attempts, on the other hand, foundered so dramatically that even my records cannot cover up the failure. In 1959, for example, Frau Christiansen, Frau Rüstig, and prosecutor Clemens organized a series of three public meetings at an agricultural cooperative to discuss the conviction of one of its members who had been prosecuted for the economic crime of feeding unsuitable fodder to the co-op's cattle (with the result that milk production fell and one cow died). To judge by the court's report, all three events were pedagogical disasters. The farmers in the audience claimed "that the cows' bloating due to wet feed was inevitable." They "exaggerated the objective difficulties of sheltering the cattle" (this was the period of the Soviet-inspired "open stabling" of livestock in the GDR, a policy that the Party would abandon in the 1960s). They defended their convicted colleague "in every respect." They refused to lodge a civil damage suit against him and declared that they would rather "bear the economic loss collectively." Yes, the new co-op members demonstrated solidarity—but of the wrong, the soft, forgiving kind by looking for excuses for their mate rather than for ways to criticize and fight his failings.

I try to visualize the meeting: about twenty farmers assembled by Frau Rüstig or Frau Christiansen in the "culture room" of their new collective farm, which the majority only recently had joined (most likely under pressure) and that the few remaining "individual farmers" in the audience still refused to recognize as their political home. In 1959, both judges were not yet forty: two young city women (a former cashier and an ex-cigar maker) who were lecturing the farmers, obstinately planted in their chairs, on how to feed their cattle. I don't know prosecutor Clemens' background (like the two judges, he was an alumnus of one of the early training courses for "people's judges"), but I doubt that he had much agricultural experience. All farmers present at the meeting must have felt the anger and resentment caused by the recent forced collectivization of East German agriculture. Is it surprising that Frau Rüstig's and Frau Christiansen's sermons fell on disbelieving ears? At the end of one of the meetings, Frau Christiansen asked the three or four remaining "individual farmers" in the room whether they now were willing to join the agricultural cooperative. No. Frau Christiansen's report on the event reflects the icy reception of her message: "Being informed of Comrade Walter Ulbricht's recent speech before the People's Chamber that linked the new Seven-Year Plan with the creation of the country's social wealth and thus the individual farmers' personal well-being, they chose to remain silent."

In later years, I find such open resistance to political indoctrination only occasionally in the statements of would-be fugitives whose arrest warrants, on the reverse side, carry the captive's own description of his attempted crime. Having been caught already, some suspects no longer took the trouble to conceal their alienation from the system. "I don't like this eternally being told to learn in our state," a sixteen-year-old boy says, who in August 1988 is apprehended, for the second time, trying to sneak across the border. But the solid citizens with jobs and families who make up the audiences that I encounter in my judges' public education sessions cannot afford to speak their minds. They deal more diplomatically with their teachers and simply say whatever they are meant to. Here is an example from a 1979 report on a court-initiated meeting discussing a spate of thefts at the convicted thief's workplace, the Phoenix shipyard: "All colleagues condemn the crimes and approve of the court's verdict and the educational measures that it entails. Each colleague considers it his or her personal obligation to strengthen Socialist property by contributing to the further prevention of crimes." And a similar report from the same year: "All members of the defendant's work collective drew serious lessons from his trial and will do their best to honorably fulfill their own obligations to society."

Who knows what a defendant's comrades thought when they pronounced assurances like these. Their statements sound more persuasive when it came to filling out that part of the court's questionnaire that asked whether members of the audience desired further lectures by a judge or prosecutor. The answer is not always "no." But if participants in court-initiated discussions about law do ask for additional information, it is always on legal topics that concern not the state's but their own personal interests, such as inheritance matters or divorce law. It also happens that an audience makes use of the presence of a judge by turning a legal propaganda meeting into a question-and-answer session on civic issues totally unrelated to the case at hand. The angry farmers at Frau Rüstig's and Frau Christiansen's meetings on state-approved methods of feeding cattle, for example, made use of the occasion to complain about the head of their agricultural cooperative, who allegedly ignored the village's concerns and already at noontime could be found in the village pub. Most answers to the question "Does the collective desire further instruction about the law?" though, are polite regrets: "Unfortunately, time pressures do not leave room for another meeting"; "not at the moment"; "no, because we already had a lecture about law two years ago." Often, the answer to this item on the questionnaire is left blank.

And how successful was the court in actually making peace between its clients? Originally, the search for what Socialism called the "material truth" was to prevent a judge from disposing of a case with legal arguments before he or she had made a thorough factual investigation of the social tensions that had given rise to the dispute. Hence the Socialist objection to default decrees and hence the judicial obligation to provide reasons even in cases of settlements or the abandonment of actions: the law wanted to be certain that the former opponents in a law suit had indeed made up. There was no way in which my judges could sustain the energy required for such an exhausting resolution of all legal conflicts. As caseloads rose, inevitably their judicial vigor began to flag. By the late 1970s, the Lüritz court, again, routinely ruled against defaulting parties without more than a cursory investigation of the issue. "Facts and circumstances sufficiently resolved," the judge would dictate for the record in these cases. Since such "absentee judgments," however, ran counter to the Socialist commitment to comprehensive justice, the court occasionally would save face by slapping the defaulting party with a fine for "flouting the dignity of the court by its provocative and unexcused absence from the hearing." Easier and less time-consuming than hauling reluctant parties, just so they could be educated, into court.

Yes, until the very end, East German judges avoided judgments and favored settlements or, as they would call it, "mutual agreements." They did so far more often than their West German counterparts. So was litigation in the GDR, after all, a warmer and more cooperative undertaking than under self-serving and contentious Capitalist justice? Not necessarily, since many "mutual agreements" seem to have benefited judges more than parties. As in the West, East German judges liked "agreements" because they saved judicial time and energy. They had additional incentives: a high percentage of non-contested case resolutions on its docket made an East German court look good to its superiors (who favored socially harmonious over zero-sum solutions), and settlements facilitated the enforcement of decrees in a legal system that was notoriously short of bailiffs. And while—unlike their colleagues in the FRG—East German judges had to support their settlements with reasons, *factual* justifications were considered good enough, and a judge presiding over the non-contentious resolution of a conflict virtually never had to produce *legal* arguments for her decision. As a result, my judges often leaned on parties to "agree." Many of the "agreements" in my files are so negligently structured and so loosely worded that they almost seemed to invite continued hostilities between the parties. A settlement in an inheritance dispute of 1979, for instance, reads: "The parties have agreed to try to reach a mutually acceptable way of dividing the estate." Or a property agreement of 1982 between divorcing spouses who, because of the general housing shortage in the GDR, had to continue life together in the marital apartment: "The parties both confirm that they have orally agreed on how to divide their common property, that they will stick to that agreement, and that they plan, in the near future, to put it into writing."

It does not look as if Herr Taddäus put a lot of effort into the resolution of the parties' quarrels. Moreover, since he and his Lüritz colleagues in almost all disputes that ended with "agreements" managed to talk the parties into waiving their right to later challenge the result in court—after first "suitably advising them" on the legal implications of a waiver, naturally—most "mutual agreements" were final and thus no longer had to worry the busy judge who engineered them. Even under their new name, East German settlements essentially were an important means of managing judicial caseloads.

I also discover that many Lüritz "agreements" (unlike most settlements under bourgeois law) do not cement a *compromise* between the parties whose negotiation, together with the required give and take, might have brought former adversaries together and fostered peace between them. Instead, in roughly one-third of all Lüritz "agreements" one side takes all, the other nothing. These are contested judgments in the garb of settlements. The reason for the disguise: the judge, after deciding for the winner, persuades both parties to reclassify the outcome of their suit as an "agreement" with the result that court costs are halved and that the judge no longer has to produce legal arguments for his decision but only a short factual description of the issue. The court saves time and effort—while the prevailing party goes home in triumph and the opposing party, I assume, is just as mad and upset at the outcome as losers always are.

I should apologize for spending so much time on so technical a subject as the different procedural avenues for terminating civil litigation. I want to show how, in the system's youth, its hopes for a brave new world, like fresh sap, made new green leaves spring from the law's every branch and how, when hopes dried up, rules that were meant to educate "new men" again took over the old function of procedural efficiency that they had held before the Socialist excursion into utopia. As a result, the East German goal of forging social solidarity by means of law over the years increasingly looked forced and artificial. Here is an example from the mid-1970s. An old lady sells a used bicycle for 150 Marks to a young man who learned of it in the "for sale" ads in the paper. Bike and money change hands. But the man's family is not impressed by his new acquisition, he regrets his purchase, and after a few days he returns the bike to the old lady and wants his money back. When she refuses, the buyer simply leaves the bicycle at her front door, goes home, and sues for the return of 150 Marks. The seller, understandably, will have none of it: "Our deal had been completed and Herr K. offers no reasons for his change of mind." But the judge, Herr Taddäus, does not throw out the cheeky suit. Instead, he talks the seller into offering the buyer a price reduction of 25 Marks (which the old lady pays on the spot) and closes the case not with a judgment for the seller but with the buyer's withdrawal of his suit. But it is unlikely that the discord between the parties has been pacified. The old lady must have bristled with annoyance as she left the court. The parties are even less connected than they were before.

My example is meant to illustrate that the legal "warmth" that Socialism claimed to have achieved was not the outcome of more friendly interactions between people but a creation—a fiction, rather—of the state itself, asserted and imposed by state actors on a largely passive public. In any case, official hopes for the transformative powers of the law were soon scaled back. Take the development of conflict commissions, for example: those lay tribunals that in the GDR adjudicated labor law disputes at the workplace. While the first Decree on Conflict Commissions of 1953 provided that the commissions' decisions had to be *unanimous*, the C.C. Decree of 1960 required only *two-thirds* of a commission's members to support its verdict, and only three years later the newly amended Decree of 1963 allowed decisions based on a simple majority of commission members. Apparently, unanimity in legal matters was too difficult to achieve even among class comrades to be a practical procedural requirement. Or take the fate of the "physical labor campaigns" of the 1950s. Here, too, reality took over after hopes had failed. In 1961, the Justice Administration in Neuburg informs my court that the annual stints of factory or farm work previously expected from every judge and prosecutor now should be performed only if they made actual economic sense. From then on, "physical labor" is no longer mentioned in my Lüritz files. I don't want to exaggerate the ideological importance of the issue. One reason for its introduction probably was practical rather than ideal: namely, the cheap procurement of labor for the state. Already in 1955, my judges could (and sometimes even had to) escape their blue-collar chores by paying 1% of their monthly salary into a "Reconstruction Fund"—a Socialist indulgence, as it were; demonstrating the judiciary's affinity with the working class. Nevertheless, the idea of physical labor obligations for everyone was borne

CHAPTER 9

from utopian hopes that wanted to imagine state officials in proletarian dress: in patched overalls and with calluses on their hands. By the mid-1960s, those fantasies had waned.

The disenchantment brought some progress, too. Here are two examples that can illustrate how the forward-looking, boisterous, and ruthless pedagogic style of the 1950s was gradually replaced by the law's cautious and circumspect didactics that insisted on keeping every aspect of a public education session under tight control. Two criminal trials, both carefully stage-managed and both almost identical as to the adjudicated violation of the law: an employee of the Lüritz shipyard was put on trial for embezzlement of union dues in one case, for the theft of work tools in the other. No heinous crimes, but nevertheless offenses that in an enterprise with 6500 workers and many opportunities to yield to temptation had to be energetically put down. Both trials were about deterrence. The first was run in a rough-and-ready, optimistic fashion. The second one, devoid of hopes to change the world, was far more moderate, but tightly regimented.

The first trial occurred in August 1952; two months before the Law on the Protection of State-Owned Property was passed and thus at the beginning of the political campaign meant to scare citizens into respecting the sanctity of public ownership. The hearing was scheduled to take place before an "extended public," and this time, for once, the term truly fit: the court convened in a gigantic hangar, holding 800 spectators, with an additional crowd of 2000 shipyard employees listening outside to the loudspeaker-amplified proceedings. I imagine the voices booming across the shipyard: the accusations of the prosecutor; the damning evidence detailed by the witnesses; the apologies of the defendant, who has no counsel but represents himself. If he had not been found out, he says—and the excuse blasts into thousands of ears—he would have returned the embezzled money by asking his mother to sell her house. The court's sentence in the Lüritz archive describes the audience's outrage at this subterfuge: "To cover up a crime with money is possible under Capitalism, but not in the GDR." "We've put an end to" the distinctions between wealthy and poor defendants. The sentence: two-and-a-half years of hard labor.

How can I possibly describe as "optimistic" a show trial that has the obvious function of driving the fear of God (in this case: of the Party and its laws) into a crowd of agitated listeners? The risks of scheduling a trial of this sort in front of almost 3000 people (of whom the two-thirds outside the hangar were practically uncontrollable) strikes me as too great to have been undertaken by pessimists. In opting for a mass event, the organizers must have been motivated by the conviction that most of the audience would side with the prosecution. In 1952, the public mood at the Lüritz shipyard was not just one of fear of further state repression, but also—especially at this place—one that must have been dominated by a new euphoria of equality that even in the last years of the GDR never quite evaporated. In other records from the 1950s, too, I find traces of the feeling that the time for the "little people" finally has come. By now, many East German citizens with social status and with money had gone West. Those who remained behind were more likely poor than rich. Many of them had welcomed the expropriation of the huge estates of the Prussian aristocracy and gentry, and the redistribution of their land among refugees and land-poor locals.[48] And there cannot have been many workers at the shipyard whose mother had a house to sell. I think it unlikely that the public scorn at the defendant's apologies for his offense was no more than an invention of the court stenographer. There must have been real anger in the crowd on which the organizers felt they could rely.

Maybe the contrast between this and the second case can spell out the differences that I have in mind. A criminal trial in November 1965, again involving a shipyard employee accused of having stolen "material" from the state and unidentified items from some fellow workers. Again, the court deliberates before an "extended public." The goal, this time, is not to persuade 3000 people of the inviolability of state property but to design a program for the three-day visit of the Vice-Chairman of the GDR Council of State, Dr. Heinrich Homann, that is to include the Lüritz District Court. The court's director participates in the planning of the event and writes to his superiors in Neuburg: on Dr. Homann's second day in Lüritz, "he will attend the trial of S., from the Phoenix shipyard, and have occasion to observe the demeanor of the social representatives taking part in the proceedings. It has been suggested that the trial should take place in front of an 'extended public' at the courthouse. As soon as we receive the dossier from the prosecutor's office, we will ask the shipyard management to select suitable participants. Prior to the visit of Dr. Homann, the comrades from the Council of State's Law Department will contact us to check on the state of our preparations, in particular, the preparations for the trial. I would recommend sending a representative of the Appellate Court to Lüritz to further advise and assist us, should the need arise."

So this was not to be a mass spectacle in open air, but a manageable hearing at the courthouse. No giant audience that included everyone, but a carefully selected group of "suitable participants." Homann's visit in Lüritz was meant to focus in particular on "problems connected with the implementation of the Justice Decree of January 1961,"—that very statute that by involving ordinary people in the work of courts was to transform East Germany's administration of justice into a civic enterprise. But already two-and-a-half years after the passage of the decree, the participation of laymen at this criminal trial is so carefully designed and staged that the invitation for Dr. Homann "to observe the demeanor of social representatives" sounds almost like an invitation to watch a performance of folk dancers. Nothing will happen at the show that had not carefully been choreographed by the producers.

CHAPTER 9

This procedural pattern prevailed into the 1970s and 1980s. The Socialist state wanted its law to be accessible and caring, but it also did not want to lose its grip on anything that happened in the courtroom. And so the human features of this legal system were carefully orchestrated and put on show. "Spontaneous" meant "uncontrolled" and thus something that had to be avoided. When in the winter of 1975, Herr Taddäus, the director of the District Court, is asked to present a report on "rowdyism" at an upcoming plenary session of the Supreme Court, the invitation is meant to demonstrate the justices' respect for the experience and the wisdom of trial judges. But that does not mean that Herr Taddäus himself decides what he will say. The Appellate Court in Neuburg sends a lengthy paper "to assist in the preparation of your contribution." "Despite inclement weather," a Supreme Court justice comes by car all the way up from Berlin to be present as Herr Taddäus' speech is discussed and polished at the Lüritz courthouse. The text that the District Court director, during his fifteen minutes in the sun, finally *reads* before the assembled High Court justices in Berlin (it would be far too risky to extemporize) no longer discusses anything but simply reaffirms, in eager platitudes, his and his judges' loyalty and commitment to official legal policies.

The event repeats itself when, in 1987, the new director of the District Court, Frau Walter, is ordered to present a paper on Lüritz experiences with trials before "extended publics" at the GDR Ministry of Justice in Berlin. Ordinarily, Frau Walter thinks that the efforts needed to round up an "extended public" are a waste of time. She'd make exceptions only in those cases in which concrete and identifiable groups of people might learn something from a specific case: such as the members of the "Traffic Safety Action Group" of a Lüritz enterprise whom she had invited in 1986 to attend the criminal trial of one of the enterprise's drivers, who had caused a serious accident. But virtually nothing of Frau Walter's first draft of her little talk—a cautious attempt to distinguish between sensible and not so sensible exercises in judicial pedagogics—survives the objections of the Regional Court and the concerns of the gentlemen from the Ministry of Justice, who, this time too, come from Berlin to make sure that Frau Walter's talk conforms to expectations. The front page of the final version of her talk (a wood-cellar find) lists the various censors who insured that nothing untoward would offend the Minister: "Based on consultation with director of Regional Court. Additional consultants: Division 3 [of the Ministry of Justice]: Dr. Christoph, Dr. Dankwarth. Inspectorate: Dr. Mücke." As usual, the text—despite its by now perfect banality—is not made public. A little note, attached to Frau Walter's talk, warns: "Attention: not to be circulated! After reading return to Division 6." Many years later, Frau Walter tells me that the Minister, for a few minutes, involved her in a very affable chat. She had felt very superfluous, she says.

But even if it is difficult to find a "new man" in my Lüritz files, the men and women who populate my legal history, at the end of its four decades, no longer are who they were at the beginning. The are not "new" but different: not more free, more self-assured, more hopeful, or more concerned about the social welfare, but shaped, nevertheless, by the political system to which they had to conform for forty years. If, at the beginning, their world had been chaotic and full of possibilities, it is now confined and orderly. As Herr Taddäus told me (and others, too: attorney Mohr, for instance, ordinarily something of a free spirit, I should think), the narrowness of life in the GDR did not trouble him. "But I was annoyed by the evidence of heartlessness." A curious choice of words, considering that Herr Taddäus was talking of the state, in whose body politic I would not know where to find the heart. But "heartless," in the GDR, was a much used term to describe how the administration should *not* treat its citizens. The justice apparatus, too, did its best not to appear heartless to its clients. A large part of my court's working hours, for example, were spent on locating the addresses of fathers in arrears with child support, whose ex-wives or former girlfriends were too helpless (or too lazy) to find them on their own. In criminal trials, East German courts investigated a victim's possible claim to compensation for harm suffered at the court's own motion and helped a victim to enforce this claim, often reminding him or her repeatedly to apply to the civil court for its enforcement against the perpetrator. Every Friday evening, judges gave free legal advice during "judicial consultation hours" at the courthouse. If someone was unable to attend these sessions, the court would advise a questioner in writing. When, in 1989, an out-of-town plaintiff writes to the court to ask for information about train connections to Lüritz and, since the hearing may be lengthy, for the reservation of some place to spend the night (hotel rooms were often hard to find in the GDR), long-suffering Judge Neumann complies, again, and finds a room for the plaintiff in the Lüritz "Seamen's Home."

Theoretically, my judges were to show care and solicitude to good people and to bad; to those observing the state's laws as well as to those who broke them. In a 1977 circular, the Supreme Court reminded its trial judges of the need to be patient in criminal trials, too: "Properly structured hearings avoid the hectic atmosphere that is the result of pushing for supposed procedural rationality and economy. Deliberations that are rushed make it impossible for the participants to speak their minds and to discuss their problems." The admonition may well have been necessary since the quest for familiar warmth in Socialist courtrooms could go hand in hand with the cold and distant treatment of those who did not fit in with the collective. My judges were patient and considerate with the old and frail; even with cranks who litigated over trifles. But not with applicants for exit visas. Socialism liked *dependent* people. The *independent* people were the ones that it found hard to stomach. Criticism was welcome if it presented itself as a plea for help. When my district court does not receive a single letter of complaint during the entire year of 1972, the Regional Court in Neuburg sends a worried letter to ask "why the citizens of Lüritz did not turn to the court for help with their concerns." This was a symbolic, not a literal question. Most complaints directed against courts in the GDR addressed delays in issuing copies of a verdict or enforcing it, problems which the courts—forever short of typists and of bailiffs—were in no position to resolve. As a result, it was not very sensible to waste one's time complaining to a court. And since the courts had nothing to give away—no money, no apartments, no political influence, no exit visas—they (unlike most other government authorities in the GDR) received few petitions and complaints. The Lüritz court had to deal with between fifteen and twenty grievances a year; sometimes even fewer. Nonetheless, its annual "Analysis of Citizens' Complaints" served as important proof of the court's closeness to its clients. Even in 1972, the year without complaints, the court submits an "Analysis" of citizens' grievances to the Appellate Court in Neuburg.

This state so greedily was looking for evidence of its own warmth. Complaints served perfectly to demonstrate official care because they offered an occasion, but not a legal obligation, for the authority complained about to help. Complaints also brought citizen and state into immediate contact. The petitioner was probably irritated and annoyed but—in the language of the system—"trustingly" turned to the parental agency on whom he knew himself to be dependent. Accordingly, it was a good idea, when dealing with Socialist authorities, to write complaints yourself, in awkward, everyday vernacular, rather than to employ a lawyer to assist you. When once, in 1986, a lawyer submitted a complaint for his client, an old lady, directly to the East German Ministry of Justice, the reaction in the Ministry resembled the flustered irritation parents might have felt had their children conveyed their birthday wishes with the help of legal counsel. "This is not my idea of a lawyer's job," the official in charge had written in the margins of the file, and his superior had agreed in an addendum: "The complaint procedure is meant to allow a citizen to personally submit suggestions, criticism, and ideas to state authorities. A submission loses its character of 'complaint' if it is placed by legal counsel acting on behalf of someone else." In other words: the personal relationship between state and citizens has no room for intermediaries and certainly not for intermediaries so well versed in contradiction and dissent as lawyers are. "Yes," the Minister himself had written with green ministerial ink beneath the comment.

Many of the Lüritzers whom I encounter in my records seem to share this view, or—put more cautiously—at least seem to behave as if they felt tied to the state in a very personal manner. They expected state care without the need to offer something in return. For instance, even well-to-do people often would pay their rent late and even then only after considerable pressure: perhaps because they thought that the state owed them housing, anyway; perhaps, too, because East German rents were kept so low that they seemed no financial equivalent for the use of an apartment but rather looked like pedagogically motivated deductions from one's pocket money. Often, debtors justified arrears with reasons that seemed to imply the creditor's indulgence. "Since moving [five years ago!] into my current flat, I had to deal with problems affecting my financial discipline," says a defendant in 1989, who was supposed to pay a monthly rent of 21.80 Marks, and the excuse sounds like the self-diagnosis of an illness that the state's housing industry was meant to cure. "The missing shifts can be explained with my personal problems," says a cleaning lady who, in a period of two months, failed to show up at work on thirty-four days. "Due to my personal unstableness and inattentiveness I often run into problems and therefore would like to ask you help me solve my difficulties," says someone owing 1003 Marks in unpaid electricity bills and the VEB Energy, having finally brought suit, indeed agrees with an installment plan allowing the defendant to pay back his debt in gentle increments. It is easy to find many similar excuses: "I already told you that my son has kidney problems" (the mother of a young man with substantial debts to his Savings and Loans); "I'm used to a more modern flat" (an *Asozialer*, complaining about the apartment that he had been assigned after his release from prison); "I think that with some good will and [a] little bit more patience with me my dismissal could have been avoided" (a driver who was fired by his enterprise after missing 150 working hours).

But a citizen who expects lenience from his state (and often finds it, too) is in no position to also insist on his rights. Parental warmth and patience come at a price: submission to the parent's authority. One example: although under East German criminal procedure the accused could refuse to testify at his own trial, I have found in hundreds of criminal case files only two defendants who actually did so—one of them a foreigner. "I would not have advised my clients to stay silent," confirms attorney Mohr. Ingenuous trust was a more useful attitude to adopt than obstinacy. And so I find withdrawals of confessions, too, only in the very last volumes of my Lüritz files. Socialism liked confessions. They were seen as the first step toward a culprit's understanding and reform: his acceptance of the moral legitimacy of the state's authority. Renouncing one's confession was equal to taking back that step and thus to making it impossible for a caring state to accept a sinner back into its arms. A criminal defendant hoping for leniency was advised not to chose so ornery a strategy. It took until 1988 for the GDR Supreme Court to even consider the possibility that some confessions might be due to pressure and thus, in one of its guidelines, to command its judges not to make light of their withdrawal.[49]

Instead of evasive actions by suspected perpetrators, I discover, in their arrest files, the very opposite technique of dealing with their captors: some of the freshly apprehended might confess to *more* crimes than the police already knew about. "I also faked two checks that I cashed in Neuburg," someone caught red-handed

CHAPTER 9

and arrested for check fraud might admit. "But that now really is the lot of it," says a petty thief in 1980 after informing the police of four additional items he had stolen when he was arrested. Now he had made a clean breast of it all.

Instead of insisting on their rights, many of my protagonists, in a blurrier and more comfortable way, hope for protection and indulgence. It happens, for instance, that the loser in a civil law suit does not *appeal* the judgment that defeated him (sometimes because he was too lackadaisical about a deadline), but instead attacks the outcome by way of a *complaint*—assuming that, after all, the state rather than the law should have the final word in matters that affect his welfare. In 1979, a woman who no longer is satisfied by the property division between her and her ex-boyfriend, which she had agreed to, complains to the Supreme Court: "I just don't understand how such a law [in this case: the procedural rules that finalized the agreement between the former cohabitants] can be valid in a state like ours where we are always told that everyone will receive the help he needs." In 1977, a woman accuses the judge who recently presided over her divorce not to have done enough to save her marriage: "Why did the court accept the behavior [of her husband and his new girlfriend] as immutable instead of using its authority to try to lead my husband back to his family?"

From counting on the state for help, it is only a little step toward accusing it of having failed to properly support or supervise a citizen and thus to have contributed to his stumbling. In a shop meeting to discuss an employee's attempted "flight from the Republic," one of the culprit's workmates says in the early 1970s: "One should have paid attention to him long ago." Another: "This act could have been prevented if only one had intervened more quickly." And a third: "We think that our city government does too little. A year ago, the City Council contracted with our enterprise to get involved in the education of three of our colleagues. But it took almost nine months before the Council did anything." In 1988, a criminal defendant's appellate brief asserts that the Lüritz judge did not assign some of the responsibility for his offense to the state's unsatisfactory reintegration efforts after the culprit's previous convictions: "The court did not consider that the lion's share of blame should go to the City Council's Labor Division."

Sometimes, the almost familiar ties between citizen and state that my files reveal can lead to surprising forms of cooperation between the two. I encountered few denunciations in the Lüritz records. But of those I found, almost all came from parents whose grown or half-grown children had gotten into bad company or were playing with the dangerous idea of going West and whose own authority was not enough to keep their children on the straight and narrow path of Socialist behavior. Yes, the parents' tips informing the police about their children's misbegotten plans almost certainly lead to their arrest and consequent conviction for "asocial behavior" or attempted flight. A better outcome, a desperate father or mother may have thought, than see your child corrupted by sloth and drink or to have it shot while trying to sneak across the border. In a state obsessed with the education of its citizens, it is not far-fetched if the authorities of family and state cooperate to reach the pedagogic outcome wished by both.

Sometimes, East German citizens' expectations for a warm and caring law even exceeded the state's own intentions. A number of complaints addressed to the Ministry of Justice in the 1980s, for example, attacked the perceived aggressiveness and greed—in other words, the "Capitalist" behavior—of attorneys. "I hope you'll steer Socialist law again onto its proper track," a recently divorced man writes in 1987, outraged by his wife's attorney's combative behavior. "In my opinion, lawyers should not act that way." In the spring of 1989, the losing party in a civil case complains about the fact that that his opponent's lawyer had been unwilling to look for an agreement: "At the hearing, he was uninterested in any compromise or rapprochement between the parties. Rather than look for mutual understanding, he claimed that the divisiveness between the parties was beyond repair. I was quite shocked to see that there is room for such behavior in our judicial system." Evidently, the authors of these letters were themselves formed by a law focusing more on social harmony than on social conflict. The Ministry of Justice—which in earlier years itself had told attorneys never to forget that they had to serve not just their clients but also the interests of society—now, at the eleventh hour, always rejects complaints about the ardent advocacy of attorneys. The statement of one lawyer, asked by the Ministry in 1987 to comment on the accusations raised against him, could just as well have come from an attorney in the West: The complainant overlooks "that I, as counsel for Herr S., have the obligation to represent, and solely represent, Herr S.'s own interests."

The popular suspicion of lawyers that my files reflect can serve as an example of how Socialist legal culture, over time, changed the perceptions of its citizens; changed them more, even, than the Party, in its final days, might have liked to see. This is nowhere more obvious than with respect to so-called asocial citizens. GDR law was extraordinarily effective in teaching widespread contempt for bums and truants. Admittedly, the social exclusion of *Asoziale* has a long, and under Hitler, a murderous, tradition in German legal history.[50] But Socialism combined this tradition with its own education-, improvement-, and work-obsession in a manner that to this day has left lasting marks on East German public opinion. Trying to reconstruct what might be called the "legal mentality" of my Lüritz subjects from the files, I am not always certain of my story: Are my sources reliable? Do I read them right? But I have no doubts about my *Asozialen* data. The texts are indisputable: most references to "asocial citizens" reflect contempt. To the good folks of Lüritz, they were outsiders and parasites.

In the last years of Socialism in the GDR, that view was no longer shared by the East German leadership. We saw in the criminal law chapter of this book that

CHAPTER 9

by the mid-1980s, justice authorities in Berlin had begun to doubt the effectiveness of a policy trying to beat labor discipline into disorganized and shiftless people with the help of law. Instead, they looked for therapeutic ways of dealing at least with those of the chronically unemployed who were too helpless and too unstable to on their own adapt to social norms. But by this time, most regular people were no longer willing to endorse reforms. The Party might have despaired over its own *Asozialen* policy. "That we just couldn't come to grips with it!" Frau Nissen, formerly director of the Regional Court, said to me, still not quite believing that Socialism should have been unable to handle a problem that so crucially affected its central values. But the protagonists of my Lüritz files were convinced that an iron hand was needed to return habitual shirkers to the workplace. The population "counts on the police and justice apparatus to address this issue," the regional court reports to the Ministry of Justice in Berlin. Especially during the usual post-mortems of an *Assi*'s criminal conviction at his place of work, the members of his former work collective call for law and order. Sometimes they mourn the fact that East German criminal law no longer uses methods of repression that might be usefully applied to work evasion. "We shilly-shally far too long before reacting to these kind of people," someone says in 1985. Another critic of state lenience toward *Assis* does not speak of "people" but of "elements": "Asocial elements are treated too humanely in this country." The faceless term is often used in the discussion. "It would be best to educate work-shy elements in those temporary labor camps which unfortunately no longer exist in our Republic," I read in another in-house debate of a workmate's conviction under §249 of the Criminal Code. In May 1981, on the occasion of an enterprise festival in Neuburg, a crowd of people gets together in a "public forum" to vent their collective anger against the *Asoziale*. It is a spontaneous and, in so far, truly democratic event—the people's wrath demanding to be heard. The speakers make no bones about their anger at the courts' excessive "lenience" towards shirkers: the judges "don't have the same experiences as we. If they did, they would deal differently with the *Assis*."

The accusation is correct insofar as the absenteeism of one member of a work collective affected the plan performance of all others, with the result that the conscientious workers in a brigade either had to work harder (to make up for the missing output of their mate) or swallow the loss of earnings that the brigade in its entirety would suffer for having missed its target. A judge's work had targets, too (so many hearings, so many legal propaganda events, etc. per month), but her plan performance did not depend on the cooperation of her colleagues. Still, the general contempt for the *Assis* in the GDR strikes me as too raw and virulent to be explained solely by the financial interests of some. The explanation, I believe, lies deeper: in people's disappointment with the broken promises of Socialism. That applies both to rulers and to ruled.

For the East German Justice Administration, the existence of an army of idle, alcohol-dependent drifters unable to hold down a job must have been a double defeat: Socialism neither had managed to reeducate and integrate some of its weakest members nor had succeeded in convincing ordinary people that *Assis*—now called "problem citizens"—needed patience and forbearance if they were to become useful members of society. A Lüritz judge once told me that she had been grateful to be able to blame her court's supposed "lenience" with truants on the guidelines of appellate courts: that way, she had been able to deflect a bit the public's anger at freeloaders and parasites. The Neuburg Regional Court, in one of its weekly reports to the Ministry of Justice, described its trial courts' dutiful attempts to follow official *Assi* policy in this way: "In cases [involving asocial behavior], the judges do their best to represent the principles of fighting work evasion as a social task."

It is difficult to say whether my Lüritz judges themselves believed in the more moderate official *Asozialen* policy of the 1980s. At least some local office-holders clearly shared in the popular disdain for *Assis*. In 1987, for example, the District Court has to decide a criminal case against seven members of the Lüritz police department who on their daily beat had used their powers of investigation to stop and frisk local drifters, pick their pockets, extort payments from drunks, and then "equitably divide" the loot among themselves. At the trial, one of the defendants admits that to them, "problem citizens belonged into a lower category of humans." He and his comrades also "hated" them because of all the trouble *Assis* caused for the police. The prosecution has collected evidence on forty-seven instances of theft by the defendants, and the court's penalties strike me as mild: seventeen months of prison for the leader of the group (of which he serves not more than half); suspended sentences and fines for the six others. Where are the "Socialist new men" among the perpetrators, or their victims?

The loathing that ordinary people felt for *Asoziale*, I believe, was rooted in the deprivations of their own lives. What had Socialism done for them? Here is the statement of a twenty-four-year-old blue-collar worker from the Lüritz shipyard, caught in September 1988 as he tries to sneak across the border to West Germany: "These are the reasons why I wanted to get out. At home, I have difficulties with my mother. I can't get an apartment. And for my wages I cannot buy things that I'd really like to have and if there is something to buy, it takes enormous legwork to get hold of it. At work, we're pressured to make 'solidarity contributions' [to various Socialist causes]. And if you don't pay, the foreman says: 'You'll see what that will get you.' I also think there shouldn't be so much pressure to join the SGSF [Society for German-Soviet Friendship]. They tell you: everyone has joined and you shouldn't stand aside. At work, people's punch-cards in the morning are punched by their buddies while they haven't even come to work."

CHAPTER 9

A potpourri of discontent, which in the speaker's case might have contained more indigestible ingredients than in the case of those of his landsmen willing to stay home, but that to all East German citizens must have tasted only too familiar. The people uttering contempt for *Asoziale*, it seems to me, looked at their own confined and modest way of life and could not understand why someone who had not adapted to the strictures of Socialism should have the same claims to be supported by the state as they did. They also may have felt envy for the freedom of bums and loiterers and for their cheeky disregard of state controls. Like in the story of the prodigal son, honest and upright citizens were filled with indignation at the father's attention and concern for the black sheep in the family.

Had it not been the father himself who, since as far back as they could think, had preached to his good children the importance of hard work and discipline? "I must work every day to earn my living," an outraged woman once says at the criminal trial of a neighbor prosecuted for truancy. "How can it be tolerated that in our social system someone can get away with never holding down a proper job?" "Why isn't someone with such enormous debts simply forced to work?" a petitioner writes in 1989. Here is the particularly illustrative statement of a participant in a work collective, asked in 1980 to comment on the prosecution of a nineteen-year-old former member who—as he did not work—could not pay his debts but who otherwise had caused no harm to anybody: "It is degrading for the colleagues who every day loyally do their work for the Republic to have to watch how a young man who has been raised in our state feels perfectly at ease while living an asocial life." It is the "ease" at which the colleagues take particular offense. They feel "degraded" because their own obedient submission is put into question by the happy parasitism of the young defendant. I can detect no hopefulness in the *Asozialen* files; only tiredness and disappointment.

There are objections to be raised to this description. Usually, East German criminal and civil records are peopled not by the successful members of society but by those with problems, who may have many reasons for their disappointments. The not-prosecuted, not-dismissed, and not-divorced good citizens of Lüritz may have been more content with life under Socialism than those coming into contact with the law (and hence, with my Lüritz project). As a result, my picture of legal life in Lüritz in the final years of Socialism may be too depressed, too dull, too conforming to what Westerners would expect in any case. I have to admit that I encountered in my sources few Lüritz protagonists with social status, academic education, money, or influence. My records do not tell me what the well-to-do and well-adjusted citizens of Lüritz thought about the law. On the other hand, my records also contain next to no evidence of any skirmishes with the law that Lüritz notables might have engaged in. Only as late as 1985—no, even later—the so-called better folks of Lüritz (*die besseren Leute*) begin occasionally to show up in the Lüritz files. Until then, they are conspicuous by their absence. My records do not tell me whether or not they made their peace with Socialism. If they objected, they objected not vigorously enough to end up making an appearance in the Lüritz criminal case files. It seems likely that Lüritzers with good jobs, supportive bosses, and harmonious families had access to extra-judicial ways of circumventing or softening the restrictions of Socialism.

In any case: up to the eleventh hour, most cases of open confrontations between citizen and state that I discover in my Lüritz files tend to involve outsiders, youngsters, or *Asoziale*. Most of their attempts to counter the broken promises of Socialism with hopes and projects of their own were unplanned, unprepared, and unrestrained by practicalities. Before the final years, even "political offenses"—such as "resistance to state authority" or "flight from the Republic"—usually were not motivated by principled and reasoned opposition to the Party. It is rare that I encounter declarations like this statement of a student who in 1984 is arrested at the border: "I wanted to get out because I have no personal freedom in the GDR; because I cannot openly ask questions; because I don't get honest answers." This is a serious challenge to the system and is treated accordingly. The young man's lawyer—it is clever Herr Arhuis from Dorndorf—admits everything, doesn't make the slightest attempt to bargain for a lighter penalty, and hopes that his client will be included in the West German ransom policy exchanging prisoners for cash.

This is not to say that the majority of flight cases in the Lüritz archive had nothing to do with the political situation in the GDR. They all were triggered by the fugitive's longing for a better life; a longing of which hunger for freedom was a powerful ingredient. The hunger was impatient and intense, perhaps because most of these defendants were so young. Socialism was harder to take for young people than for old. People with jobs and families experienced not only the limitations of the system but also its blessings: health care, job security, child benefits. The young and unattached saw only the limitations and controls preventing them from following their hopes and dreams. A bricklayer, accused (together with two friends) of having engineered a poster campaign intended to force the state into granting him an exit visa, says in 1984: "I am now twenty-three years old and have not had a lot of good things happen to me so far. One can't reproach young people like us for the past. We live now, and that's the only thing that counts for me. I hate this entire system. I almost hate myself because I cannot move freely where I want to." The reader senses the despair of the young man; understands his rage against a state that will not let go of him. He describes precisely what is wrong with it: "Here, you don't have the right to be yourself. Everyone has to submit to the Socialist community." But the speaker has illusions, I believe, about not having to adapt in other societies. Most fugitives

CHAPTER 9

whom I encounter in the files long for unrestricted freedom. They hope to find a land of endless possibilities on the Wall's other side. Go West, young man! "In the GDR, I am not allowed to build the life that I imagine," says a sixteen-year-old girl, who in 1982 attempts to flee in order to "run a horse farm in Texas." One of the lay assessors at her trial asks where she would look for Texas on the map. "In America or Africa. I am not sure."

How can the West fulfill such boundless expectations? In the late 1970s, a young mason tries twice to escape across the border, lands in prison both times, is finally ransomed by the Federal Republic, is allowed to emigrate, and finds a job and an apartment in Hamburg. But the apartment is small, the job is more confining and monotonous than he had expected, and in 1978, the East German People's Police arrests him for the third time as he tries clandestinely to cross the border, this time from West to East, to return to the GDR. A picture is stapled to his file: a young man with a head of black curls laughs into the camera of the police photographer. He is bare-chested, so the photographer can also make a record of his various tattoos: across the young man's chest sails a tall ship, fully rigged, and on his arm, a skull, pierced by a dagger, displays the caption "Better Dead Than Slave." This time, he is sent to the *Stasi* prison in Berlin. As in many cases involving *Asoziale*, I cannot find the white sheets of a post-1989 rehabilitation judgment in the folder: perhaps because, like other would-be fugitives from the days of Socialism, the young man, now released, could not afford a lawyer to represent him in a Capitalist court; perhaps because, even under the rule of law, people like him remained too marginal to turn to the law for help.

Not all East German fugitives were quite as unrealistic and impetuous as the young horse farmer and the mason. But most runaways who actually tried to cross the border fortifications between East and West (the *Sperrbrecher*) resembled those two rebels in their youth, their impatience, their complaints about the boredom in the GDR ("Everything here is so boring and so normal," says another sixteen-year-old caught at the border), their yearning for "all the nice things" in the Federal Republic, and their unwillingness to adapt to the crusty rules and regulations at home. I have the strong suspicion that they would rather not adapt to any regulation. Many would-be fugitives have records of previous collisions with the state; mostly for petty theft or truancy. A surprising number of the apprehended wanted to escape because in the GDR they were not allowed to go to sea. In the 1960s, it was the Foreign Legion which to these young people looked like the embodiment of worldwide adventure and of freedom. In the 1980s, it is the life at sea. "In the Federal Republic, I would be doing deep-sea fishery," says someone with 5500 Marks of unpaid debts and three previous convictions when he is arrested. Would he indeed? In 1988, a hapless runaway explains his plans to the examining judge: "Here's what I thought: that they would assign me an apartment, I'd get a job, and start a new life." The following year, a seventeen-year-old apprentice described his pie in the sky: "I thought if only I got out, that all my problems would be solved." The Federal Republic as the land of milk and honey; as *Ultima Thule*; as Peter Pan's Never-Never Land in which one can escape the compromises that the grown-ups make.

So that is the lay of the land in Lüritz shortly before the tolling of the bell: a justice administration conscious of the failure of its hopes; a population that is both dependent on the state and angry at it; and a reservoir of fantasies about the West that are no more realistic than the utopian hopes of people's judges had been during the early years of Socialism in the GDR. But my judges are still expected to busily promote the blessings of the East German legal system. In 1984, the Lüritz District Court, besides taking care of its annual caseload, makes four reports on legal developments to the District Assembly; arranges one conference on law and order, twenty-one trials before an "extended public," twenty-five post-conviction discussions at the defendant's place of work, seven debates with work collectives, fifty-three talks about the law at various venues, and twenty-two training sessions; composes seven court censures and fifty-eight letters to agencies and enterprises advising them of legal errors they committed; and organizes seventeen "other" events to propagate Socialist legality. Add to that the continuing legal education efforts judges had to engage in, such as judges' conferences, training sessions, delegations to Party courses, and the like; the voluntary sign-ups for programs fostering efficiency and thrift (which then were undermined by the consumption of time and paper necessary to report on them to one's superiors); the Socialist competition between courts to increase performance ("such idiocy," Frau Nissen called the efforts which she herself, pre-1989, had to promote); the many birthday parties at the courthouse (after all, this was a legal system that propagated human warmth!); the common demonstrations on the First of May and other political high holidays—I'm sure that there were other duties that I have omitted.

Since by now all this busy work was done without the proper political conviction, and since my judges would have much preferred to save their time and energy for their judicial work, they tried to dispatch their ideological chores with as little time and effort spent on them as possible. I find the minutes of a four-and-a-half-hour-long in-house meeting at the District Court at which the assembled judges discussed, in 1986, how they could improve their monthly legal propaganda output simply by better *reporting* on their efforts. "We must tally everything we do, including responses to inquiries, and any other activity," suggests Frau Neumann. "In family law matters, no more telephone information, but only written communications," says another judge, because a written note can be counted as a "letter of advice" and thus improve the court's statistics. As

CHAPTER 9

Frau Walter tells me, she now occasionally cheated and reported a hearing attended by some curious friends or colleagues of a defendant as a "trial before an extended public."

Which brings us to the lies we started out with in this chapter. If, in the early years, lies were needed to convince the public of Socialism's feasibility, they are now necessary to cover up its failures. Everyday legal life in Lüritz is as overgrown with lies as a meadow is with weeds. Frau Walter lied when padding her legal propaganda reports for the Ministry of Justice. The Lüritz prosecutor lied when sidestepping a question by a member of the public about whether one could attend the trial of the six policemen accused of robbing *Asoziale*: he was not authorized (thus the evasive answer) to comment on proceedings *sub judice*. His Neuburg boss promoted what boils down to lies when he prosecuted the policemen not in Lüritz but, behind closed doors, in Neuburg in order to avoid the embarrassing story making the rounds at home. Even Herr Taddäus lied when he wrote his moving letter to First Secretary Erich Honecker, in which he talked about his shame of having followed Party rules and broken contacts with his parents in the Federal Republic. It wasn't true: the family continued to visit in restaurants along the transit *Autobahn* running from West Germany across the GDR to West Berlin. Herr Taddäus told me so himself.

Many of these lies were necessary to protect a speaker from getting into trouble. Many were superfluous and were spoken or acted out like reflexes within a legal system that had forgotten to be truthful. Sometimes I come across a lie by some official intended to field a question that, ten or twenty years earlier, a citizen would not have dared to ask because he would have feared the state's reaction. To some extent, the increase in official lies in the 1980s is a sign of progress: GDR citizens have become more inquisitive, and state officials less ready to respond to challenges with raw oppression. Take the log book of the court's information office, which handled legal inquiries by citizens free of charge. In the final years of Socialism, the office was flooded with the brazen questions of would-be emigrants about the ins and outs of obtaining exit visas. But the log book reflects nothing of the desire of so many to leave the country; it lists the topics of inquiries only in code, by number, and so stays mum about the growing discontent that sweeps the country. Or take the questions of that citizen who in 1987 inquired at the prosecutor's office about the Lüritz police scandal. His wish to attend the trial was an act of political chutzpah: asked by the prosecutor for his reasons, he answered: "Because I'm generally interested in getting to the bottom of this kind of rumor." But the prosecutor is too uncertain of his own authority to openly reject the challenge. He gets rid of the questioner with a seemingly mild-mannered subterfuge, then turns around and sends an internal memo about the incident to "Department BVfS Neuburg," that is, to the Secret Police. I doubt, though, that at this late date the memo got the questioner into serious trouble.

Because, by now, there is some evidence suggesting that the East German Justice Administration itself is beginning to tire of its own dishonesty. In the 1988 files, for instance, I find not only the usual didactic trials before an "extended public," but also a number of politically *embarrassing* cases that Lüritz judges discuss with various audiences in and out of court: collective suits of groups of employees banding together to complain about decisions of the management; a case of four young rowdies who had toppled gravestones in a churchyard; the prosecution of two accountants from the State Procurement Agency who had embezzled 30,000 Marks by manipulating sales and purchase documents. At these discussions, there is open disagreement in the room, on one occasion "an extensive, even controversial debate with lively audience participation." The public anger vented at events like these occasionally seems to bear fruit: as one report by my court to the Ministry of Justice claims: "The District State and Party leadership have already taken action to address the issues raised in the debate." East German legal language is becoming a bit more honest: in some letters from the Ministry of Justice, for example, the old euphemism "extended public" is replaced by the more accurate "focused public" (*gezielte Öffentlichkeit*). On January 1, 1988, the Ministry of Justice orders the classification "confidential" (*Vertrauliche Dienstsache*, or VD) to be dropped from internal use. All courts are told to accordingly scale back the classified materials under their control.

But after so many years of secretiveness, it is not easy to all of a sudden open up. The declassification takes its time and, by September 1988, has not yet been completed at the Lüritz court. In December 1988, the Ministry of Justice sends a "Directive" to its courts, informing them that even without the former VD stamp, communications containing "classified information that does not contain state secrets" must be registered, numbered, and signed for upon receipt and may be duplicated only if "absolutely necessary." The order applies to calendars, work notes, weekly reports, analyses, "statistical and other data of a confidential nature," and the like, including the "Directive" itself, which as "Official Matter—Copy no. 979/7 pages" is kept under lock and key. If anyone at the Lüritz court would have passed it on to the outside world, the source of the indiscretion would have been easy to identify.

It is too late; East German justice cannot reinvent itself. Even the reformers' liberalization efforts—conceived with optimism only to be timidly withdrawn—reverse from hopes to lies. I discover in one of the weekly reports to the Ministry of Justice a handwritten remark by Under-Secretary Wolfgang Peller (himself a man open to reforms) that shows how difficult it has become to leave the

CHAPTER 9

system's inbred dishonesty behind. The report deals with a corruption case involving large state assets in Berlin that would be prosecuted in a trial closed to the public. "Why? §211 [of the] Code of Criminal Procedure," Herr Peller has written next to the dutiful account. ("Trials are conducted in public," says the Code.) But Herr Peller knows the answer to his question: because forty years of dishonesty in East Germany's administration of justice cannot be undone by glib ministerial comments in the margins.

CHAPTER 10

THE END

Judging from my records, the end begins around 1985, the year in which Michail Gorbachev rises to power in the Soviet Union. But his name does not come up in my Lüritz story. It is no sudden event that brings about the change but the slow addition of factors that existed long before: a jug is being filled and finally runs over; a virus, initially harmless, spreads and causes an epidemic; a rumor, at first just whispered, spreads and grows until it is shouted from the rooftops. Frau Nissen, ex-director of the Regional Court in Neuburg, confirms my dating of the turning of the tide. In the second half of the 1980s, she and her judges had noticed a change of public attitudes toward the judiciary. If before, the courts' clients had behaved in a friendly, even "affectionate" manner toward judges, she now began to sense a "cooling" of the air. Not a lack of interest but "defiance." "We no longer were in step."

Everywhere, the writing is on the wall. The Justice Administration is losing volunteers: between 1984 and 1988, 9.2% of all members of the dispute commissions in the Neuburg region (lay courts adjudicating minor civil disputes and administrative offenses in the public housing sector) resign from office, but less than a third of the lay judges needed to replace them can be found. The Regional Court reports "considerable recruitment problems" to the Ministry of Justice. In Lüritz, only 60% of the lay judges still on the books show up for the regular training sessions. It "cannot be denied that the number of objective reasons for citizens' unwillingness to get involved have grown," the Regional Court informs the Ministry. "Objective reasons"? Those must be the same reasons as those that in 1986 motivate a Lüritz lay assessor not to vote (a scandalous behavior for a civic volunteer) and that, by the year 1989, have moved twenty-two other lay assessors to submit their resignations to the Lüritz Court. Several lay judges simply return their court ID cards in the mail. Some of the accompanying letters of the drop-outs offer tactful excuses: "For personal reasons..."; "for reasons of personal health..."; "asking for your understanding...." "I do not want to talk about the reasons that caused me to resign my office," one lay assessor writes in the fall of 1989 and thanks the court "for the excellent cooperation and the trust shown." He has renounced a job that meant a lot to him.

Not that the mood among the judges is much more sanguine. In one of Frau Walter's notebooks ("Meetings and Conferences. July 1987–July 1988"—a

CHAPTER 10

wood-cellar find), I discover on the last pages, behind all the professional bits, a number of disrespectful notices and doodles that she must have scribbled during lulls in the official program and that seem to mock whatever important messages the speaker of the moment must have tried to get across. "We are storming ahead but are advancing very slowly," I read, for instance. At a judicial conference in July 1988, Frau Nissen reports on the many complaints, particularly of young judges in her region: about the insufficient technical equipment at the courts; the "lack of respect for judicial authority among state agencies"; the absence of a shared mission and of role models for judges. "We must provide answers to the questions of our young colleagues and comrades," Frau Nissen says.

But where to find such answers? The judges are tired, and whatever respect the citizens once might have felt for them appears to be evaporating. One bit of evidence: it happens frequently in these last years that civil parties and those criminal defendants not already under lock and key fail to show up for hearings. In 1986, two carefully prepared trials "before an extended public" cannot proceed for lack of the defendants. Thankfully, court authorities manage at least to locate and "fetch one of them." But as Frau Nissen reports two years later to Berlin, the incidents of "citizens' negating state authority by missing court dates have not abated in the recent past." The kinds of excuses parties offer for their absence seem to confirm Frau Nissen's statement. In January 1988, a Lüritz litigant who missed her hearing explains that "she is currently in the process of wall-papering" her new apartment. In 1989, a witness admits to having falsely testified in favor of a plaintiff who had promised to tile her roof: "We had terrible difficulties with our building project." First things first. Instead of the proper people to attend the trial, now, in the final years, there may be not-so-proper people in the audience: the friends and drinking mates of a defendant prosecuted for "asocial behavior" whom an accused occasionally brings along—perhaps for entertainment, perhaps just so they might enjoy, for a few hours, the warmth and comfort of the courtroom. As I can tell from a number of worried "weekly reports" by district courts to the Ministry of Justice, this is not the "extended public" that the system had in mind. But *Assis* always were notorious for their disrespect of state authority. Their contempt for rules seems to spread to other groups in the GDR. The "weekly reports" of trial courts are filled with stories of Fascist or racist insults or assaults. They also tell of the increasing, and increasingly brazen, use of alcohol at work. The black market grows and prospers. The law seems less and less capable of enforcing Socialist good manners in daily life.

One place where the weakening of old rules of social interaction and the slow emergence of new ones can most easily be shown is civil law, and within it, that most bourgeois area of law: the law of contracts. Actually, civil law—though seemingly more innocuous than public law—is a far more sensitive barometer of changes in a country's legal culture than, say, criminal law. Criminal law is an instrument of power; it is unaffected by the interests and desires of those whom it condemns, and it is employed by governments with as much ruthlessness or sensitivity as their respective plans and ideologies require. But civil law governs the relationships of citizens among each other. The use or non-use of its mechanisms by its addressees may tell us something about their attitudes toward the law, their fellow citizens, and the state. The law of contracts in particular—that very institution at the heart of civil law that enables people to arrange their own affairs as they see fit—can serve as a touchstone to reveal perceptions about individual autonomy and the legitimacy of self-interest. If I trace how my Lüritz protagonists, over time, changed their contractual habits and beliefs, I may be able to measure how much they distanced themselves from their bourgeois past, and whether, at some point, they actually turned around to at least temperamentally rejoin it.

From its beginnings, East German law mistrusted contracts. That does not only hold for economic law, where obviously the Plan left little room for self-determined legal relationships between state-owned enterprises. Legal relationships between individual citizens, too, increasingly were controlled and limited by rules and targets set by state authorities such as rationing, price fixing, rent controls, and the like. Although the contract law of the old German BGB (*Bürgerliches Gesetzbuch*) of 1900 stayed in force in the GDR until 1975, and although the new East German ZGB (*Zivilgesetzbuch*) that followed it contained a contracts chapter, the Lüritz case records show little sympathy for the idea that every citizen should be entitled to arrange his own affairs with as much individual autonomy as possible. The early people's judges did not care about contractual *freedom* but about contractual *justice,* and they defined that justice not by what the contracting parties had *intended* but by what Socialist morality would have *required* them to do. In 1953, Frau Rüstig affirms the validity of a sales price for a horse (which the buyer now disputes) not by consulting the agreement between the parties but by pointing to the fact that both the village mayor and the Chairman of the Land Commission had be present at the sale, and that they would have interfered if the price had been unreasonable. "Our agricultural functionaries must see to it that contracts are just, conform to the needs of our time, and are concluded without advantaging one or the other side."

In this view, contract law no longer is supposed to enable parties to advance their interests by way of cleverly negotiated deals but is simply a means of co-ordinating socially desirable exchange relationships. If after the conclusion of a contract the parties later disagree about its meaning, the court will search not for the intent and expectations of the parties but for that interpretation most in line with overall political and economic goals. Here is a case in point. In 1954, a Lüritz landlord sues his tenant for the reimbursement of maintenance costs that under the rental agreement were to be paid by the defendant tenant. The tenant,

CHAPTER 10

sensing that the political wind has turned, claims that the agreement is no longer valid as far as the costs of the apartment's upkeep are concerned. "We now have a new social order," he says. "We are too old for those kinds of excuses," responds the landlord with, I assume, a heavy sigh, and the court secretary, taking down the minutes, considers the objection to be central enough to be recorded in the protocol. And she is right: this is indeed a conflict between "new" and "old," with the judge, Herr Steinmetz, safely siding with the "new." He holds the maintenance clause of the rental contract to be in violation of a rent freeze (passed *after* the conclusion of the contract!); declares that under the GDR Constitution of 1949 ownership is linked with obligations; states that the tenant therefore cannot be expected to maintain the owner's assets; and rejects the landlord's suit.

I find a number of similar decisions disregarding contractual agreements in the civil case files. Most of them date from the 1950s and 1960s. Some are well argued, some are not. But none seem very interested in what the parties actually agreed on. Instead, the judges try to bring about that outcome to a legal conflict which in their view, would best serve society's welfare. With the consolidation of a planned economy in the GDR, private contractual leeway shrinks. By and by, the state proceeds to close those legal loopholes that for a while allowed enterprising people to make a living by contracting along the outskirts of the economic plan. In 1966, for instance, a poultry expert loses his suit against his agricultural cooperative by which he wanted to enforce a so-called specialist's agreement entitling him to wages above the collective norm. Originally, the specialist's agreement had lured the plaintiff into joining the collective farm at a time when middle-class technocrats still needed to be wooed to cooperate with Socialism. But the contract had to be reapproved each year by the Regional Agricultural Authority in Neuburg, and by 1966 it refuses to do so. The plaintiff claims that the Agricultural Authority was not entitled to withdraw its consent without a reason. But my Lüritz judge loses no time over this argument. To him, the collectivization of East German agriculture now has been completed (I might add: and the Wall keeps even technocrats at home), and specialist's agreements therefore have become redundant. The new East German contract law should advance collective cohesion. It should not help some parties to secure advantages over others.

This also is the lesson that a Lüritz tenant has to learn in 1982 when he sues the Communal Housing Agency for the costs of renovating his apartment, a claim clearly supported by his rental agreement with the Agency. But the tenant's contract dates from 1972, when the apartment house was still in private hands, and although the renovation clause expressly was included in his new contract in 1977, when the house was taken over by the state, it runs counter to the usual contractual practice in public housing that makes the *tenants* responsible for the upkeep of their flats. Moreover, as the Housing Agency's attorney reproachfully points out, the Agency had agreed to the plaintiff's unusual conditions only because in 1977, when with the change of ownership the contracts were re-drafted, he "categorically refused to sign the usual version of the contract."

Such obstinacy also seems suspicious to the court. Although the new East German Civil Code in §104, para. II explicitly allows contracting parties to deviate from the standard rule assigning renovation costs to tenants rather than the public landlord, the judge leans on the plaintiff to accept a settlement with the defendant under which he is paid only two thirds of the costs to which he is entitled and, moreover, has to promise to consent to a rewording of his present contract to bring it "in line with current practice." *"Nur keine Extra-Wurst,"* as Germans say; "no extra sausage" and no special treatment for anyone. Socialism wants its contract law to be unselfish and cooperative. As late as October 1989, Frau Neumann writes in a judgment concerning the sale of a used car: "The plaintiff wanted to buy the car at any price and the defendant wanted to sell it at the highest price he could obtain. Such behavior is not acceptable under Socialism."

In this legal climate it can come as no surprise if citizens forget that contracts are promises meant to be kept. Especially deals involving scarce and desirable goods such as cars often are recklessly rushed into, with parties giving little thought to the contractual obligations they incur. "Although we signed the sales contract, we didn't really understand the meaning of its terms," a buyer says in 1988. A few years earlier, the seller of a shed no longer wants to honor the agreement because in retrospect he thinks that he obtained "too low a price" and now has found another potential buyer willing to pay more. Many Lüritzers have only vague ideas of what it means to conclude a contract. "We only have an oral rent agreement because the landlord refused to sign a written contract," says a tenant in a case in which it is quite doubtful whether the parties agreed on anything. Many cites in my files suggest that my protagonists do not distinguish between substantive and formal justice. "It shouldn't be allowed to benefit from a mistake a colleague made in formulating an agreement," a manager says in 1971 who no longer wants to pay the price for weekend jobs farmed out to one of his enterprise's work brigades. A plaintiff's brief in a dispute over an apartment swap—composed by an attorney!—boldly states in 1979: "The plaintiff does not want to base his claim on this or that specific section of the code but wants to point out that the interests of society require that the agreement must be honored."

Arrangements for long-term relationships such as rent or labor contracts often are never formalized at all. This makes sense insofar as many of the details—rents, wages, causes for dismissal, etc.—are predetermined by public law and thus not subject to the parties' bargaining. But even issues that the parties could determine on their own are rarely even talked about when the relationship begins. Nor does it seems to matter if they are discussed, but the parties cannot

CHAPTER 10

agree. Contract or no contract: the tenant will move in, the employee will take up his job without the details of the mutual rights and obligations ever being settled. So it can happen that a tenant lives for twenty-one years in an apartment without a lease because the terms and conditions suggested by the landlord "always ran counter to the tenant's interests" and therefore were never signed by him. A Lüritz rent dispute of 1989 reveals that the tenants at no point received the keys to the apartment from the landlady (they had been borrowed from the public housing agency to view the flat and never been returned), that they moved in a month *before* the housing authorities had approved of their tenancy, that the tenants began to pay rent only nine months *after* they had moved in, and that they ordered costly renovation work without ever checking with the owner of the house. The case finally comes to court because the tenants want their landlady to pay for the work done and she refuses. So the tenants sue. But even at this point, the judge does not address the failure of the parties to agree but simply tries to disentangle the various factual interests of the parties in a way that furthers overall social welfare.

But while in East Germany's public economic life individual contracts are increasingly neglected, they gain in number and significance in the shadow economy. Contracts about the after-hours and weekend work of enterprise brigades (frequently teetering on the brink of illegality) and the clearly illegal contracts structuring black-market deals look like the old-fashioned Capitalist contracts that we are familiar with: unregulated by public law and driven only by the private interests of the parties. They follow rules that also guide the business relations under bourgeois law: *do ut des*; *pacta sunt servanda*; "you get what you pay for"; and whatever other wisdoms of the market you can think of. Black-market contracts are always oral and insist on immediate performance because the parties cannot later go to court. "Why the orality?" I asked a Lüritz architect who under Socialism had done quite a lot of building work in his off-hours. "Because in those days, an honest handshake was enough," he said. He did not mention that it also was a good idea to not leave written traces for the prosecutor. But his use of the word "honest" strikes me as significant. He did not mean honesty toward the state (whose laws both parties were ignoring) but honesty toward one's partner in crime (to whom he felt he owed performance of the promised work). The shadow economy was ruled by a private moral code.

Because this code was not backed up by public law and order, private black-market morality was fragile and likely to disintegrate under the pressures of that other Capitalist feature of black-market interactions: private greed. The development of East Germany's black market for used cars can serve as an example. By the mid-1980s, these markets had become so common in the GDR that I learned of their existence from a prosecutor in Erfurt who in 1986, matter-of-factly and without the slightest trace of outrage in his voice, explained to me how these markets worked. Since all cars in the GDR were covered by state price controls, they could be sold—legally—only at their officially estimated value. For used cars, that value would be even lower than the (equally artificial) state price for a new car produced by the East German auto industry. In an economy in which you had to spend ten years and more on an official waiting list before being allowed to purchase one of those new cars, the official car prices were ludicrous. Nobody in his right mind would have been willing to part with such a desirable object as a car, even a used car, at the legal price. As a result, black-market prices for used cars surpassed their officially determined values by at least 100%. If an illegal car deal later came to light, the prosecutor could reclaim the illegal surcharge from the seller. Theoretically, the seller also could be prosecuted for speculation. If the buyer of the car was in "good faith" as to its exaggerated value, he could himself sue the seller, under civil law, for the return of the sum exceeding the official price-estimate for his new jalopy. Since by the mid-1980s neither police nor prosecutors were willing to exert themselves by combating illegal car deals, most "surcharge" cases show up in my civil-law records: as suits by disappointed buyers who, after having purchased a particularly ramshackle and expensive car, apply for its official valuation and then turn around to sue the seller for the return of the excess price. In most of these cases, the court sided with the buyer.

The Lüritz used car market took place once a month on a big empty field behind the remnants of the city wall. Sellers would drive their car onto the field, roll down one of the front windows by a couple of centimeters, lock the car, and wait. Buyers would inspect the parked cars from all sides and, if they were interested, would drop a little note containing a price offer through the window slit. In the evening, the seller would select the most desirable offers and approach the buyers. The resulting negotiations usually led to *two* contracts with the winning offerer: one oral contract, specifying the black-market price agreed upon, and a second, written contract listing a much lower price, presumably conforming to official price scales. This second contract could be used in later contacts of the parties with the state.

For a number of years, the oral contracts usually were adhered to. But this was a market where demand exceeded supply by a considerable margin. Much more than elsewhere, cars in East Germany stood for luxury, mobility, and freedom, all yearnings that in a closed and regimented country were not easy to fulfill. Often, prospective buyers of a car were so keen on calling it their own that they threw caution to the wind and agreed to prices for moribund Wartburgs or rattling Trabanten that I can only note in wonderment. In December 1988, for instance, at 5:30 in the evening, a Lüritz man at the Berlin car fair sells a twenty-year-old Trabant station wagon for 10,000 Marks. Since it is already dark, the buyer inspects the car, as best he can, under a street light and discovers

CHAPTER 10

"numerous defects." But the seller is unwilling to negotiate; "all attempts to bargain for a lower price were unsuccessful," and the buyer, afraid that the deal might fold, finally agrees to pay the asking price. Of course, when he examines it in the cold light of the next morning, the car is even more ramshackle than expected. But isn't the buyer himself to blame for his own impetuousness and folly?

No, because he can ask for an official estimate of the car's value (4100 Marks, say the experts from the State Bureau for Motor Vehicles) and sue the seller for the "excess value" he was asked to pay. It must be said that now, in January 1989, the buyer does not get the entire 5900 Marks that he allegedly was overcharged. Frau Neumann who presides over the case takes into account the well-known "everyday experiences" of car buyers in the GDR and talks the parties into a settlement that awards the buyer only a third of the illegally charged (and grudgingly, but voluntarily accepted) excess price. Still, even this "agreement" relieves the buyer of the full responsibility for his own deals. "You don't have to pay all that much attention," says the court in its decisions that reduce insane and recklessly paid prices for used cars to their legal non-market level. "We will protect you." And to the sellers these decisions say: "Don't be too greedy. Don't charge the price your customers are willing to pay, but ask for no more than what the state in its infinite wisdom considers equitable. Don't think that buying low and selling high is the right way of accumulating wealth." Very Socialist admonitions all of them.

In due course, the illegal car sales case law of East German district courts caused contract practices on the black market to degenerate. Buyers who knew that they could retrieve a good part of the sales price that they had agreed to, did not even go to the trouble of obtaining official estimates of a car's value but, without asserting any flaws in their purchase or misunderstandings in their deal, went straight to court to sue for the return of the "excess price." Some buyers even avoided the circuitous route of litigation and took the law into their own hands, as it were. Pretending to accept the seller's black-market price, they handed him an envelope that was filled with enough bills to pay for what would have been the car's legally permissible price but otherwise was stuffed with sheets of paper (and, on one occasion, with two packages of cacao). One can imagine the wads of money (real and pretend) exchanging hands behind the Lüritz city wall. Once a hopeful buyer brings 60,000 Marks in cash to the car fair. With such high stakes, the rules of the game become more frenzied. Both sides, buyers and sellers, take muscular friends along to observe the deal who can protect them, and, if need be, can serve as useful witnesses in court. Sometimes, a transaction gets out of hand and turns violent. On those occasions, the police prefer to look the other way. In October 1989, a buyer, conned in a chain-sale, sends an angry letter to the court: "Everyone with open eyes knows what's going on at our auto fairs, and elsewhere, too, when cars are changing hands. This is a market governed by supply, demand, and a maximum of legal insecurity." Another malcontent writes: "What kind of contracts are these? People use them as they see fit." On the black market, too, the "honest handshake" counts less and less.

And then, something amazing happens. In 1987, Herr Zaster, an illegal car dealer in town who runs such a booming trade that even the prosecutor can no longer ignore him, is charged with "speculation" and is sentenced to repay 71,800 Marks of "excess" gains into the city coffers. Where will he find such an enormous sum? With the help of clever Herr Arhuis for attorney (whom else?) he sues one of his middlemen for the return of the "excess price" that he—Zaster—had to pay to obtain the car that Herr Zaster then, in turn, sold for the illegal gains that he now owes the state. It is a sum of 6800 Marks. My Lüritz judge is outraged: in this fashion, car speculators could retrieve their penalties and duck their punishment! She asks the city to confiscate Herr Zaster's earnings by way of administrative decree, but the City Council is uncooperative. She wants to know the official estimate of the car's value, but too much time has passed for the Motor Vehicle officials to undertake that job. She finally, with effort, manages to persuade the prosecutor to participate in Herr Zaster's hearing (the prosecutor barely speaks a word) and dismisses the suit. But Herr Arhuis appeals, and the Regional Court (which has, of course, long been advised of the affair) in an anxious note to the Ministry of Justice admits that Herr Zaster's "claim under §§ 68 II, 69 of the Civil Code is probably well-founded." So the Court of Appeals encourages a settlement between Herr Zaster and his middleman under which the Lüritz dealer is paid back half of the "excess payment" he himself had to shell out to obtain the car. Herr Arhuis successfully brings suit against two other suppliers of Herr Zaster, and by and by, the dealer collects much of the sums he needs to pay his penalties for "speculation." The black market has entered the courthouse. The legal culture of the shadow economy has stepped into the light.

In the late 1980s, I find quite a few other cases of citizens resorting to the law to enforce claims that must have looked provocative to a judge. Lüritzers were always willing to use the law, if possible, to prevent invasions by the state into what they considered their own territory. Herr Boehnke's fight for the "Cooperative Hotel" was a case in point. In 1971, the custodian of the Lüritz "House of Pioneers," of all places (a state-run club for children preparing them for later Party membership), went to court to prevent the dismantling of the building's antenna, which allowed him to watch Western television. Since for job reasons he had to live in the "House of Pioneers," he said, and since the company apartment in the house was his to use, he could do with it what he wanted. The custodian's wife joined in the battle by locking the attic door and so prevented a group of "young pioneers" from climbing on the roof themselves to point the offensive antenna, away from Western channels, to the East. Surprisingly, the dispute was resolved not by an exercise of Party power but by law. The "Pioneer" organization sued the custodian to have the antenna removed and won the suit—and rightly so, I regret to say, since the custodian's rental contract with the "Pioneers" conditioned the installation of an antenna upon the house-owner's consent. But the case shows that even under Socialism, citizens insisted on what they deemed to be their *"gutes Recht"*: their proper rights. What counted as a "proper" right changed in the course of East German legal history. Work, a roof over one's head, a modest number of personal possessions were always part of what East Germans thought their due. Since the main codes that regulated daily life in the GDR—Civil Code, Labor Code, Family Code—were clearly written and accessible to laymen, many Lüritzers could and did research their legal problems on their own and as "weekend lawyers" managed their own litigation, if it should come to it. Civil and Labor Codes were published in large editions and were personally owned by many ordinary citizens. The GDR television show "What's Right?" was so popular that it was frequently quoted by plaintiffs and defendants writing their own briefs.

But what made the legal assertiveness of Lüritz citizens different in the final years were the political undertones and the new aggressive style of lawsuits brought not just to protect personal territory but also to embarrass and attack the state and its institutions. In 1982, for instance, a member of an agricultural cooperative sues his collective farm for its consent to his withdrawal from the cooperative. The court rejects the suit as inadmissible. I find civil law suits in the 1980s in which a buyer, sometimes over the span of several years, fights so heroically for the quality and service to which his contract with some state-owned store entitles him that I can explain the plaintiff's obstinacy and endurance not by financial interests but only by his anger against an insolent and apathetic state consumer industry. In 1986, a citizen asks the Legal Information Office of the Neuburg Appellate Court against which state agency he could bring suit if his application for an exit visa were, again, rejected. The Appellate Court, clearly unsettled, reports the incident to the Ministry of Justice in Berlin: "Although we informed the citizen repeatedly of the inadmissibility of a lawsuit, he persisted in citing international agreements." Agitated clients of the court demand compensation for false legal information provided by court officials (and seem to get it, too), complain about having to rise when they address the bench of the Neuburg court ("why should judges ask for reverence from the people who elected them?"), and show suspicion when, in Lüritz, prospective members of an audience are refused admission to a trial because of lack of space. Again, the court reports the incident to Berlin: "The citizens who could not be admitted expressed their annoyance. Some voiced the conjecture that a small courtroom had been intentionally chosen in order avoid spectators at the trial."

Not all of these critics were political dissidents. Most of them look like cooperative, inconspicuous citizens whose patience has worn thin. By the way: even actual dissidents, who begin to show up in my Lüritz case files around 1987, were not always enemies of Socialism. Many of them are successful citizens, with offices and titles, sometimes even with Party badges, who simply are no longer willing to adjust. Even in their resistance to the system, they are disciplined and rational. A Supreme Court study from 1988 revealed that in the entire GDR, only 7.5% of the offenders sentenced for "defamation of the state" were also applicants for exit visas. In contrast, two-thirds of these defendants had been drunk when they shouted their political abuse, and 42% of them had uttered neo-Nazi or Fascist slogans. Dissenters usually were no rowdies; rowdies were no dissenters. But neo-Nazi illusions of grandeur and the widespread flight into alcoholism, too, were signs of the corrosive discontent that was spreading through the GDR. It affected all citizens; the solid and the not-so-solid ones.

Some of the politically touchy lawsuits of these years simply seem to say: I am fed up. In November 1988, for instance, a Lüritz woman brings a tort suit against her own sister for having spoiled her impending visit to West Germany. The defendant, allegedly, had spread the rumor that her sister would use the trip to defect to the Federal Republic and the police, in due course, had taken away the temporary travel visa that would have enabled the plaintiff to cross the border. My District Court and the Appellate Court in Neuburg worriedly report the matter to Berlin: might this be an inadmissible lawsuit to obtain a visa under the disguise of a civil damage action? But I think the case should be read differently: as the story of two sisters who in their different ways struggle against a no longer bearable confinement. The plaintiff, dutiful and proper, asserts that her sister's "slander" has cost her a coveted trip and (so she claims) her reputation. The defendant, herself an unsuccessful applicant for a permanent exit visa, is angry because not she, but only her obedient sister was allowed to travel West. The fact, though, that even the "good" sister used the law to vent her anger must indeed have been unsettling for the system. Remember: until now the rule had been that courts stay out of politics. For many plaintiffs, that rule no longer seems to hold. If nothing else works, why not try the courts?

The public mood-change, it appears, has also affected Lüritz judges and lawyers. I find a case from 1982 among my civil records in which attorney Mohr (as far as I can tell, for the first time) cites *precedent* to support his client's viewpoint in a dispute over the sale of a defective car (he relies on a 1977 Supreme Court decision under which a buyer who was acquainted with the car's condition at the time of the sale could not, at a later date, claim restitution for the flaws he was aware of). Why should it be remarkable that an attorney cites Supreme Court case law? Because precedents were not decisive in a legal system that did not look to the past but to the future. Socialist judges were to be guided not by

CHAPTER 10

old wisdoms but by the most recent insights and decisions of the Party. To claim that a judge should take account of precedent in her decision also implied that she should *not* be swayed by the Party line. Also new in the files these years: a rising number of instances in which a lawyer (again: in most cases Herr Mohr) advances purely formal arguments to win his case: claiming, for instance, that opponent counsel, when bringing suit, had not yet obtained the necessary power of attorney; that compensation for damages could only be awarded upon application by the victim, which was lacking in the case at hand; or that an undated photograph was inadmissible evidence in a criminal trial. In the past, the whiff of formalism was something that a lawyer would have wanted to avoid. Another first: in 1985, Herr Mohr and Herr Arhuis, in two separate trials, assert that their clients were bullied by police intimidation into giving incriminating evidence against themselves. In 1988, in a prosecution for asocial behavior, Herr Mohr asserts police brutality against his client, and with insistent questions during oral arguments elicits evidence of the insulting manner of the officers. The Lüritz prosecutor is so incensed that he informs the political department of the Neuburg Regional Prosecutor's Office (the *Stasi* branch of the judicial system) of Herr Mohr's "presumptuous and provocative behavior." But the Lüritz judge at least takes note of the attorney's accusations, and even the Lüritz prosecutor admits that the police "did not behave entirely correctly." In these last years, judges and prosecutors at least are willing to consider the possibility of coerced confessions. Unlike in previous decades, occasional freshly apprehended suspects *deny* their guilt. As the GDR drifts towards its downfall, the state, no longer a protective parent, is also no longer owed the honesty that parents can demand. As public lies collapse, individual lies are gaining ground. The law becomes an instrument for the defense of personal interests even in confrontations with the state.

The justice authorities in Berlin seemed to agree. On December 14, 1988, the People's Chamber passed the "Law Regulating the Authority and the Procedure of Courts to Review Administrative Decisions" (*Gesetz über die gerichtliche Nachprüfung von Verwaltungsakten*, or GNV), which introduced the right of citizens to sue the state not only in its civil law persona (as landlord or employer, for example) but also in its capacity as sovereign. The new law was prodded not so much by domestic as by foreign law concerns: in the wake of the Helsinki Conference, the GDR feared that without some judicial protection against the executive, it would be isolated during international talks in Vienna. But the country was ready for change, and lawyers at the Supreme Court and the Ministry of Justice were keen to get involved in the reforms.

There was not much time. It was impossible to develop a home-grown East German jurisprudence of judicial review in the one short year between the Central Committee's first "suggestion" of reform in December 1987[51] and the law's passage in December 1988. Of the two central issues that any system of judicial review of executive decisions must address, the GDR law expressly dealt with only one: the *reach* of court review. Some legal systems use a "general clause" that allows a citizen to attack *any* act of government authority that affects his rights by suing the interfering agency in court—the Federal Republic, for instance, uses this approach. The new East German GNV, not surprisingly, chose the more restrictive method of *enumerating* the specific instances in which an aggrieved citizen could sue the administration. As Minister of Justice Hans Joachim Heusinger said in November 1988 in a speech intended to calm the worries of high-level GDR administrators: only a small, "manageable" group of government decisions would be subject to court review. Admittedly, the most explosive issue East German administrators daily had to rule on—awarding or denying exits visas—under the GNV belonged among the group of reviewable executive decisions.

The second crucial question any legal system must resolve that wants to enable courts to monitor the legality of government behavior—what about *discretionary* decisions by administrators?—had not even been properly articulated in East German legal literature by the time the GNV was passed. How far should judges go in checking up on the legality of government decisions? The answer is relatively simple in cases in which the law exactly dictates what should happen in a specific case. The rule that "a citizen can vote when he has reached his eighteenth birthday," for example, does not leave much room for doubt: whether someone is eighteen years old and a citizen can fairly easily be determined, and an election officer who excludes an eighteen-year-old citizen from the ballot has broken the law. But what if a statute regulating government decisions intentionally has left administrators in the field some leeway to chose the course of action that in a specific case would be most advisable? Should judges be allowed to tell administrators how they should have used that leeway? And does it make a difference whether a legal rule that authorizes administrators to take action gives them discretion in a general way (for instance: "the application for a hunting license *may* be denied") and thus leaves room for several different decisions that would *all* be legal, or whether the rule gives some direction for the administrator's decision in the field (for instance: "the applications for a hunting license may be denied for *important reasons*")? West German administrative law has called the latter type of legislative term, which gives some—roundabout— instruction for its interpretation, an "indeterminate legal concept" (*unbestimmter Rechtsbegriff*). West German administrative courts have held that "indeterminate legal concepts," when applied, can have only one correct interpretation in each case, and that the legality of their de facto application, therefore, can be fully checked by the reviewing judge. But what, actually, is an "important reason"? And how can a judge in the cool and quiet of his courtroom determine

CHAPTER 10

which reasons truly were "important" for an experienced administrator acting under the pressures of the here and now, and which were not?

The Federal Republic sometimes has been criticized for being not just a *Rechtsstaat* (a state under the rule of law) but a *Rechtswege Staat* (a state with too many roads leading into court) that gives its judges more authority for second-guessing its administrators than is healthy in a democracy (whose officials, after all, are supervised by an executive that is dependent on an elected government). When it promoted its new law on the judicial review of administrative decisions, the East German government had the opposite goal in mind: it wanted to give its courts as little control over executive decision-making as it could get away with considering the country's international reputation and its rumbling people. In an authoritarian state, the second branch of government is far more crucial to the maintenance of power than the third. When the Central Committee's Department on Questions of State and Law endorsed the introduction of judicial review of administrative acts into the East German legal system, it had decreed that judges "should only examine the observation of legality" by the administration. "The discretionary leeway of local government bodies will not be restricted." In his speech of November 18, 1988, Minister of Justice Heusinger had told his audience: "Again, I want to stress that this reform *is not about* dividing the branches of a unitary government, *it is not about* placing local government bodies under the tutelage of judges, and *not about* replacing the exemplary cooperation of courts and local state agencies by a new, possibly even confrontational, juxtaposition." A judge who was present at that meeting told me that "a sigh of relief" ran through the assembly of administrators when they learned that there was still no need to fear the courts.

The Minister's statement sounded clear enough: no judicial review of discretionary government decisions. Only: the words were spoken at a time when no one in East Germany's administration of justice seemed to have much of an idea of how this rule would be carried out in practice and what its implications were for the success or failure of the new GNV. How else could one explain the eagerness and bustle with which the Ministry engaged in preparations for East Germany's new administrative courts? Minister Heusinger predicts a "considerable increase" in judicial caseloads when an estimated litigation wave of 55,000 administrative lawsuits per year would hit the courts. In the Neuburg region alone the Ministry plans for fifty-nine new positions for administrative judges. My Lüritz court expects to add to its current staff of five judges two new judges plus five supporting personnel such as secretaries, typists, and the like. Frau Walter, the new director of the court, despairs of finding office space for all the newcomers. Humboldt University in Berlin (where East Germany's judiciary is trained) prepares for the admission of 200 additional law students. New training courses for administrative judges are arranged: in March 1989, a meeting for district court directors preparing them for the expansion of their duties; in May 1989, the first get-together of administrative judges in the Neuburg region.

And what happens, when on July 1, 1989 the new GNV comes into force? Not much. No wave of administrative lawsuits hits the courts. Four months after the GNV has become valid law, only seventy-four administrative suits have been filed in the Neuburg region, seven or eight of them in Lüritz. Why this amazing lack of public interest in a reform that was supposed to turn the GDR into "a Socialist state governed by the rule of law"? Because the drafters of the GNV had studiously avoided any rule that might allow a court to review the substance of administrative acts. The drafters also had ignored the fact that right-holders only go to court if there is no easier and less expensive way of enforcing their entitlements. In a market society, for instance, customers do not go to court if something they just bought turns out to be defective. They simply complain about their purchase to the seller, and that way, usually get better and quicker satisfaction than if they had brought suit. Socialist citizens, too, were used to defending those rights that the state approved of—to housing or to health care, for example—by way of complaints, and if the state was able and willing to accede to their request, complaints, as in a market, were an easy and often successful method of salvaging one's rights. The new GNV would have been useful to complainants if it had allowed them to enforce those rights against the state that the state was *unwilling* to grant them on its own. But the one, the so fervently desired right that citizens would have been glad to wrestle from the state's hands—freedom of movement—was not subject to court review.

Yes, the new "Decree on Citizens' Travels" of November 30, 1988, was included in the list of statutes that under the GNV entitled a citizen to go to court if he could claim that the administration had violated his rights under the decree. Section 10, paragraph II of the "Travel Decree" allowed the granting of a permanent exit visa to the West if "humanitarian reasons" so required. But under GDR doctrine, those reasons were too vague to be assessed by judges far removed from the administrative context in which the original decision had been made. Instead, the term "humanitarian reasons" was said to give discretionary leeway to the administrator in the field who could interpret it as he thought fit. That meant that it was useless to attack a visa denial in court. The Interior Department that rejected a plaintiff's application simply could claim that it was not supported by "humanitarian reasons." Theoretically, even in the GDR administrative discretion was not limitless but could, again theoretically, be exceeded or abused. If Socialism had survived a little longer, it is conceivable that, over time, an energized GDR judiciary might have been able to find some chinks in the Interior Department's armor. But time was running out, and East German judges, unschooled in confrontations with the state, could not be expected to aggressively interpret their new powers. Thus, most of the potential plaintiffs trying to enforce their emigration with the help of lawsuits apparently were talked out of their rebellious plans. Of the seven or eight such suits in Lüritz, all but one were dropped. The files on these cases are very slim. I find a few handwritten notes by Judge Neumann, who seems to have interviewed prospective plaintiffs about why they wanted to turn their back on the GDR. Reading their answers ("political and economic discontent," "loss of trust in the state and its representatives," "objections to economic and social conditions in the country"), I can understand why the judge was not particularly eager to examine whether these motives were supported "by humanitarian reasons."

That was in the early fall of 1989. By October, even the Justice Administration seems to notice that a system of judicial protection against the executive that does not protect anybody harms rather than helps the legal reputation of a state. A letter from the Regional Court of October 18, 1989, advises its trial courts to seriously consider whether some denials of exit visas might have been in violation of the law and whether suits challenging the denial therefore should be granted. The Regional Court offers its trial judges no doctrinal explanations for its change of policy. The appellate judges must have seen the writing on the wall because the letter adds, almost desperately trying to preserve some remnants of executive authority: "Do not strike down visa denials at all costs." But now, the dike has broken. Prospective runaways no longer go to court but simply leave. Even solid and settled people are infected by the epidemic. "I thought of fleeing when my apprentice in February 1988 was allowed to leave. From then on, I just couldn't take it anymore," says a stone mason when he is arrested in the fall of 1989. "I wanted to make it by way of Hungary because that is the way a lot of young people get out these days," says a boiler worker. "I decided to escape last week, when one of my colleagues did not return from the Federal Republic and I watched all these flight stories on [West] German television," says a trucker who is caught, with birth certificate and work credentials in his pocket, at the Lüritz railroad station.

By now, even the justice system does not seriously attempt to stop the avalanche. I still find twenty-five arrest warrants for "flight of the Republic" in the Lüritz records of September 1989, and twenty-seven warrants in the October files; the last Lüritz arrest warrant for flight is issued on October 25, 1989. But most of these warrants apply to fugitives who have left the GDR by way of "illegal non-return," which means that they are safely in the West and that the warrant is not intended to assure their capture. Instead, it rather looks like an official seal to the escapee's change of residence. Of the thirty criminal prosecutions for "attempted flight" initiated at the Lüritz court in 1989, twenty-one are dropped and five end with suspended sentences. At the Appellate Court in Neuburg (which used to handle the politically more explosive cases of "flight of the Republic") these cases now are almost always transferred to the Neuburg District Court, and by the end of August 1989, are all discontinued. On October 29, 1989, the GDR government issues the first and, only six weeks later, the second amnesty for border-crimes. In a letter to the country's regional courts, the Ministry of Justice explains the large-scale pardon with "the extremely tense situation in our prisons which is part of the profound political crisis our country is experiencing."

In late January 1989, the crane operator who had tried to hang himself on the Lüritz market square if he were again denied a visa had been paroled and released from prison; he had served half of his fourteen-month sentence. By the fall of 1989, some political trials are not terminated or suspended: they simply stop. One gets the impression of a car running out of gas: the motor coughs and splutters a bit and then falls silent. On September 4, 1989, for instance, a thirty-year-old electrician is prosecuted in Neuburg for "seditious agency" and sentenced to two years in prison. On September 6, his lawyer appeals the sentence. On November 1, the Supreme Court voids his arrest warrant. Then nothing. There are no more pages in the file.

East Germany's machinery of justice, too, is running out of steam. On a "weekly report" describing one of those grass-root activities to promote the law that trial courts regularly announced to the Ministry of Justice, I discover a handwritten annotation by Minister of Justice Heusinger: "Good, but do we still have the strength?" That was written in March 1988. Now, a year-and-a-half-later, the answer is clearly "no." The system no longer has the strength to successfully defend itself. But that does not yet explain why Socialism in the GDR did go so gently into that good night. Why, for instance, did East German courts not use that tool that still was at their disposal—the criminal law—to ruthlessly repress the critics of the government? Why, in the face of imminent disaster, did the Party and the state not send legality and justice to the devil and use injustice to regain their footing? Instead of responding to pressures from below with pressures from above, they backed away. My records suggest that at least both the Ministry of Justice and the Lüritz SED leadership wanted to avoid violence at all costs. Minister Heusinger, for instance, justifies the second East German amnesty of December 1989 by arguing that overcrowded prisons might lead to a situation where "massive prison riots could only be contained by the force of arms." That "absolutely must not happen." When on October 20, 1989, the Lüritz District Party Leadership debates how to react to the numerous protest demonstrations that spread like wildfire throughout the city, the comrades suggest several flexible, even devious, measures of self-defense—conciliatory gestures, a willingness to talk, the infiltration of opposition meetings with Party people, discrediting well-known dissenters by spreading rumors about them, etc.—but no violence. The Party rejects an application by the dissenter group *Neues Forum* to stage a demonstration on November 7, 1989. But since everyone expects that their denial will be disregarded, the comrades, simultaneously, also resolve to let the planned event take place, "despite its illegality, without official intervention." Above all, no violence.

I know: this book only tells a local story, and the political decisions in the final days of the GDR were made in more important places than Lüritz and by more important people than the judges of my District Court and even Minister of Justice Heusinger. What happened in Lüritz need not have happened in Berlin. Still, law played a role in the events even beyond the modest framework of my town. The legal developments in the GDR, I think, can help explain why East German Socialism collapsed so rapidly, and without putting up a serious fight for its survival. The attempts at law reform in the country's final years (whose impact on my little town I have described in these pages) more or less all failed. The moderation of East German criminal adjudication did not persuade young people to stay at home rather than yearn for an escape. The redefinition of "asocial behavior" as, possibly, an illness rather than a criminal offense did not lead to the social integration of the county's numerous *Assis*. The introduction of court review of at least some administrative acts did not increase popular trust in the government and in the Party. But even failed reforms set milestones that governments cannot easily ignore. A state that had just promised its citizens, with the passage of the GNV, to establish a "Socialist rule of law" cannot, a few months later, use its army to disperse political demonstrations. As half-hearted as they were, legal reforms in the GDR had set the country on a path on which it was difficult to turn around.

My chronicle of forty years of justice (and injustice) in my town is marked by two different developmental lines. The first line traces what happens to the *faith in Socialism* at the Lüritz District Court. This curve begins at a high point on the y-axis of my imaginary graph, dips slowly, rises a bit on one or two occasions, and, in the end, drops to the very bottom. From the convictions of the early people's judges that they were serving a more just society than Germany had ever known, to the ideological pretenses and lies that my judges resorted to in the final years of the system, the first line illustrates the loss of political faith in the GDR.

My second curve follows the professional convictions and practices of my judges; it traces the ups and downs of their *faith in law*. This line starts at the bottom of the graph, beginning with the poor legal education and the lack of formal instincts of the early people's judges; then, over the decades, the line rises as the East German judiciary becomes increasingly professional, and by November 1989 has reached the level of a legal system that increasingly puts its trust in legal formality and professional routine.

There is a connection between these lines that one might call the inverse relationship between political and legal faith. The more utopian a society, the more expectant of political salvation, the less its need for law. If you are certain that the Party unfailingly will lead the country into a better future, objective and neutral mechanisms of decision-making are not just superfluous, they are suspect. And on the other hand: if civic trust decreases and if the disaffection of the judiciary is on the rise, the need for law will grow. People who no longer believe that there is only one right answer to each question (namely: the Party's) will have to rely on the neutrality and formal precision of a legal system that can mediate between conflicting interests. In my Lüritz story, the two developmental lines cross each other: my judges' *legal* faith increases as their *political* faith declines and, in the end, comes close to resembling cynicism.

I don't want to exaggerate the rule-of-law instincts of East German judges in these final hours, neither in Lüritz nor elsewhere in the GDR. They still were children of the legal system that produced them: positivists (because what one West German judge once described to me as "interpretive courage" was not in demand in an autocratic state); unschooled in doctrinal elegance and savvy (because law mattered little in the GDR and therefore could stay simple and accessible); more caring social workers than combative lawyers. But they were lawyers *enough* to make bad Socialists. "Lawyers make bad (literally: *böse* = evil) Christians," Martin Luther said: because they are too well trained in subterfuges; in linguistic hairsplitting; in doubts, objections, on-the-one and on-the-other-hand deliberations. Luther's condemnation of lawyers must be shared by all religions that expect unconditional faith from their servants. My judges were not "evil," but they were definitely unreliable Socialists. When the end arrived, they were intellectually better prepared to function under Capitalism than almost any other professional group in the GDR (black-market dealers possibly excepted).

Already in the first days after the fall of the Berlin Wall, judges and prosecutors in the GDR thus easily adjusted to the conventions of a rule of law. In my files, the change-over appears almost seamless. The biggest difference I notice between the days before and after November 9 is a change in the tone of interactions between court authorities and citizens. Rumor in Lüritz has it that, under the new rules, the citizen is king and judges are there to serve him, and so I find examples of absurd politeness in communications from the court and of occasional rudeness on the side of citizens. "I would be obliged if you could acquaint yourself with the relevant provisions, acknowledge gratefully your cooperation, and hope that you will follow this suggestion," Judge Rodewaldt writes on November 21, 1989, in a letter to a party in a civil suit, and, two weeks later, for his part is accused by attorney Möller (unjustly, it seems to me) of running a criminal trial "in a military style." "And this kind of behavior happens after November 9, 1989!" Herr Möller complains in court.

But tempers calm, and relations return to normal by October 1990, when West German judges take over at the Lüritz Court (which after Reunification will

CHAPTER 10

become, again, a traditional German *Amtsgericht*). In the first weeks after the *Wende*, judges and prosecutors from Berlin to Lüritz work on the renewal of the East German judicial system. Their eagerness seems fueled by a mixture of euphoria, hopes, and fears. Already on December 9, 1989, the Lüritz prosecutor launches an investigation against "unknown" suspects for the misuse of public office for private gains. On December 14, 1989, the director of the Regional Court in Neuburg writes to the city's mayor to request the transfer of a former *Stasi* building to the Appellate Court, which currently is bursting at the seams. Frau Nissen speaks as one whose sails are filled by a fresh wind: "It cannot be disputed that in the future, courts will be assigned considerably more authority than they enjoyed in the past." On November 24, 1989, a position paper from the Ministry of Justice mentions the need for an East German Constitutional Court and states that "the entire issue of high courts guiding lower court decisions must be reconsidered." And in December 1989, the Ministry drafts its first Half-Year Plan for 1990, aiming for "the restoration of justice in our country."

There is something surreal about all these deliberations. In the winter of 1989, the planners still operate as if time were on their side. In late December, for example, the organizers of a new East German Judges' League still worry whether membership in the new League should be compatible with union membership (which in the GDR was needed to gain access to state-owned vacation facilities and spas). But the speed of political developments in the GDR soon outpaces the reformers. New undertakings are already out of date at the moment of conception. What started out as bold and hopeful plans of self-reform begin to sound like whistling in the dark to keep up spirits in unfamiliar and threatening surroundings. By the spring of 1990, the justice administration in the GDR no longer concentrates its energies on political change but on its own survival.

Initially, the judges in the Neuburg region are worried about the creation of citizens' committees investigating the preferential treatment of state functionaries and of Party bosses in the days of Socialism. In Lüritz, too, a "Privilege Committee" begins to scrutinize the careers of local notables. To me, it seems absurd to think of Lüritz judges who commanded neither influence nor money as "privileged" in any way. But in the frenzy of post-*Wende* change, West German allegations against Socialism and East German shame over the many humiliations suffered under it combine to produce such a potent brew of public anger and resentment that its different ingredients can no longer be sorted out. Admittedly, the Lüritz "Privilege Committee" unearths little infamy and greed: no Finnish sauna in the headquarters of the Lüritz Party leadership; no special fund of Western currency at the disposal of the city government; no reduced income taxes for Party bosses—and only those, perhaps excessive, expenditures for city functions and PR-events that one might find in many other cities, East or

West. But judges know that they were, after all, the representatives of a regime that is now the object of the people's scorn. A rumor makes the rounds according to which some Neuburg colleagues found funeral wreaths, with their names, on their doorsteps. On December 5, 1989, the *Sentinel* publishes a "Declaration" signed by sixty-eight judges from the Neuburg region that "supports wholeheartedly the process of democratic change" in the GDR, but mainly serves to defend the judges' own position in the process: "We dissociate ourselves from citizens who, for personal reasons, take advantage of current public debates and demonstrations to vilify judges for having rendered decisions based on law, and declare our solidarity with those colleagues."

Two Lüritz judges whom I ask whether they signed the declaration cannot remember whether they did or not. Their memory gaps are not surprising: after the feverish euphoria of the first few weeks, East German judges suffered many humiliations in the *Wende* months, and nobody likes to remember his own shame. Under the pressures of the fears for their professional survival, the solidarity of judges in the GDR collapsed. Given its many hierarchical constraints, that solidarity never could have been very strong. Already on December 6, 1989, two statements—one originating in the Ministry of Justice, the other in the Supreme Court—had tried to place the blame for the courts' failings under Socialism on the Party. An "Open Letter," signed by many jurists working in the Ministry, admitted that in the GDR, "political conflicts were managed with the instruments of criminal law. That meant that courts in those cases had to function as executors of the former Party and government leadership and of the Secret Police." On the same day, a declaration of the Plenum of the Supreme Court accused "misguided security concerns of the former state and Party leadership" of having been responsible for judicial developments in the GDR.

But declarations such as these were of little use to local judges who had to face the wrath of their constituencies *in situ*. Hence the attempts of lower courts to distance themselves from their superiors in Berlin, which in December 1989 resulted in plans for the creation of a "Judges' League" to represent the interests of the GDR district and regional court bench. "The Ministry of Justice and the Supreme Court have been unable to strengthen the position of the judiciary and to bring it in line with democratic and rule-of-law requirements," asserts a letter from the City Court in Berlin-Hellersdorf that wants to enlist my Lüritz judges in the foundation of the "League." The accusation is correct but not quite fair, since in the forty years of East German legal history *both* the authoritarian restrictions *and* the impetus for liberalization and law reform had originated at the top of the country's legal hierarchy. The rank and file of the judiciary had gone along with both. But as my files on the creation of the "Judges' League" reveal, its future members soon are less concerned about establishing a rule of law than

CHAPTER 10

about saving their own skins. The minutes of a preparatory judges' meeting in Neuburg on January 13, 1990, reveal how difficult it is to reflect upon your own role in a national catastrophe when its rising waters are about to reach your neck.

The meeting was convened to discuss the tasks and organizational structure of the future "League"; some Lüritz judges, too, were present. But all contributors to the debate speak to the one issue that is on everybody's mind: the prospect that, under the rule of law, East German judges might become marginal and ostracized. "We can't always allow ourselves to be pushed against the wall," says a judge from the District Court Neuburg/City (which in the past had dealt with the overflow of political offenses coming from the Neuburg Appellate Court). "We must clearly and unambiguously let them know: either all of us stay in office, or nobody does," declares a judge from that Appellate Court. "I think that some change of personnel at the level of the Supreme Court and the Ministry of Justice will be needed," he adds. "But at the base nobody is responsible for the situation." "I think that, if necessary, we should go on strike to make our interests clear and to show citizens who it is for whom we're working," says another, and the assembled judges vote unanimously to include strikes among the future League's legitimate bargaining strategies. None of the Lüritz judges present speaks in the discussion. No one directly talks about the reasons why a judge who spent his professional life dispensing justice under Socialism might be considered a liability under the rule of law. "As long as someone did not actually break the law we must show solidarity," says a presiding judge from the Neuburg Appellate Court. "We must fight against the cherry-picking of individual judges who are fired one by one. Our apparatus continues to be needed, and they will not want to demolish it."

"They" are the West German observers and managers of law reform, whose un-brotherly self-righteousness when dealing with their Eastern colleagues makes it all the more difficult for the new arrivals to the rule of law to muster the moral energy needed for reflecting upon one's own role in a repugnant past. Under the critical eyes of Western-run and largely Western-staffed "Judicial Selection Committees," every judge in the GDR who wants to stay in office is now scheduled to be examined for his or her suitability in a democratic state. The committees are slow to take up their work; by September 1990, the judicial staff of the Lüritz District Court has no yet been vetted. But that they "will continue to be needed" in a united Germany increasingly seems questionable to my judges. So they leave on their own, one after the other. Frau Neumann is the first to go: in June 1990, she accepts a job offer from the Legal Department of the Lüritz shipyard. Two other colleagues follow in September 1990. Only Frau Walter, still director of the court, and its two youngest judges (Herr Rodewaldt and Frau Nissen) continue to hold the fort, until on October 3, 1990—Reunification Day —a new crew of judges from West Germany takes over.

THE END

Of the Lüritz bench, only Herr Rodewaldt (who only joined the court in 1987 and therefore hoped to look innocuous enough to West German examiners to be acceptable to the rule of law) decides to apply for continuation in his job and to face the vetting. The Judicial Selection Committee rejects him. He had done what a decree by the GDR government in February 1990 expressly had permitted him to do: namely, to remove all Party commentaries and evaluations from his personnel file. The East German government had hoped to cleanse survivors' resumés from now damaging associations with the Party. To no avail: Herr Rodewaldt's professional resumé—now reduced to a few nondescript pages—only increases the suspicions of the vetters. But he manages to retrieve the discarded documents and after Reunification makes good use of the new *Rechtsstaat*: he sues the German Justice Administration for continuation in his job. He wins his case. In 1995, Herr Rodewaldt is the only East German among the eight judges of the former District Court, now renamed *Amtsgericht*. Today, he handles the juvenile offenders at his court, an area of law in which the socially protective instincts of Herr Rodewaldt's Socialist past stand him in good stead. His former colleagues from the court open up law offices in town and have to face the fierce and savvy competition of the many new attorneys now arriving from West Germany. Frau Walter's life has taken the most symbolic and most hopeful turn. Together with her son (already educated at a West German law school), she has founded the Law Offices of Walter & Walter, located just behind the Lüritz town hall, that today combines the generations, the experiences, and the East and West German views of "justice" in uncomplicated and familiar fashion.

What else is there to report? On June 1, 1990, the first West German attorney opens his office in Lüritz. On June 18, 1990, the *Sentinel*, until then a Party-paper, declares its independence from the SED, a move foreshadowed by the newspaper's critical and aggressive reporting in the *Wende* days. I should have included journalism among the professions that would find it easiest to adjust to the change from Socialism to Capitalism: like money and like law, words, too, circulate easiest in the marketplace of ideas. In 1993, the former "Cooperative Hotel" (now again "Hotel Stockholm"), over which Herr Boehnke litigated from 1963 to 1967 to gain the equivalent value of a taxi cab, is sold to an insurance company for thirty-two-million Deutschmarks. In January 1999, Herr Kosewitz, the man who as First District Party Secretary governed the town for 28 years, dies of a stroke. The *Sentinel* publishes a death notice placed by the family but no obituary. Twelve years after he left office, ten years after the Turnabout, nobody wants to publicly remember the most important man in the Lüritz district. Judging by all I know about Herr Kosewitz—both good and not so good—he has not deserved to be so totally ignored.

It is too late now, but I, too, ought to apologize to Herr Kosewitz. I thought that he had lied to me when, back then in Lüritz, I spoke with him about the

CHAPTER 10

disappearance of Frau Christiansen from the Lüritz case files. "Wasn't that a promotion?" he had said, and I had mentally discarded his question as a subterfuge. But Herr Kosewitz had been right—or, rather, he also had been right. Frau Christiansen's removal from the Lüritz court was both a punishment and a promotion. I had paid insufficient attention to my dates and had not noticed the two-and-a-half-year gap between the drowning of Frau Christiansen's son in the Mediterranean and the last time that her signature appeared on a Lüritz document. It is true that, by Party standards, Lars Christiansen's attempt to jump ship and his subsequent death had meant that his mother could not remain in her position as director of the Lüritz District Court. But the East German justice administration and the Party did not want to lose so loyal and so responsible a judge. It took two-and-a-half years to find a post for Frau Christiansen as director of a bigger and more important district court than the Lüritz *Kreisgericht*. A banishment *and* a promotion. I noticed my mistake only when interviewing Frau Christiansen's daughter. That's when I learned that Frau Christiansen had died of a heart attack in the fall of 1989. She was about to sew a dress when the attack occurred; a dress meant to be worn at a ceremony to celebrate the fortieth birthday of East Germany's Supreme Court, at which she and other deserving judges in the country were to be honored with a medal for their work. That birthday party, set for December 8, 1989, did not happen either: it was preempted by the Turnabout. But it is fitting, I believe, to end this book that wants to trace human experiences of justice and injustice under Socialism by remembering someone whose own life was marked by the successes and the failures of East German law, by its hopes and disappointments, and by the most desperate and devastating decision of the Party: the building of the Wall.

NOTES

[1] *Zur Geschichte der Rechtspflege in der DDR*, ed. Hilde Benjamin, 3 vols. (Berlin, vol. 1: 1945–1949 [1976]; vol. 2: 1949–1961 [1980]; vol. 3: 1961–1971 [1986]). Here: vol. 1:71.

[2] Ibid., 1:44

[3] Bauerkämper, "Von der Bodenreform zur Kollektivierung," in Hartmuth Zwar, ed., *Sozialgeschichte der DDR* (Stuttgart, 1994), 119, 122.

[4] *Oberstes Gericht* (Supreme Court), Judgment of August 1, 1951, *Neue Justiz*, 1951, 464.

[5] Bauerkämper, "Die Neubauern in der SBZ/DDR 1945–1952," in Richard Bessel/Ralph Jessen, eds., *Die Grenzen der Diktatur. Staat und Gesellschaft in der DDR* (Göttingen, 1996), 108, 123.

[6] Benjamin, *Zur Geschichte,* 1:249, 253.

[7] Benjamin, "Volkseigentum ist unantastbar!," *Neue Justiz*, 1951, 61.

[8] Klaus Müller, *Die Lenkung des Strafjustiz durch die SED Staats- und Parteiführung am Beispiel der Aktion Rose* (Frankfurt/Main, 1995).

[9] Benjamin/Becker/Görner/Schriewer, "Der Entwicklungsprozess zum sozialistischen Strafrecht der DDR," *Staat und Recht*, 1969, 1112, 1129.

[10] Dieckmann, "Kündigungsklagen und Konjunktur," *Zeitschrift für Rechtssoziologie* 5, 1984, 79.

[11] Markovits, "Pursuing One's Rights under Socialism," *Stanford Law Review* 38, 1986, 707.

[12] Paul, "Nochmals: Zur Frage der Beweislast bei der materiellen Verantwortlichkeit der Arbeiter und Angestellten," *Neue Justiz*, 1953, 201.

[13] Bredernitz/Kunz, "Für eine höhere gesellschaftliche Wirksamkeit der Arbeitsrechtsprechung bei der Bekämpfung von Inventurdifferenzen im Handel," *Neue Justiz*, 1964, 358.

[14] *Oberstes Gericht* (Supreme Court), Judgment of April 8, 1954, *OGA* 1, 84.

[15] Nathan, "Eheschliessung, persönliche Rechte und Pflichten der Ehegatten, Beendigung der Ehe," *Neue Justiz*, 1954, 358, 361.

[16] *Oberstes Gericht* (Supreme Court), Judgment of December 1, 1950, *OGZ* 1, 72, 78.

[17] *Oberstes Gericht* (Supreme Court), Judgment of November 24, 1952, *OGZ* 2, 50.

[18] Benjamin, *Zur Geschichte*, 3:347.

[19] *Oberstes Gericht* (Supreme Court), Judgment of December 1, 1950, *OGZ* 1, 65, 67.

[20] Ostner, "Slow Motion: Women, Work and the Family in Germany," in Jane Lewis, ed., *Women and Social Policies in Europe. Working, Family and the State* (Aldershot, 1993), 92, 110–112.

[21] Norman Naimark, *The Russians in Germany*, (Cambridge, MA, 1995), 89.

[22] Falco Werkentin, *Politische Strafjustiz in der Ära Ulbricht* (Berlin, 1995), 174ff.

[23] *Oberstes Gericht* (Supreme Court), Judgment of October 4, 1950, *OGSt.* 1, 33.

[24] *Oberstes Gericht* (Supreme Court), *OGSt.* 1, 33.

NOTES

[25]"Brief der Richter des Obersten Gerichts an alle Richter der DDR," *Neue Justiz*, 1952, 348.

[26]*Oberstes Gericht* (Supreme Court), Judgment of June 27, 1955, *Neue Justiz*, 1955, 425.

[27]Andrea Feth, *Hilde Benjamin—Eine Biographie* (Berlin, 1997), 453.

[28]Hilde Benjamin, "Zur Strafpolitik," *Neue Justiz*, 1954, 453.

[29]My figures are based on Ammer, "Stichwort: Flucht aus der DDR," *Deutschland-Archiv* 22, 1989, 1206f.

[30]"Über die unmittelbare Mitwirkung der Bevölkerung im Strafverfahren," Beschluss des Präsidiums des Obersten Gerichts of April 21, 1965, *Neue Justiz*, 1965, 337.

[31]*Statistisches Jahrbuch der DDR*, 1989, 399.

[32]*Oberstes Gericht* (Supreme Court), Judgment of November 8, 1987, *Neue Justiz*, 1988, 467.

[33]Wolfgang Ayass, *"Asoziale" im Nationalsozialismus* (Stuttgart, 1995).

[34]*Oberstes Gericht* (Supreme Court), *Schulungsmaterial zum 3. Strafrechtsänderungsgesetz, Informationen des Obersten Gerichts* (Sonderdruck, June, 1979), 73.

[35]Luther/Weis, "Zur Anwendung des Strafrechts in der Deutschen Demokratischen Republik," *Recht in Ost und West* 34, 1990, 289, 292.

[36]Wendt, "Die deutsch-deutschen Wanderungen—Bilanz einer 40-jährigen Geschichte von Flucht und Ausreise," *Deutschland-Archiv* 25, 1991, 368, 388.

[37]Köhler/Ronge, "Einmal DDR—einfach." Die DDR-Ausreisewelle vom Frühjahr 1984," *Deutschland-Archiv* 17, 1984, 128.

[38]Wendt, *Deutschland-Archiv* 25, 1991, 390.

[39]Köhler/Ronge, *Deutschland-Archiv* 17, 1984, 128.

[40]Figures based on Wendt, *Deutschland-Archiv*, 25, 1991, 386, 390.

[41]Rottleuthner, "Zur Steuerung der Justiz in der DDR," in Hubert Rottleuthner, ed., *Steuerung der Justiz in der DDR* (Köln, 1994), 9, 40.

[42]Daniel Meador, *Impressions of Law in East Germany: Legal Education and Legal Systems in the German Democratic Republic* (Charlottesville, 1986).

[43]Inga Markovits, *Sozialistisches und bürgerliches Zivilrechtsdenken in der DDR* (Köln, 1969).

[44]Marcus Mollnau, *Die Bodenrechtsentwicklung in der SBZ/DDR*, (Berlin, 2001), 470.

[45]*Informationen des Obersten Gerichts* (Berlin, 1977), 1:3.

[46]Civil law suits in the entire GDR dropped from 78,315 in 1956 to 29,313 in 1968. See *Statistisches Jahrbuch der DDR 1969* (Berlin), 484.

[47]*Statistisches Jahrbuch für die BRD 1990* (Stuttgart), 337.

[48]To illustrate this point: In the 1946 communal elections in Mecklenburg-Vorpommern (then one of the states of the still federally structured Soviet Occupation Zone), 49% of voters in cities and 75.2% of voters in rural districts voted for the SED. Reported by Bauerkämper, "Die Neubauern," in *Die Grenzen der Diktatur, Staat und Gesellschaft in der DDR*, 108, 120.

[49]On the issue of confessions in the GDR, and their withdrawal, see Jörg Arnold, *Die Normalität des Strafrechts der DDR* (Freiburg/Breisgau, 1996), vol. 2.

[50]Sven Korzilius, *"Asoziale" und "Parasiten" im Recht der SBZ/DDR* (Köln, 2005).

[51]Johannes Raschka, *Justizpolitik im SED-Staat* (Köln, 2000), 274.

GPSR Authorized Representative: Easy Access System Europe - Mustamäe tee 50, 10621 Tallinn, Estonia, gpsr.requests@easproject.com